GUIDEBOOK IN THE FORM OF A LIFE TRANSFORMATION NOVEL

I REDISCOVER *myself*

CELINE WALASIK

Edition: Joanna Sosnówka Limitless Mind Publishing
Translation: Maria Pogwizd
Cover and graphic design: Anna Gajowniczek
Text Compostion: InkWander

ISBN: 9788397031876

Copyright © 2023 by Celina Walasik
Copyright © 2023 by Limitless Mind Publishing
All rights reserved.

Limitless Mind Publishing Ltd
15 Carleton Road
Chichester
PO19 3NX
England
Tel. +44 7747761146
Email: office@limitlessmindpublishing.com

Dear Reader !

Find us on Facebook/Instagram: limitless mind publishing
And visit our page on Amazon: limitless mind publishing

♥We would greatly appreciate your opinion. It means a lot to us.

Dear Reader,

I invite you on the most beautiful journey. A journey within yourself.

Life is like riding on a speeding train. You may not even know where it's heading or what's driving it. It's worth getting off that train for a moment and taking a walk. That one step will give you a sense of relief.

In that pause, you have a chance to see who you truly are. How much potential, worth, and richness exist within you. You will understand where emotions come from and how to deal with them. You will learn where to find happiness.

The book you hold in your hands is full of valuable guidance that will make this journey easier for you. Step by step, towards greater self-awareness. Take from this book as much as you want, as much as you need. Give yourself a chance for a better tomorrow.

- Celine Walasik

CHAPTER 1

I was sitting in a cafe, right by the window. I had a perfect view of the main square of the town. I smiled and felt the peace flowing through my body. I knew it was only temporary, so I enjoyed it while I could. On the other side of the table sat Simon, a handsome dark-haired man. He looked at me happily and talked about his next trip. His green shirt harmonized with tanned skin, and the delicate lines at the mouth, from the eternal smile, only emphasized his current attitude to the world. I listened to him with interest and I envied him a little about his travels around the world. He wanted to take me with him on one of his trips, but I always refused. I had many excuses - final exams in college, work, and now preparations for the wedding. Always something. And so I were in Piaseczno near Warsaw, facing doubts, decisions and problems every day. It was not easy. And lately, I haven't been particularly laughing because I felt like my life was getting more and more complicated.

"Okay," Simon said, and touched my hand. I was playing with a teaspoon. "I talk so much and you hardly say anything. How is the wedding preparation going?"

"All right. There's still some time left. Just don't forget to be with me that day." I looked at him hopefully. "I'm counting on you."

"I will be there, no worries. I heard that you moved to Greg…"

"Yes, he was very insistent. We have a whole floor in the house at our disposal, we are just finishing the renovation."

"I wish I had the chance to meet him," said Simon. "You decided to get married pretty quickly."

"Quickly? We've been together for two years. You're the one running around the world and you're out of space-time a bit."

"Maybe, but tell me, are you happy? Are you sure that Greg is the right guy for you?"

"We will see."

"If you know something ... I'll even come from the other end of the world" he said, carefully looking into my eyes.

"Thanks. I've always had your support." I smiled.

Simon is my close cousin, we are the same age, we used to live on the same street. We have always had a sister-brother bond. I could be honest with him, say everything that was on my heart, and I wondered if I should tell him my doubts this time too. Instead, I took a deep breath and leaned toward him.

"And I'm really glad you came here to see me. And thank you for the gift."

"It's your birthday, my love, I will never miss this."

I felt someone's gaze on me, I instinctively glanced to my right. Through the window I saw an elegantly dressed blonde. That piercing gaze fixed on me, lips tightly pressed together. I froze. We stared at each other for a moment. I nodded my head slightly in greeting. The blonde turned around and I breathed a sigh of relief. I glanced at Simon, apparently he also saw the woman outside the window.

"How's the hotel? All right?" I asked. "I just sold my apartment a few days ago, if it weren't for that, you'd be staying with me."

"The hotel is fine, and the apartment is not a pity for you to sell? You could leave it as an investment and rent it out. Great location, well kept…"

"I even thought about it for a moment, but Greg persuaded me to sell."

Suddenly, I heard a rough, firm, female voice next to me.

"Natalie, isn't Greg waiting for you? You should be home with your future husband."

I turned my head to the left and looked at the elegant blonde, my future mother-in-law.

I felt uncomfortable with her. Soon we were going to be a family, living under the same roof, and I was overwhelmed by this woman. Always haughty, confident in her motives, pursuing her goal. Maybe it was the fact that she was mayor of the town that made her so inaccessible.

"Greg works longer today" I explained in a calm voice.

"Then you should wait for him at home. Won't you introduce me to your friend?" She looked suspiciously at Simon.

"Of course, this is my friend Simon."

Simon got up and said hello. He also shook hands with the man with whom the mayor had come.

"Mr Simon, do you know that Natalie is getting married soon? It's a bit awkward that she meets other men" said Evelyn in a haughty voice, looking meaningfully at the gift lying on the table.

"Of course, I know that, but I also know that Natalie is a free human-being. She is nobody's property" Simon replied, and sat back in his set.

I felt the pressure rising. I just wanted this woman to go away.

"I'm not suggesting anything like that" Evelyn was indignant "I just think that a wife's place is with her husband, not in pubs with strangers. Natalie, please, say goodbye and go home."

"Mrs. Evelyn, I have an important meeting here, which I intend to continue"I said indignantly. I felt my face burn.

"Really? Do not forget, my dear child, that you live in MY HO-USE…" she emphasized the last two words. "I don't need to explain what that means."

She turned on her heel and waved her hand toward the coffee tables.

"Henryk, we're staying here." She strode ahead in search of a free space. Henryk, of course, followed her without a word.

I looked at Simon. His expression was priceless. I was fucking stupid for the unnecessary remarks of my future mother-in-law, and Simon was nervous.

"What was that supposed to be?"

"My future mother-in-law," I replied. "Let's get out of here, shall we?"

Simon looked disapprovingly at Evelyn.

"And who is this guy?" he asked.

"I have no idea. I'm sorry for her."

"You are apologizing to me? Really?" He stared into my eyes. "You should apologize to yourself. What are you getting into girl?"

I returned home on foot. Despite the incident with Evelyn, it was a good evening. Simon did not come back to the subject, he looked at me worried for a while, but then he got over it. We went for a long walk along the river. We talked, we laughed, no one bothered us there. In the end, he just asked me to take care of myself and go through life bravely and not be afraid to make the right decisions.

I thought I was taking good care of myself. For a slender brunette with blue eyes and long, manageable hair, I looked pretty good. I was tall enough not to wear heels. I felt better in sneakers, jeans and a shirt. The delicate make-up emphasized the regular features of the face and the smooth complexion.

Many times I persuaded Greg to live separately. I had my own apartment, small, but no one would disturb us there. Greg did not even want to hear about moving out of his mother's comfortable and large house. I don't know why I gave in, why I agreed to sell my apartment to live with Greg's parents. And that's before the wedding. We were supposed to invest the money in the renovation of the floor, our living space. I stood in front of the gate and looked at the house. I didn't want to go in there. It was late. Evelyn must have been standing by the window checking what time I got back. She crossed the line today. I was so damn ashamed because of her. There, in the cafe, I downplayed the matter, we left quickly and arranged the topics of conversation in such a way that they were far from my future mother-in-law and my future home. But if that's what it was supposed to look like...

As expected, after crossing the gate of the house, I immediately came across Evelyn. She stepped out into the corridor wearing a silk robe. She waved the index finger of her left hand at me.

"Come here, my darling." It didn't bode well.

It was a hard journey. No one has ever humiliated me like she did tonight. Contemptuous words falling from her mouth, exorbitant demands and an attempt to subjugate me in the most impudent and rude way. I didn't even argue. I had nothing to reproach myself for. I listened with tears in my eyes to what she had to say to me, and then, trembling, I quickly entered Greg's room. I started packing. I pulled out two suitcases from the closet and threw all my clothes, shoes and cosmetics into it.

Greg was lying in bed, propped up on pillows. Laid back, content. His blond, slightly overlong hair, not yet dry from the shower, was sticking to his forehead and sunken cheeks. A slim, almost skinny chest and bony arms stood out clearly against the navy blue bedclothes. He set the TV remote aside on the duvet and looked at me in surprise.

"What are you doing?" He asked.

"I'm packing, I need to get out of here. Right now. You're coming with me?" I looked at him carefully.

"Don't be kidding me," he said, then jumped out of bed.

"I am quite serious. I can't live here any longer. Are you coming with me?"

"But where?"

"Let's go to the hotel for now, and then we'll find something."

"You know I can't leave my mother alone. My father is always on the road. Anyway, I am to inherit this house. When I move out, my mother will leave it to my brother or sister in her will."

"But they have their fancy houses, what do they need this one for?"

"But I won't risk it. They will finish the renovation in a month, we will have a separate floor."

"But I'm not staying here, you understand? Are you coming with me or not? I won't ask a third time."

"You just moved in. You'll get used to it. Give yourself some time."

"No, not after what your mother told me."

"Don't overdo it. She's annoying and so what? Don't worry about it," he said lightly. "She was always picking on you about everything, even before you moved in here. Really."

"What?" I looked at Greg carefully.

"Let her say what she wants." It is like that already.

"And you allowed it? You listened so calmly to all these insults addressed to me and you did nothing?"

"What was I supposed to say? She's my mother."

I had absolutely no doubts anymore. I just sped up the pace of gathering my stuff. It was a good thing there was a hotel in town, and it certainly had plenty of spare rooms.

And so a week later, dragging two large suitcases, I stood at the door of my older sister, Eve's apartment. She opened the door in surprise.

"Seriously?" she asked, looking at me and the suitcases.

"Till I find something. For a few days, eh?" I asked in a tired voice.

"Come in, please," she said, stepping away from the door so I could go inside.

I left all my possessions in the hall and followed her into the living room. A cream leather sofa, two armchairs, and a glass coffee table stood by the window. There was a forty-inch TV on one wall and a long chest of drawers on the other. Just above it hung abstract paintings of models in colorful dresses.

Eve was a fashion designer, had excellent taste and on such a solid basis she arranged her nest on the second floor of a Warsaw apartment building. She looked like she was on the cover of Vogue. The fitted dress with poppies emphasized her perfect figure. Black hair, slightly wavy, reached almost to the waist. She was obsessed with her hair, I didn't know what she was doing with it, but it was shiny and healthy. Few people could boast of such a flawless complexion. Add to that a deep look from under mascaraed eyelashes and no one could resist her.

"Tell me." She sat down on the couch and looked at me curiously.

"I don't even know where to start" I felt terrible and didn't even want to talk about what I'd been through the past few days.

"I'll make it easy for you - So you kicked Greg in the ass. Knowing life, you messed with your mother-in-law, luckily she didn't make it, and you're down."

"More or less. My would-be mother-in-law, when she found out that I had moved out of her house and settled in a hotel, decided to play on my nerves. I didn't want to live there. Greg did not want to live any-where else, so I gave him an ultimatum: either he comes with me or we break up. He watched me pack my bags, so without a word, so simply, as if he was sure I'd be right back. But none of that. Well, I went my-self. Evelyn came to school on Monday. I saw her enter the principal's office. I got fired from my job the same day. The director said there was nothing he could do. I wanted to stay until the end of the school year so as not to leave students just like that, some classes are before their final exams. I got a notice and it's over. I am unemployed, lonely, I have no-where to live."

"Hmm, what a pig!" Eve got up and nervously began to pace the room. She got pissed. "How could she do that?! And the money for your apartment, I hope they didn't take it from you? They didn't take everything from you, did they?"

"They didn't. I had to pay for the repair. Now I don't have to."

"Fortunately. What a family! I can not believe. This Greg is an ass, not a man."

"I don't even want to think about him."

"You did well." Eve hugged me for a moment. "You did really well."

"So now what? There, in the town, I have nothing to look for any-more. I can't find a job anywhere.""Do not make dark scenarios" said Eve "something will come up. Give yourself time. You can stay here for now, and then something will be arranged."

"I only know one thing, I'm not going back to my parents' house, no way," I said, devastated. I associated my family home with pain and longing.

"Do not even think about it."

For the next two weeks I wandered around Eve's apartment like a shadow. I was down, shaky and unhappy. I didn't know what hurt me more - Greg's behavior or his mother and how she treated me. For these two years, I was convinced that Greg and I made a harmonious pair. We didn't argue like our friends, everything between us was orderly, predictable. We had a similar sense of humor, the same passion for travel. We often took short trips. Greg was so compliant, everything suited him, he agreed to everything. He was consistent in only one thing - he couldn't cut the umbilical cord and make a life for himself without maternal supervision. In this one he was very firm. Or should I actually stay with him? Maybe it would work out somehow? Then I chastised myself for such thoughts. It felt like there were two people in me and they were saying completely different things. I wanted to bang my head against the wall just to silence these insufferable thoughts for a moment. I couldn't sleep at night, even sleeping pills didn't work.

Eve was hardly ever home. She left early in the morning and returned late in the evening. She was preoccupied with preparing for the fashion show - this is a very important event for her. She claimed that her future career depended on this show. She didn't pay much attention to me, so I didn't bother her with my problems. I was so grateful to her for letting me live here.

I don't know if I was depressed or just hurt pride, but I didn't feel like doing anything. I didn't feel like going out, I ate little, I didn't need to get dressed, a bathrobe was enough. I felt like nothing. Where to look for a job? Who needs a teacher in early May, when there are a few weeks left until the holidays? I browsed some classifieds on the Internet, then closed my laptop with an even greater sense of hopelessness.

One day Eve came to me. It was evening.

"I have a present for you," she said with a smile. She was wearing a short dress with small colorful flowers.

"What?" I asked grimly. I was sitting on my bed with a book in my hand.

Eve sat next to me and enthusiastically presented a wonderful, from her point of view, way to improve my well-being.

"I have booked a three-week stay for you at a lovely guesthouse in the mountains. What do you think? You'll go, you'll rest, you'll distance yourself a bit from what you've been through recently. It will be fun. That's what you need" she handed me the voucher.

I took the envelope and pulled out an elegant card with colorful prints. I looked at it more closely. I had neither the desire nor the intention to leave and rest, especially not so far from Warsaw.

"But your name is written here," I pointed out.

"It's only on this invitation. In the guest house everything is already booked for you. Just go and have fun."

I eyed my sister suspiciously.

"I do not understand" I thought for a moment "If I have to move out, then tell me right away, and don't mess with it."

"That's not the point. I just got it from one rich admirer. We work together sometimes. He sent me this as a "thank you" for helping him, and you know I'm having a show right now and I can't leave. Not now, not in a month or two. This is not the best time to rest. I need to get on with my job and career. And I thought of you. You will go, rest and tell us how it was. A little detail, not too much. You know, if that guy asked if I had fun."

"It's not fair. If he invited you, he paid for it..."

"And what, should I give it to him now?" He would be offended. And yes, we both benefit from it.

"I don't know."

And that's how my life's journey, an interesting adventure, began. Like a coincidence... A coincidence? Are there cases? I don't think so. Everything is for something.

CHAPTER 2

I parked my old Opel in the parking lot and looked through the window at the guest house. A huge two-story building. It must have been a hundred meters wide. Wooden balconies were visible against the background of white walls and a sloping roof. Right next to the wide entrance, pots with large-leaved plants stood on the stairs. I was intrigued by the terrace at the entrance. On the wooden logs, up to the roof itself, sprouts of ivy were winding. It was certainly nice to sit there on a bench on hot days.

I got out of the car and looked around grimly. Space, greenery, somewhere in the distance I saw a wooden bridge, so there's probably a lake, and an orchard full of fruit trees on the right.

"And what am I supposed to do here for three weeks?" I thought. Pension off the beaten track, views of the mountain range in the background, but nothing else. I passed the shop about two kilometers away, no other attractions. If only this guesthouse was at least in the center of Kościelisko, but not at the very end of the village. I stood there and wondered if I should get back in my car and drive away. Realizing I had nowhere else to go, I went to the trunk and pulled out my suitcases. I was in no hurry. I saw my reflection in the car window. I frowned. Tousled hair, a silhouette bent in a gesture of resignation. I sighed and dragging my suitcases behind me, I headed towards the main entrance of the guest house.

Suddenly I was terrified. A man on a horse was coming towards me. I stood still, unable even to scream. The rider stopped the galloping animal literally less than two meters from me. My heart was pounding like crazy in my chest.

A man, about seventy, a withered but very lively old man jumped down from the saddle. I stood and stared at him dumbfounded.

"Good morning, Beautiful Girl," he greeted, extending his hand. He let go of the reins, and the horse ran freely towards the yard.

"Good morning," I choked out.

I held out my hand mechanically. The old man kissed the back of my hand, then grabbed the suitcases and began to drag them lightly into the building.

"Welcome to our humble home. How was the road? We're having dinner in an hour, so you'll have time to freshen up, darling." He glanced at my baggy pants. "Only we have a rule here, for many years anyway, that women, especially young girls, must wear only shorts or skirts here."

I looked with surprise at my clothes, then at the grandfather, and finally for other guests of the boarding house, but I did not see anyone. Am I the only visitor here? I felt tense. That I didn't check online reviews about this place either. Where have I come? What is this strange place?

Grandpa briskly carried my suitcases in and I followed him, wondering if it was a good idea to stay here. Full of reserve, I entered the reception. An elderly woman was sitting behind the counter, talking on the phone. I looked around. On the wall, there was an inscription drawn in large, ornate letters, surely a quote: "It's time to move on and give yourself a chance."

"I see you came alone, if you need company, I'll be happy to take care of it" Grandpa offered with a smile on his lips and fire in his eyes. "I'll take you to your room right now."

"Thank you, but I can do it alone. I'm just checking in. You've helped so much already."

"But, dear, I'll show you why you have to search and wander around the corridors. I'll show you everything. And there is much to show, I assure you. And what's your name?"

"Natalie."

"What a beautiful name. A beautiful girl with a beautiful name" he stood and looked at me with delight.

I felt really weird. I looked terrible, my face puffy, after a night of tears and self-pity. Dirty clothes, messy hair. And he has these words. This guy scared me.

"Anthony, leave the girl alone, don't show off!" the old lady behind the reception desk admonished him.

"What are you up to, good woman?" Grandpa was indignant at these words. "I make sure that our beloved Natalie feels very comfortable with us from the very first moment."

"Come on now, storyteller one! Please, come closer. Can I have an ID card please?"

"Yes of course. Here you go." I pulled the documents out of a small backpack and handed them to the woman.

Later, after checking in, I walked quickly towards where my room was. I just looked to see if the old man was following me. Apparently the front desk lady gave him another job to do.

I set the suitcases against the wall and sat on the bed. I looked around. The room is quite practical. Pastel colors of the walls, good quality furniture. Sheer curtains and curtains. There were several bottles of mineral water on the dresser. I laid down on the bed and looked at the ceiling. I lay there for an hour, wondering what I would be doing here for the next three weeks. And I had very interesting visions. A walk in the dark forest where I got lost, my whole body in blisters from biting mosquitoes by the lake, being trampled by a horse running freely around the boarding house, or just sitting in the room with the TV. I really didn't have the strength or the inclination to do anything.

I wasn't planning on going down to dinner. I took a bath and went to bed. My head was pounding, I felt uncomfortable, hoping that a long sleep would make me feel better.

Suddenly I heard a vigorous knock on the door. I sat up quickly and looked over there. Another knock. I didn't expect this.

"Hello, Natalie, are you there?" I heard a man's voice from behind the door.

"Who's there?" I asked as the knock came a third time.

"Anthony, we've already met."

I tensed up.

"What do you want from me?"

"You didn't come down to dinner. It can't be. I'm here to personally show you the way to the dining room. I invite you, today our Maggie did something special."

"Thank you, Anthony, but I'm not hungry," I said firmly.

"That's why you're so skinny. I understand. And now I'm inviting you to dinner, and I don't take no for an answer."

"When I really..."

"When I insist."

I analyzed the situation in seconds. Grandpa wouldn't let go and was going to torment me, which I absolutely wanted to avoid. I got up from bed.

"Okay, I'll just get dressed."

"Oh, that's better. I'll wait," the man replied, and began to sing an Italian song.

I pulled out a white shirt and jeans from my suitcase. I dressed quickly and left the room.

Mr. Anthony, with a smile on his lips, continued to sing, I must admit beautifully, with a nice accent. He also looked elegant in a blue shirt and black pants.

"I think those beautiful blue eyes will be happier after a hearty dinner," he said, and pointed the way.

I walked fast, erect. I wasn't usually that uptight. However, it is these recent events that have changed me a bit. I just wanted to sleep and be at peace, and at the same time be far away from myself, from the problems and thoughts flooding my mind. Until recently, I was a teacher, I worked in a high school, I taught young people English. It's quite a contact job, always among people. I liked it. I was involved in teaching. Being a teenager is a difficult time, so I tried to support and understand my students as much as possible. And so, day by day, it was taken from me. Literally everything – a sense of security, a home, a sense of belonging, dignity. This situation very clearly showed me that I am nothing, something worthless to throw away. It completely took my strength away.

I was thinking that I would sit somewhere in the back at a table, alone, eat quickly and go back to the room. That's what I was planning until I entered the room. There were no small tables in the dining room, just three very long tables, literally like at a wedding. In order to sit down, I had to have at least five companions next to me and in front of me. The meal is served on a buffet basis.

"Well, go ahead, darling, no one will eat you here" said Anthony with a smile.

I grabbed a plate and put some rice on it. It looked quite appetizing. Then I turned and looked at the gathered people. I was surprised how well everyone felt there, cheerful conversations, laughter, pats on the shoulder. I felt like everyone knew each other well. Age range from thirty to eighty years.

"Sit down, dear, you will be comfortable here" Anthony showed me a place next to the laughing ladies. "They're so amused they won't notice you," he said, gesturing to the women.

"Thank you," I replied and started eating. Moments later Anthony brought me a glass of red wine.

"Drink, my dear child, it will make your head roar a bit, it will drive away your sorrows" he said and left.

I took care of the food. Sometimes I glanced over my plate at the company. And then I actually tasted some wine. I was surprised by the taste. Delicate, subtle. I haven't had such good wine in a long time.

I felt I was being watched. I discreetly looked around. At the next table sat a very pretty dark-skinned woman with long black curls. She was wearing colorful clothes. She looked at me curiously but kindly. She didn't look away when I looked at her. She just smiled and nodded in greeting. I gave her a faint smile, the best I could manage today. Then I got up from the table and went to my room.

I had to walk past the front desk.

"You're not staying at the show?" said the old lady behind the counter, barely visible. "The cabaret is performing today."

"No no. I'm tired." I explained and walked away.

The next day I got up early in the morning, a few minutes after five. I got dressed and not really knowing what to do with myself, I went outside. Just off the huge terrace was a tasteful flowerbed of flowers and shrubs. There are several wooden benches with backrests nearby. I kept walking, towards the lake, only glancing to see if there wasn't a stray horse galloping wildly somewhere from the side of the field. Fortunately, it was quiet and peaceful, only the sound of crowing roosters could be heard from the neighbors. There was dew on the mowed lawn, soaking my sneakers a little. I slowly made my way to the lake. I felt cold from the water. The lake wasn't too big. Three boats tethered to it bobbed by the wooden dock. I stepped onto the dock, the boards creaking, but the whole thing felt solidly built. I stood motionless for a moment. After a while, I realized that I felt an incredible peace within myself. I stayed like that for quite a while until I heard a noise behind me. Someone was running. I turned around and glanced behind me.

Slim female silhouette, colorful tracksuit, dark sports shoes. And that storm of black curls tied in a ponytail. I immediately recognized the woman who had watched me at dinner last night. I didn't want to watch him go for his morning jog, so I turned back to the water.

But the woman ran up to me. She was out of breath.

"Hi," she greeted and held out her hand, "I'm Olivia."

I squeezed her hand.

"Natalie."

"Nice to have you here. I didn't have a chance to say hello yesterday, you left the company quickly."

"Journey fatigue," I explained casually. I looked at the woman, she must be in her forties. She had so much energy and joy that many teenagers could envy.

"I hope you'll find what you're looking for here," she said, which I didn't quite understand. "It's quite a special place."

"I haven't looked around yet."

"Very well, everything is ahead of you." You will definitely not be bored.

"I just need…" I hesitated, because what could I want here except a comfortable bed and food? "I just need peace." I added.

Olivia smiled understandingly.

We have a rule here. As you have noticed, the guests are of different ages, with different marital status, and the rule is that we are all equal here. Regardless of age, position, bank account balance. All equal. We call each other by name, so don't mind the familiarity of our other guests. I'm just warning you. We are like one big family here, living in friendship.

"I see, that's where the long tables come from..."

"Exactly. Just for people to talk to each other, get to know each other. Now we have times where everyone is closed in themselves and does not want or is afraid to show their true self, and friendship is needed for everyone."

"A noble idea," I admitted.

"These were my intentions when creating this place and I succeeded" said Olivia.

"Are you the owner of this boarding house?" I was surprised.

"Yes. We have a horse farm here. You like horses?"

"I don't know. I've never ridden a horse."

"Great, give it a try, maybe you'll like it? I'll check the timetable to see what time Lena can take you to study. Every day we organize something interesting. The bulletin board is in the reception area. I encourage you to use it."

„Thank you very much."

"Then hold on, I'm running on," she trotted away towards the building.

I went to breakfast first, ate quickly so as not to meet too many people and not get into unnecessary conversations. I noticed that people there were very nice and open, and I wasn't ready for that yet. I held my sadness and pain deep in my heart, I was at a stage where I needed solitude, not companionship. I felt bad about it. I knew I hadn't been myself in the last few days, which made me even more sad. It will pass, I repeated to myself. Everything will be back to normal in a while. I hoped so.

After breakfast, I walked around the guesthouse and explored the building. I wandered slowly through the corridors, sat on the terrace for a while. Upstairs I saw two huge training rooms. I entered one of them. One wall was dedicated to displaying videos and training materials. The screen was huge. Tables and chairs are lined up in a row. I sat on one of the tables and looked sadly around the room. I remembered my job. I should be at school now, the fourth graders were taking their final exams, they needed me. I should be there with them now. And here I am, in an empty training room. It would be nice to teach in such a place someday – I thought. I walked over to the lecturer's desk. I touched the smooth tabletop. I turned to the empty tables and chairs. If my disciples were here right now... What would I say to them? What could I say in such a situation? I couldn't think of anything, absolutely nothing. I sighed and took a few steps towards the exit. I looked at the big screen on the wall and then left. The other room was a bit smaller, one long narrow table with comfortable chairs around it. I only peeked through the open door, surely training sessions or meetings of important businessmen were also held here. I wonder if they used to come here.

I went down the stairs to the first floor, heading for the terrace, when a crying woman passed me. She left one of the rooms. She walked forward and sobbed, and at the same time she had so much joy in her eyes. She looked at me for a split second.

"It's good that I came here, really good" she said to herself, because it wasn't to me, I didn't know her.

I looked at her surprised. The woman descended the stairs to the ground floor, while I glanced at the plaque on the wall by the door of the room she had just left. There was an inscription on them: "Olivia's office." Well, Olivia didn't seem like the type to make a fifty-year-old woman cry, I thought. But I didn't care about it any longer. I went out onto the terrace and sat in a wicker chair. The weather was pleasant, warm and windless. I saw how many people were walking around the vast area of the yard, others went for a further hike to the lake or to the forest. Three people led the saddled horses out of the stable. Mr. Anthony greeted the next guests in the parking lot. I stared at it for a long moment, without much interest, then closed my eyes. And as soon as I closed my eyes, the nightmares and immense regret returned. I kept replaying that conversation with Evelyn, my would-be mother-in-law, in my mind. How could she say that to me, how could she treat me so badly? I didn't deserve this! She ruined my life. She destroyed my future, she humiliated me. And Greg. His behavior hurt too much. Does he regret not going with me at all? Do you miss? Was our relationship just a farce? a lie? Is he mad at me? Does he care about me at all? He didn't take my side, he let me go. Just like that, without a word. He didn't even call to check on me.

I felt tears under my eyelids. But as I pulled myself together, I heard someone coming. Two women entered the terrace. They were giggling, talking to each other with enthusiasm. I didn't care. I didn't even look at them. They sat on two of the five armchairs, it was a small terrace on the first floor, there was no room for anything else. After a few minutes the women left and I was alone again. I closed my eyes again and thought. I was thinking back to the day I met Greg, to our first meetings. He seemed like such a nice, laid back guy. He wasn't conceited, he was rather aloof. Smart, hardworking. I thought that together we would build something cool, durable… How was I supposed to trust others from that moment on?

I sat there for a long time, tossed with emotions, when I heard a voice:

"It's such a beautiful day, it's a waste of sadness."

I looked behind me. Olivia was standing in the doorway smiling and looking at me.

"Probably so," I replied. I hoped he had a lot of work to do and would be gone soon. However, that did not happen. Olivia sat down too. She focused all her attention on me. I sat up straight in my chair, suddenly uncomfortable.

As promised, I checked. Lena can take you for riding lessons at

3:00. She will be waiting for you, she said.

"Is it already? Should I start today?" I was surprised.

"Whenever you want. Why wait? We have plenty of attractions here, later there may be no time."

"All right. Thank you."

"The best way to cope with sorrows is to set the body in motion. It's the best medicine."

"Do you see my sorrows in me like that?" I asked, downcast.

"Yes, half a kilometer at least, but don't worry. Everyone has their worries. It's just a matter of how you approach them" said Olivia.

I looked at her questioningly.

"The problem will not be solved by such constant dithering and brooding. Let it go for a day or two, and maybe then the solution will come by itself...

"It's not that simple," I replied. What could this woman know about problems, having a beautiful boarding house full of guests? She also looked blooming, joy in her eyes, a smile on her face. What could she know about me and my problems? I got a little nervous.

"Each of us always has a choice" said Olivia.

"I had no choice," I replied, full of emotion. I felt anger rising in me. I didn't want to talk to this woman at all. What did she come here for? He won't understand me anyway.

"You always have a choice," Olivia said gently. "Even now. You can sit here and grieve, trying to control the galloping thoughts in your head, or you can go to the lake and go boating. You can go for a walk. You can tell yourself that you are resting from everything today. You have a choice. And you are the one who decides what your day will look like right now. Nice or hopeless."

I didn't answer. Olivia got up and left, leaving me alone. More precisely, not alone, but with my sadness, regret, anger, hopelessness and fear for the future. What was I supposed to do next? Which way to go? What was Olivia talking about here?! About the choice? And what choice did I have in the way my life turned out? How could I do anything? It was Evelyn who decided for me. I was just an insignificant pawn in this damn game.

I jumped to my feet and walked to my room. I threw myself on the bed and let the tears fall as much as they wanted.

I washed my face with cold water. I really didn't give a shit what I looked like - puffy eyes, gray complexion, blank, expressionless look. I cried out the worst emotions, so I was quiet. I put on jeans and a T-shirt and left the room. I'm mandatory, so at three o'clock I showed up at the stables. I stood for a moment by the wide open, huge, wooden door and stared into the space ahead. I smelled the horses, heard them neighing. I've never been to any stables. I didn't care now. I will fall off the horse, I will fall, I will hold on, I will hold on, no one will cry for me. With that attitude, I took it a step further. It was quite dark there.

"Good morning," a young girl called from the back of the room, "I'm on my way."

I backed off slowly. A girl was coming towards me, leading a horse. I watched calmly as the huge animal, neighing happily, stepped out of the dark stable into the sun.

"Natalie, right?" the girl called out friendly "My name is Lena. I will teach you riding. Please, come closer." The horse was so big.

"Have you ever ridden a horse before?" she asked.

"NO. I've never been on a horse" I confessed.

"All right. I'll keep the mare on the rope the whole time, so you have nothing to fear. If you want, you can stroke her muzzle. He loves it."

"What is her name?" I asked, reaching my hand carefully to the horse's mouth.

"Tina"

Tina let me pet her. Weird feeling. When I was a little girl, I had a dog at home, but a horse is definitely not the same.

"Remember, don't force anything, if you feel any discomfort, we can stop immediately and stop studying," Lena said. "So, shall we jump in?" I'll help you. Here, put your foot in and push yourself off the ground. Oh yeah, great.

I got on the mare and gripped the reins tightly. Tina tilted her head down slightly, and I felt like I was about to fall. I instinctively leaned back.

"Calm down, everything's fine. Relax," Lena told me.

Well, that's easy for her to say, I thought. I sat tense and controlled every little movement. There was silence for a moment. Lena looked at me kindly.

"Where are you from?" she asked after a moment.

"That's a pretty hard question," I replied. "How about a different set?"

"I can see you're tense." I just wanted to distract you. We don't have to talk if you don't want to," she said in a pleasant voice.

"Sorry. It's not that I wanted to be rude" I said because I felt stupid. "I just don't have a home anymore. Now I live here, later I don't know yet."

"I see."

I looked at Lena. She might not have been twenty years old. Shapely, with a dark complexion and a storm of black curls tied in a ponytail.

"How long have you been working with horses?" I asked. Lena was nice to me and kind, and didn't want to be intrusive. And driving in silence was a bit uncomfortable in this case.

"Eight years," she replied, glancing at me happily. "I love horses. They are wonderful. At the beginning there were only two mares in this stable, now we have a total of eleven horses. They are of different ages."

In the evenings, after I finish work, I drive my White Arrow on a crazy trip. I feel freedom then, the wind in my hair - a great feeling. If you enjoy horseback riding, maybe someday you'll gallop into such open spaces.

The mare kept walking slowly, and I tried to stay straight on her back. I was relaxing a bit. Somehow it was hard for me to imagine an independent expedition on any horse. Sitting in the saddle for the first time was quite an interesting experience. Will I repeat it? Hard to say.

After a few circles I felt pain in the ass and all the muscles, so I jumped off the horse with relief.

"Thank you very much. Do I have to pay for driving lessons with you?" I turned to Lena as she happily patted Tina's rump.

"Learning to drive is such a bonus for staying with us in the guesthouse. You don't have to pay anything extra" she replied.

"Oh, that's nice," I said, surprised, "Is it like this for all guests?"

"Of course, only in moderation, horses also need to rest. Therefore, you need to make an appointment for lessons or rides in advance. Sign you up for tomorrow?"

I looked at her confused. "Another lesson?"

"I don't know."

"One lesson isn't enough to tell if you like it," Lena said.

"Okay, that could be tomorrow."

"I'm free at three o'clock, so come on over."

"Great thanks."

I walked towards the boarding house. I didn't look around, just stared down at the freshly mowed lawn. I didn't even realize when Mr. Anthony approached me.

"Natalie my dear, do you remember our most important rule?" he asked in a very serious tone. "I mentioned it the day you arrived."

I stopped and looked at the man in surprise. He was not much taller than me, today wearing short jeans and a sleeveless shirt. Plus flip flops.

"What rule?" I asked, searching my memory for some rule book, it was actually hung on the walls of every floor, but who would read it? Have I forgotten something or have I behaved in the wrong way?

"Today is an exceptionally warm and sunny day" Anthony continued, looking at me disapprovingly "and as I mentioned earlier, the most important rule, for many years, has been that women, especially young girls, must wear only shorts or skirts. You need to tan your legs, show them to the sun. And you in jeans again, baby!"

„Have a nice afternoon, Mr. Anthony" I said and left. I was climbing the stairs quickly, then suddenly I turned around for a moment. The older, withered man was obviously enjoying my ass.

In the evening, after dinner, I lay in bed and looked at my mobile phone. No one has called in the last few days. Nobody. The whole world has forgotten about me. Even my own sister, Eve. I understand, she had the most important show in her career to prepare, but not to send one text message? What about work colleagues? I made friends with some. Greg was also silent. Several times I wanted to text him, I had already entered the text of the message, and then in moments of uncertainty I deleted it.

Downstairs, on the ground floor, after dinner, a dance party began. Of course I didn't, because why? What would I do there? Watching other people have fun when everything pissed me off? I heard music, laughter, screams. I lay in bed, staring at the ceiling. I could not fall asleep. It was still early, it was light outside the window, the setting sun cast a red glow on the slightly cloudy sky. I wasn't in the mood for anything. I was suffocated by a great depression, which grew stronger by the minute, I had the impression that I was about to run out of breath. I sat on the bed. I started breathing deeply through my mouth. It didn't help. I got up and went out to the balcony. The crisp air swept over me, making me shiver. What is happening with me? Why do I feel so strange? What is it about? Nothing hurts, just this feeling of lack of air, as if the lungs are about to refuse to obey. The heart was beating fast. I got scared. I leaned against the wall and tried to catch my breath. I focused completely on the signals coming from my body. It was a little better now. The legs stopped shaking. I stood like that for about half an hour until I felt fine. I went back to my room and closed the balcony door behind me. There was no way to sleep, I was still slightly aroused. The room seemed too small to me, I needed space. I quickly changed into jeans and a long sleeved shirt. I walked out into the hallway and then briskly down the stairs to the exit of the building. I stopped only at the flower bed. I sat on one of the wooden benches. It's better now. A few very deep breaths and finally calm down. I rested my elbows on my knees and hid my face in my hands. I sat in this position until the sounds from around me began to reach me. Music from the party from the guesthouse, conversations of walking guests, a slight hum of the warm wind.

I straightened up and looked around discreetly. A couple nearby me was arguing fiercely, someone else chuckled in amusement. An elderly couple walked past me. The man had clear sinus problems. He was sniffling heavily. The woman pulled out a pack of tissues from her purse.

"Here, take a sniffle," she handed one.

"No need," replied the man, "I've already taken a sip."

"Behave yourself," his wife snapped. She was giving a lecture on culture when they moved on.

I was left alone, in blissful peace. I stared ahead intently. The sun had already set, it was getting dark, only the lanterns illuminated the darkness. I thought the environment suited me very well. The large space, few buildings and proximity to nature made me feel closer to myself. A little mongrel ran up to me, looked, wagged its tail, then curled up on the ground at my feet. I stroked him gently.

"Good evening, may I sit down?" I heard a voice behind me. I leaned back and looked behind me. It was Olivia.

"Good evening. Of course, please. But let me warn you that I'm a lousy conversationalist today."

Olivia sat down. She wrapped her shawl more tightly.

"Sometimes it's nice to be silent," she said, "and sometimes it's good to talk. Just to let out all the unwanted emotions."

"Who would want to hear about my confused emotions?"

"I am," she replied honestly, and looked at me expectantly.

"Really? Got nothing else to do?" I wondered, glancing at the fun-filled boarding house.

"Mom, I like helping people, each of my guests is equally important. You are important to me too. Will you tell me what's going on?"

I eyed Olivia suspiciously. Nobody has ever talked to me like this.

I didn't know this woman. Why should I trust her and open up to her? Why would I say anything about myself? And yet I did. One look at her, a warm smile. She didn't talk unnecessarily, she just waited for me to start.

"I got a little lost in life" as I said the first sentence, then it was better. "I'm at the point where I don't know what to do next. What should I do, how should I live… I no longer have a home, job, fiancé, my own family doesn't give a shit about me. Everything fell apart within three days. I thought I was a good person and it's hard for me to accept that."

"What was built on illusion crumbled" said Olivia. "That's good sometimes. You're suffering now, and it's quite natural. See, you can now build a new future based on truth. This is a point from which you can exit in any direction. Do a lot of fantastic things in life, be happy and fulfilled. I guarantee you it will."

"Where do you get that confidence from?" There was a lot of pain and disbelief in my voice. "I'm a hopeless case."

"You are not. I assure you." She smiled slightly. "What happened in those three days?"

"I was going to get married. Everything was ready, the wedding, the beautiful setting… I moved in with him and his mother in their big house. The would-be mother-in-law tried to subdue me in a very blunt way. I couldn't agree to it. She wanted to break me mentally. And my would-be husband sided with my mother. Without saying a word, he watched as I packed up and ran out of there. As revenge, my mother-in-law got me fired immediately. I have no more to look for."

"And what are you grieving about now?" Olivia asked softly. "About standing up for yourself?" Do you mourn that you didn't let your future go to waste? That you didn't marry a boy who hadn't yet grown up to be a man? You fought for yourself dear! You are young, you have your whole life ahead of you. You don't understand it yet, but you did the best you could! You should drink champagne and celebrate your freedom with joy!

"But…" I was choked. I was shocked by Olivia's statement. Not what I expected, not words like that. "But I am distraught. Everything collapsed on me…"

"What everything? Imagine you stayed with them, and what would your everyday life look like? Would you be happy and content?"

I sat still, thoughts running through my head.

"Right," Olivia commented.

"But it's not like that…" I whispered and stopped the sentence.

"Celebrate your freedom, love! And build your life boldly and in harmony with yourself. It's your life, you decide how it will look like. Living with toxic people will never bring happiness, it will only ruin your self-esteem. You need to run away from such people quickly, which you just did.

I didn't answer. We sat in silence for a moment, then Olivia patted me gently on the shoulder, then walked away leaving me alone with my thoughts. I would never view my situation that way.

I wasn't so naive as to believe things would change after marriage. How long could I endure them? Who exactly was Greg? I felt like I didn't know him at all. He's been showing some kind of fake mask all these months, and I fell for it. And I wanted to start a family with someone like that! Have children. Greg always listened to his mother and fulfilled her wishes immediately. Sometimes he would suddenly interrupt our meetings because my mother needed something. I saw nothing wrong with it. I had little contact with Evelyn before. Greg rarely took me to his house, and when we were at his place, it was so strange that my mother was not there at the time. It was Evelyn who insisted that I move and renovate the floor with my money. I felt bad there. When I moved in with them, Evelyn constantly scolded me and corrected me, I thought that there was something wrong with me, that I was behaving inappropriately. It was her home, her habits, and I had to adapt. I tried to understand it. What I couldn't understand was the scrutiny, the inquisitive questions, why I came home later, what kept me, who I met. And that scene in the cafe, when I met my friend Simon - it lit a warning light in my head. Greg was submissive, but I wasn't going to. I didn't want to be anyone's slave!

I suddenly realized what Olivia had said. It came to me! She was right! I felt so relieved that I almost cried. Enough tears, enough despair!

I smiled. I happily took a few deep breaths. I did the right thing. I took care of myself, I fought. I woke up full of enthusiasm.

And then I sat down right away. And how am I supposed to build this new future of mine without a home, without a job? With what? The money for the sold apartment is not enough even for the smallest studio apartment in Warsaw. Nice perspective. Rent something? Maybe in another city? But where? I don't know anyone, anywhere except

Piaseczno. And the depression returned again.

I'll think about it tomorrow, I decided, and went to my room. On the way, I swiped half a bottle of red wine from the party table. I was going to celebrate my freedom.

I slept quite well there. Peace, quiet, clean, crisp air. I would get up early, just wake up and go out on the balcony to watch the world go by. The view from the balcony was quite nice. A playground for children, a well-maintained green belt, garden thujas, and further, above the fence, you can see the outline of the mountains. One day I'll get in my car and go on a day trip to the mountains. As soon as I get some strength. Recent experiences have greatly weakened my body and psyche. I had the feeling that time flowed completely differently there, although I didn't glance at my watch very often. I just was. For the first time in so long, I was alone with myself. With your sorrows and regrets. Before, I was distracted all the time, there was work, meetings with friends, shopping, cleaning, television. And there I had nothing but peace and quiet and my own company. I haven't been able to pinpoint if it's good for me or not yet. Then I really saw that I was. I noticed myself. It was a strange feeling for me. I looked at myself kind of sidEveys and I didn't like what I saw - a scared, depressed girl trying to make her way in the world. It was all me.

After what Olivia told me recently, I felt calmer. Despair was completely gone, but questions arose, why did this happen to me, why did I have to meet Greg? Why did he come in my way, why this whole situation? Couldn't it have been avoided? Why has it gone this far? It was so humiliating when Eve texted her family canceling the wedding invitation. After receiving the letter, everyone called her with questions.

To distract myself from my thoughts for a while, I dressed warmly and left the building. It was very early. There was an opportunity to make a coffee in the cafeteria, so after a while I sat down on the terrace with a cup of double espresso. It was reasonably warm, but I had zipped up my hoodie - recently I needed an extra layer of clothing, as if I wanted to keep warm for the future. An additional sweater or sweatshirt was a protective armor for me. The terrace was large, wooden, there were two solid benches with backrests, made of high-gloss oak boards. There was a long table in the center. I was quite comfortable. A light breeze blew around me, and I could feel the moisture in the air. From here I had a perfect view of the entire yard, the flower bed, the paved path winding through the ornamental bushes. I knew there was a lake beyond that wide strip of lawn. Metal benches with ornate ornaments lined the alley, inviting you to linger. The whole composition was complemented by garden lamps in the shape of lanterns. In the backyard, closer to the fence, there was a stable and an outbuilding. I glanced to my right, at the row of neatly lined cars, the rest of the lot blocked off by the guesthouse. My car was no longer visible from there.

Two hours later, I was still stuck in the same place. The sun was shining brighter now, and it was a beautiful day. From the main entrance of the guesthouse, I heard a buzz of conversation. I looked in that direction. A group of women dressed in sportswear was approaching. Each of them held an exercise mat and a bottle of mineral water in their hands. I watched them with interest. Olivia was last. She was talking on the phone. When she saw me, she exclaimed:

"Will you join us? You're welcome. Just take the mat from the reception" after these words she continued the conversation. But she watched my reaction.

"Maybe another time," I said, because I didn't feel like practicing. I preferred to stay on the terrace with my cup of coffee. Besides, my inner thighs and butt hurt, probably from the soreness from yesterday's riding lesson.

I watched the women go. They moved on to the lawn, closer to the orchard. They spread the mats, positioned themselves and waited for Olivia's first move. Olivia started exercising, it turned out that she was teaching yoga. From a distance, I could see how fit she was, how some of the older women were doing fantastically, as if they had been working out for years. Maybe it was? All movements smooth, precise. It was nice to look at. I admired these women for wanting to get up earlier and treat themselves to such an active start to the day before breakfast.

Moments later, I entered the building. I stayed at the front desk. Straight ahead was furniture made of light wood, the front plate in the shape of a semicircle. On one side of the counter was a white blooming orchid, and on the other a ceramic bowl filled with small candies. The walls were a warm shade of cappuccino, their only decoration was the quote "It's time to move on and give yourself a chance." I read that text every time I passed that way and wondered what wisdom it was supposed to convey. Somehow he didn't speak to me. To the left of the reception desk entrance, right by the window overlooking the parking lot, were six brown armchairs with small tables between them. I liked the place, it felt like a warm, cozy room.

I glanced at the bulletin board on the rack. Pinned to it was a piece of paper with the schedule for the next three days. At 7:30 yoga, in the evening a bonfire for the ladies, the gentlemen were supposed to watch the match at that time. The next day in the morning at 7:30 meditation and in the evening a barbecue. It looked interesting, and I was thinking about trying some attractions. There were also leaflets on the board about organized trips to the mountains or to nearby attractive tourist destinations. I also learned that the guest house has a tennis court, gym, jacuzzi and sauna. And then, without much emotion, I went to breakfast.

I spent the morning on the terrace. There was a bookshelf in the main hall with books you could borrow. So I picked up one, a historical novel, and started reading. Moderately addictive. My face must have been blurred because a woman came up to me and asked if I was okay.

"Okay," I replied, surprised. "Do I look like there's something wrong with me?"

"I'm sorry," the woman replied. "But you're so sad." It's over 26 degrees outside and you're wearing this thick sweater. Are you really cold? Maybe you have a fever?

The woman looked concerned, she certainly had the best of intentions.

I looked at my clothes. In fact, I didn't even notice that I was still wearing the thick sweater I had put on early in the morning. Plus jeans and sneakers. And everyone around was wearing summer clothes.

"I'm fine, I assure you." I smiled. "Yeah, I forgot to get changed." I'm sitting in the shade reading a novel set in winter in Russia. I forgot about the whole world - I was trying to be nice.

"Then I don't mind," the woman replied, and headed toward the stables.

"Thank you for your concern," I said louder so she could hear. She turned for a moment and nodded.

I closed the book and placed it on the wooden table. I sighed. I had to manage. Everyone saw my sadness. It didn't make me better.

A few minutes later, Olivia came over to me. As always, full of energy and good humor.

"I'd like to take you to one nice place, what do you say?" she asked.

"And where is this place?"

"Very close, only you'll be more comfortable in leggings and a t-shirt," she suggested. "Maybe fifteen minutes?"

"Sure," I replied. What else had I to do?

I went to the same place on the terrace. I was dressed for sports. I waited a while. Olivia suddenly appeared at my side, out of nowhere she came.

"Come!" she yelled.

We walked to the other side of the long boarding house. There was a separate entrance.

"Did you know that unexpressed emotions stay in the body and after some time cause discomfort or even pain? If stress accumulates over many years and finds no outlet, it freezes in the body and can lead to serious illness. When the body is tense, so contracted, the flow of energy is blocked and everything in the body functions worse. If anything bad happens in your life, you react emotionally, suppress your feelings, and a moment later it reflects physically in your body. This can be very easily observed as the stomach contracts, the muscles tense. You just have to learn to let go and get your emotions out of your body as quickly as possible. I know that sounds weird, but it's true. We're already there."

We entered the mini gym. A few basic devices, a stationary bike, exercise benches, barbells, a treadmill, and at the end there was a punching bag for the box, and that's where Olivia took me. She picked up the gloves from the floor and handed them to me. She put on the second one.

"Don't make such a surprised face" she laughed "It will help you, you'll see. Have you boxed yet?"

"No," I answered truthfully. I put on gloves.

"Okay, I'll show you how to hit." First thing... there are papers and a pen and duct tape on the windowsill. You can draw a caricature on a piece of paper, write a name, or whatever you want and stick it on the bag, it gives an extra kick, or without a piece of paper. It can be too. See, you punch like this, but not with just your hand, but hard, with your whole body, so that the force comes out of your shoulder, and you hit. Oh yes, she delivered the first punch. "See, same with kicks, you hit your leg like this, the power comes from the hip. Give yourself a break. There's no one here yet, so scream your heart out and box, give it your all. Any questions?

"No, I have no questions," I replied. I was looking at the punching bag, just what I needed. I've had enough of apathy, regret, anger and sadness, maybe this will wake me up from this lethargy. Three cups of double espresso failed, so how about some training? Why not ?

"Then I'll leave you alone, enjoy yourself," Olivia said, then left.

I stood still for a moment, then I tapped the sack lightly, it rocked, then I tapped again. I thought about Evelyn, about how badly she had treated me. Immediately I felt a huge anger, I kicked the bag hard. Then again and again. In my mind, I saw the figure of Greg, anger intensified. Then the headmaster of the school - why did he allow it? I was a good teacher, I wonder how Evelyn made him fire me from work? Or was she blackmailed? She needed less than a quarter of an hour to get things done. Incredible.

I was pounding my fists like crazy. It was very exhausting. After more kicks, I gave short whoops.

I fell to the floor helpless. I sat down and leaned against the wall, breathing deeply. However, I got up after a while and faced the punching bag again. I looked at him as an enemy, I was throwing punches and he couldn't hit me back.

During another break, while I was leaning against the stationary bike, all sweaty, a man entered the room. He looked around and greeted.

"Hi, can I join? I will not disturb?" He asked. He looked to be in his forties, slim, tall, dark brown, with a few days' stubble on his face. His sincere gaze and slight smile made him trustworthy.

"There you go, I'm done anyway," I said, and took off my gloves. I put them on the floor by the wall. I felt my body tremble from exertion.

"Do you box?" the man asked.

"Just started today. And I think I'll train tomorrow too. Have fun." I went away.

After lunch, at three o'clock, I had an appointment to go horseback riding, so I arrived at the stables on time. Lena was already waiting.

"Hi," I greeted.

"Hi, what's that?" we start? she asked with enthusiasm in her voice.

"Yeah, just saying hello to Tina." I walked over to the mare, touched her muzzle, and stroked her lightly. I jumped on the saddle. It was weird again. I tensed my body, which immediately began to feel the effects of training in the gym and yesterday's horse ride. I straightened up.

I talked to Lena for a long time about her work, about her great love for horses. I admired her for the passion with which she spoke. She had amazing knowledge and was able to convey it in such a way that I listened with curiosity. I saw the animal world from a completely different perspective, and as a result, I patted Tina's neck with affection and gratitude.

Finally, I wanted to know a bit about the attractions offered by the guest house.

"I saw a lot of women practicing yoga this morning. I admit it impressed me. Interesting plans for tomorrow. Is it always like this here? I asked. "I've never seen a guest house like this before.

"Yes, it is quite a specific place, different from all the others. My mother is amazing, she created this unique place and people come back here, they feel good here..."

"Your mom?" I was surprised.

"I'm Olivia's daughter," she smiled.

How could I not have guessed? Same curly black hair, dark skin, demeanor, amazing. I would never have guessed that Olivia had an adult daughter.

"Mom tries to make each of our guests find themselves here, that's why she organizes yoga, meditation, meetings, talks ... but I won't reveal all the details. I encourage you, it's really worth using."

"And all this in the price of the stay?" I asked.

"You got a paid voucher, right? Lena looked at me with a smile and understanding."

"Exactly. How did you know?"

"Because if you were paying for your stay yourself, you wouldn't be asking this question," Lena explained.

"I do not really understand."

"The price per night is so high that you have access to everything."

"Do you have any seasons here? When are there fewer people?"

"We have guests all the time, as I mentioned, this is a special place. You'll understand it soon. you will see. In three weeks, when you leave here, you'll want to come back here."

"Sounds intriguing."

"So next time I suggest going to yoga."

Focused on my sore ass, I was coming back from riding lessons. I wanted to massage it, but it might look a bit weird. I preferred not to risk it.

I saw an interesting event. A group of men of different ages and abilities organized a wood chopping competition. I stopped to look at it. I was quite far away, but the view was perfect. Gentlemen undressed, with bare torsos, brandished axes and split a prepared, cut tree trunk. Anthony gave instructions, flexed his emaciated, seventy-year-old body and showed others how to hit wood with an axe. Apparently the other gentlemen didn't know that. I noticed that they were having a great time doing it - a bit of competition, joking, all in a good, friendly atmosphere.

I thought it was amazing how easy it was to get a large group of people together and do something cool with them. Do you need any special abilities to be charismatic? I lay in bed all afternoon and rested. I looked at the inn's website. Nicely done, the main photo with the name "Bella Vita", several smaller photos showing groups of people having fun around a campfire by the lake, horseback riding and other activities. The price for the stay was nowhere to be found - do you want to know? call. I read guest reviews. All positive, full of delight. Olivia was even described as a miracle worker, a wonderful woman who created a unique place. Delights over food, surroundings, fantastic organization of additional attractions. The list of opinions was very long.

I was glad to find such a place. I was still resting on my bed when my mother called. I stared at my phone screen for a long moment, debating whether or not to answer. But finally I did it:

"Hi, Mom," I said.

"Natalie, darling, how are you feeling?" Eve said you were resting. "That's good. Tell me, what's up with you? I heard in the handset."

"All good. And with you?"

"Ah, you know how it is with me, I'm always working, I don't have time for anything. You know, I was very concerned about canceling the wedding. You've never been impulsive, but maybe you should reconsider? Greg is a pretty good match, from a rich family. You'd have a comfortable life, you wouldn't have to travel abroad for money like I do."

"Mom…" I started reproachfully, but she cut me off.

"I know, I know, I'm not supposed to interfere, you're right, but you're already twenty-nine, my dear. What are you waiting for? When are you going to start a family?"

"This is not a good time to be thinking about it," I said dejectedly.

"You have to think about the future. is to think about the future.

Guys make mistakes, but you have to forgive them. Think about it. Guys get lost, make bad decisions, and we women are there to straighten them out."

"I do not agree with this theory, there are plenty of valuable, smart men."

"Then why are you alone?"

"Because I made a mistake, I chose wrong."

"You can't just write people off like that. Will you try to forgive Greg?"

"He hasn't heard from me since I moved out, he obviously doesn't care."

"I will talk to him."

"NO! NO!" I almost screamed into the phone. "Do not do this. There will be no wedding. Forgive me, but I don't care about the wealth of Greg's family. I never want to see them again. Goodbye, Mom, have a nice afternoon" and I hung up. I sighed.

The relationship with the mother was difficult. We both tried, but sometimes it didn't work out. My parents left to work in Germany when I was nine. They left me and my six-year-old sister in the care of my grandmother. I had to grow up very quickly. Learn to cook, clean, take care of the house and take care of all the basic duties. Grandma had her life of a happy retiree and she didn't like moving into our house and taking care of two adolescent girls. She had her own company, gossip, wine meetings and generally a very light approach to life. We couldn't count on it too much.

My parents rarely came. They always sent lots of money, gifts, beautiful clothes. We didn't need that. It was a very difficult time for me and Eve, we took care of each other. After a few years, the parents separated. The father was in a relationship with a younger woman, they raised a son together. So I had a brother that I only saw in uploaded photos. My mother had been alone for two years. Parents still lived in the Munich area and neither of them planned to return to Poland.

In the evening, I learned the motive behind the gentlemen's hard work chopping wood. It turned out that they were preparing a bonfire for the ladies, which was to take place after dark, and at that time they sat down with the whole male group in one large hall to watch an important match. Four cases of beer were already waiting for them chilled on the table. I went to the planned bonfire. I just wanted to sit for a while, see what would happen and go back to my room. However, that did not happen. What happened there stayed in my memory for a long time.

The fire was burning, sparks flying high. All around, on wooden benches, were sitting laughing women of different ages. They had a great time. I've already met them. We met in the dining room for meals, sometimes we passed each other in the corridor or yard. I didn't talk to them, I even avoided contact with others, I needed solitude. Now, however, I decided to loosen the wall I had built around myself a bit. When I came to the bonfire, I sat in an empty seat and greeted everyone in general. Someone was still coming.

Olivia played the guitar. Apparently, she also listened to the conversations, because at one point she caught how one woman addressed the other very formally, showering with the titles of doctor.

"Darlings, I remind you, we are all equal here. We call each other by name, no matter who has what achievements, titles, riches and who he doesn't know. We're pulling out, dear ladies, a stick from the ass, do we understand each other?"

There was a buzz of contentment and agreement all around.

"This is our holiday, we play, relax, make friends" Olivia continued. She continued playing the guitar. "Thanks to the kindness of your husbands, we have a wonderful bonfire. They, as you probably already know, prepared the wood, benches and all the comforts that we have here. And may the team they support win today! she exclaimed the last sentence.

I smiled at the happy company. The energy that floated there made the mood improve and all worries disappeared. I relaxed a bit.

"My dear," continued Olivia. "We are gathered here to remember how great we are! Important! Smart! So many women forget about it, it is underestimated. There is so much beauty in us, love - Olivia stopped playing and looked at the gathered. "I wanted to talk to you about this. I would like each of us to remember who we really are: a wonderful, wonderful woman. So that each of us, looking in the mirror, smiles happily at her reflection. May we always remember and be completely convinced that we are valuable. Always. We are perfect as we are now. I see that not everyone agrees with me" she said, looking at the women's reaction. Some sighed, others became sad, others exclaimed "yes! We are great!"

"It's not that easy being thirty pounds overweight," my bench neighbor said.

"Right," said someone from behind.

"Hilda, remind me how many children you gave birth to?" asked

Olivia.

"Three."

"Exactly, you gave life to three beautiful creatures, you breastfed your own, your body had to gain strength to cope with raising children, work and taking care of the whole house.

Your legs are strong because you had a long way to go in life, your arms are extended because you cradled your children in them. You carried heavy bags of groceries to feed your family. Love your body, it's strong, it's beautiful, it's yours, just the way it is. There is no need to compare yourself to others, because each of us is different, everyone has a different path to follow and different problems to overcome. You have a healthy body and it is the greatest treasure, so love it. It's great to take care of yourself, it's great to dress in nice dresses, to do makeup. The main thing is a smile, good mood, kindness. It determines whether we are liked and accepted. The most important thing is that we accept ourselves. This gives us strength and power. Each of us has it here, inside" Olivia put her hand in the middle of her chest. "Incredible power that some people don't even know about, and I assure you that this power is in each of us. Do you know what is the cause of most of the world's problems?" She paused for a moment, watching the ladies' reactions. "Lack of love, lack of self-understanding. This is the basis. We are not talking about vanity and haughtiness here, because fear is hidden behind such behavior. Loving yourself is support at every step, always standing by your side, setting boundaries and not allowing others to cross these boundaries. It is allowing ourselves to rest when we are tired. It's saying "no" if you disagree with something."

"And indulgence with sweets," someone shouted from behind.

There was laughter, jokes.

"I assure you that if a woman truly loves herself, she will think twice about reaching for a donut. Healthy, conscious eating is one of the side effects of loving yourself."

You know that we eat our sorrows with sweets. Where do sorrows come from? From the feeling of lack. What are we missing then? Love. Whatever we do in life, everything is lined with it. Are you familiar with bad days, fatigue? Trying and still nothing works out, constant failures and problems? Annoyance, longing for something we can't even pinpoint exactly? The feeling that every day is the same and basically nothing changes? Going around in circles like in a spinning wheel? That happy moments happen so rarely and last only a short moment? That others look happy, but it's just so hard and senseless for us.

.. we know that, don't we? And we don't really know how to get out of it to feel better ... I'll tell you that there is only one medicine to get out of this state, not for a moment, but forever. Very effective. It's about accepting yourself, loving yourself, understanding who you are, giving yourself what you need. Understanding that you are a valuable person, that you deserve the best. Even if you have a demanding husband and a bunch of children, taking care of your own needs is very important. What does it give us? When we love ourselves, we are more understanding, calmer, and more confident. The feeling of emptiness and meaninglessness disappears. This, of course, applies to every person on earth. If we love ourselves, fear and fear disappear, no one can hurt us. Do you want to feel like this?

There were nods, some comments.

"You can, I assure you! It's a matter of looking at yourself differently, letting go of what holds us so tight, letting go of criticism, letting go of worrying about what others will say. Let others say what they want! You know best what you need, my dear ones, and do not let others tell you what to do, what to do. You hear texts like this all the time: because it's not appropriate, because it's necessary, that's what everyone does, you're too old, too young, too thin. Let everyone do what they want, but I live as I want" she pointed her hands at herself. It's my life and I decide what it looks like. And let me tell you that my life, after I understood all this and truly loved myself, looks really great. I have a question - when were you on a walk alone? Just to be together? I know it's very difficult, people usually run away from such moments, they are afraid of it. They immediately reach for the TV remote or cell phone. Or they do whatever it takes to take their minds off what matters most. Such a look inside yourself is terrifying at first, because we never know what we will find there, we may not like it. And this is a very important step to self-acceptance. We need to get to know this wonderful being that we are. Find out what is important to us, what we like. For example, are Thursday teas at my mother-in-law's really fun, or am I doing it because it's expected of me? Do I really like donuts or do I eat them because all my friends eat donuts? Do I watch the show because I'm interested or because my neighbors watch it and talk about it all the time? Do I like walking? Why didn't I sign up for the dance class I've been dreaming about? Do I want more? What makes me happy? What really moves me? - Lots of questions to be answered.

She paused for a moment, looked at the audience, then continued.

"Tomorrow, before lunch, I invite you to take a lonely walk and ask yourself these questions. See what answers come to you. Don't be afraid of it. My beloved women, say warm words to each other, such as: I am beautiful, I can handle it, I am smart and wonderful. After all, you say such words to your children, husbands. You give so much, support, help ... And when will you take care of yourself? When will it be time to fulfill your dreams? You are worth it! That's why you say kind, supportive words to yourself up to 150 times a day. Until you believe that it is. It will feel weird at first, but it will quickly become a good habit. Just talking to yourself in this way will make a difference in your life. And don't criticize yourself, because why? Each of us tries our best every day, we always do everything with the best intentions. And if something goes wrong, you have to remember one very important rule: there are no failures, there are only lessons, opportunities to learn something new.

I felt a tightness in my throat. I was very encouraged by Olivia's speech and I wanted to believe that what she said was true. I looked around, I wasn't the only one affected by her words. The neighbors from the bench sighed with hope.

The fire was burning red, warming the already warm air. Above us, the stars shone scattered in the navy blue sky, the wind stopped completely. It was so peaceful. I took off my shirt and put it on my lap.

Olivia, after a sip of water, continued her speech, so I focused all my attention on her.

"Now I'm going to say something to each of you. Each of you has the right to build a happy, joyful life. Live your life the way you want, do what you want no matter what others say. Because really, only you know what you want, what is important to you. Nobody else knows. Friends can give you good advice, your mother wants the best for you, your husband will suggest something, they all have the best intentions, they want you well. But you have to listen to yourself. You can't listen to one thing and then the other, be like a flag, go where you're told. It's not supposed to look like this. Enough of this uncertainty and letting others decide for themselves. You will never please anyone no matter how hard you try. Enough already. Shake off pleasing others, live for yourself. Start to see your power, your beauty, just yourself. I know that comments will be pouring in soon, because the husband, because the children, because you have to be there for them ... yes, but to take care of them, you must first take care of yourself. If you are happy, your children and husband will be happy. What do you think happens at home when a woman is always whining and complaining? Is there room for such an important joy in this house? For proximity? Believe me, a happy woman can give a lot of herself and create a real, loving home. So be for yourself, discover your possibilities and love yourself as you are. Don't judge, don't criticize, just be and enjoy it. And stop being afraid. Now you know that you can look at your life differently. Now you have great knowledge. Are you relieved?

- Of course!

"Thank you for sharing this with us. It's fantastic."

"I didn't know that before either."

The women were talking one after the other, and one of them even cried.

"I feel guilty all the time!"

"And I'm mad at myself." Non-stop, about everything and others.

Olivia picked up on the last sentence.

"Exactly, my dear women, there was a very good example here. see. Getting angry is punishing yourself, taking away your right to peace, to happiness, to being a support for yourself. Why are we doing this to ourselves? Because we feel not good enough? Not smart enough? Not important enough, needed? For whom? for others? Or maybe for themselves? This is so important, pay attention to it. Think about it. We get angry at ourselves because we lack love. And only we can give it to ourselves. We can be loved by a thousand men, but if we don't have love for ourselves, we can't accept it from others. Or give it truly to others. Therefore, my dear, let's be understanding, generous, let's support each other, because we create this world! It is us women who give life, go through many difficult moments and give advice. We do several things at once, we embrace the whole family. Everything is on our heads, sometimes we don't sleep well, but we manage anyway! Let's appreciate it."

There were a few comments and nods.

"One more very important point," Olivia pointed out, gesticulating with her hands. I wanted to draw your attention to one very important fact. There are a lot of pretty people around us in the world, we all know that. See how few beautiful people there are... The beauty of a person does not come from beauty, but from authenticity, from the way of being, from the energy we have inside. This is what attracts other people, it makes others feel good in our company. Interest in the other person, showing him kindness. Look, when choosing your friends, what are you guided by? I'm listening, I encourage discussion.

"You have to trust a friend," said one of the elegantly dressed ladies.

"A friend must be supportive, must be wise, helpful, understanding" added.

"So that you can count on her, but also to do stupid things, laugh, go shopping."

"She should be cheerful."

"An interesting person, so it wouldn't be boring."

"Exactly," said Olivia. "Look, no one said a friend had to be pretty or attractive. Why?"

"So that her husband doesn't look back at her," one of the women joked, and the rest of the ladies laughed loudly.

"Or maybe the appearance of a close, trusted person is not so important?" asked Olivia.

"Because what does the size of your ass or breasts matter in a friendship? Or height or hair color?"

"Well, it doesn't really matter," replied an elderly woman in the front row, closest to the fire.

"Exactly, Theresa. So the next time we stand in front of the mirror and look at ourselves with criticism, let's remember what is most important - not what we look like, but who we are. And instead of whining in front of the mirror that there is too much here, too little there, we just put on a colorful dress, put on a smile, kindness and sincerity. And then we are not only pretty and well-groomed, but also beautiful. So I am telling you here today: you are unique and beautiful! And let none of you dare to doubt it even for a moment!

"How nice of you to say it," said Theresa. How much truth and wisdom there is in this.

"And now, to feel great, we're having a party!" Let's dance a little, let's move our lovely bodies, let the whole world see how beautiful we are! See it yourself!

Olivia grabbed the guitar and started playing lively music. Someone knew the words of the song, someone joined in, and after a while the whole choir was singing.

"Come on baby, let's dance!" Olivia stood up and moved her hips to the music as she played. – We thank ourselves for being so wise, we thank each other for our patience, for our beauty. For our sexy bodies. For the fact that we are hot, for the fact that we do not have to compare ourselves to skinny models who eat only a leaf of lettuce a day. Hooray! We are free!

I was delighted with what was happening. Women danced, jumped, clapped, sang. Such joy emanated from them. I also felt light on my soul, I smiled, but I did not leave the bench. I was just watching.

"We're great! We are free! Our bodies are beautiful! Cellulite is already there. And we're not ashamed of it. We are not ashamed of our bodies! We love our bodies! My dear, it's a warm night, let's do something crazy. Who wants to swim in the lake? Who wants to splash? Who is not afraid to show their beloved body in underwear only? Or maybe no underwear?! Today is madness day! It's our day, our party! Lets play! Let's feel young! Alluring! attractive! Today we are light as a feather. Let's let go of control!"

One big madness. A huge bonfire, sparks shooting up to the sky, warmth, the smell of wood and over fifty naked knuckles both jumping lightly, like teenagers, into the calm lake reflected against the night sky.

"What about you? Don't you dare?" Olivia called me.

"I can't, I can't," I replied. It was enough for me to watch this phenomenal event.

Olivia threw a drum at me.

"You'll help me!"

"But what am I supposed to do?" I was surprised, holding the large wooden instrument in front of me.

"Hit the beat with your hand from above. You are driving! That's easy."

What was wrong with me? I put my knees on the drum and started pounding on it with my fingers. I liked it. Not to the rhythm at all, but loud and the effect was extraordinary. I smiled broadly. I looked at the splash in the water. Some women actually jumped naked. They were not bothered by overweight, sagging skin or other imperfections. It was a moment of total freedom and self-acceptance. Children's joy. It's possible that they haven't experienced something so crazy and wonderful in a long time. I noticed that a young girl was quickly spreading white bath towels on wooden benches. So it was all intentional, great idea. And what an effect! Certainly none of us will ever forget that evening. I concentrated on the drumbeats, feeling my joy grow. I felt a connection with this place, with these people.

"Hope I don't lose all my fish," Olivia joked and glanced at me as she continued to play her guitar and sway to the music. The songs were very lively and energetic.

All the ladies came back beaming and giggling. They were delighted with the towels waiting for them. They quickly wrapped themselves around each other and began exchanging impressions. The music didn't stop even for a moment. Two young girls very efficiently served each of the ladies a mug of mulled wine.

I watched the whole company, I haven't seen so much joy in the eyes of such a large group for a long time, such delight, connection. I realized we had all just met. Amazing.

The next hour was drinking mulled wine, talking, joking, singing songs. Women were not ashamed to talk among themselves about dilemmas or joys. There were countless topics. I talked to some of them for a while, exchanged kind words or just got to know each other's names. I also approached Olivia for a moment, she was sought after, but I managed to accost her and express my appreciation.

"Olivia, it's really fantastic what you're doing," I said admiringly.

"Thank you, I have a lot of cool ideas, so as you can see, it's worth using. I do all this for you. And how do you feel? Have you already boxed the greatest emotions?

"A small part, for sure."

"Then I invite you to continue your journey, a wonderful journey of self-discovery. Tomorrow 7:30. Don't be late." With these words, she reached for her drum and began to play.

I went to get my feet wet. I held a cup of mulled wine in my hand, I felt a pleasant warmth radiating from my stomach. I was looking at the lake in the dark. The water swayed slightly, you could hear its roar. I lifted my head up and looked at the sky, I saw so many stars. I heard the sounds of the party. I sighed contentedly, I haven't felt as good as I do here and now in a long time. I wanted to enjoy that moment as much as I could. Suddenly, several giggling women ran past me and jumped into the water again. Fortunately, they didn't go far, they were playing right by the shore. Two young employees of the boarding house stood guard and made sure that nothing unforeseen happened to anyone.

I smiled at the scenes before me. Someone came from my right. I looked curiously.

"Nice party," said a pretty brown-haired woman of medium height, with braids braided like a little girl's. I'd noticed her earlier in the crowd of talking ladies.

"I am surprised, I did not expect such attractions here" I replied.

"Do you think we'll play like this when we're that age?"

"I hope so," I replied honestly.

"Marlene." She shook my hand.

"Natalie." I shook her hand for a moment.

"Thank God there are a few of us a little younger here. I came with my father to catch up on relationships, and I was afraid that it would be terribly boring here, and here's a surprise. My father insisted that he absolutely wanted to come here, so I agreed. I spent half a day in the Jacuzzi, now swimming in the lake. And this wine is so delicious, I don't know where they buy it, but it's a firecracker. And you came here alone?

"By myself."

"By yourself? So if you don't mind if we spend some time on girl gossip?" I will be very pleased.

"Sure, why not."

"Are you going to meditate tomorrow?"

"A little early, because 7:30, but I'll see, I'll try, maybe I'll like it."

"Perhaps so," I replied. I heard huge screams from the guest house. Cheers, whistles and shouts. I looked over there.

"Well, we already know who won the match" commented Olivia with a laugh. "My darlings, remind me what tasks you have for each day of your life? she exclaimed so that she could be heard clearly."

"Appreciate yourself!" the women shouted one after the other.

"Do not criticize!"

"Be nice to yourself!"

"Find time to rest!"

"Love yourself and take care of yourself!"

"Accept your body! accept yourself!"

"Don't worry about what other people say about us!"

"We're great!"

"A hundred times a day tell yourself: I love myself, I'm great!"

"Yes it is," cried Olivia. "You obviously listened carefully to what I was saying and took it to heart. You are cool. And now the second round of music and dancing. Show what you're capable of. We drive!

Guitar sounds, dancing and singing. I don't know what worked - maybe a cup of mulled wine, but I went jumping and dancing with everyone. No one sat with a stick up their ass on a bench by the fire anymore. All of us, without exception, were in a party mood.

CHAPTER 3

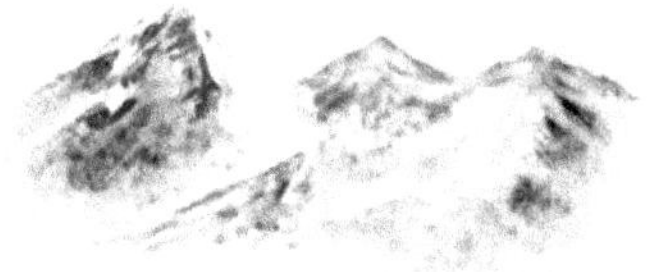

I woke up with a smile on my face. I opened my eyes and for a moment savored the feeling of contentment and lightness. I felt great after yesterday's party. It was such an uplifting experience that I felt like I was a different person for a moment. I just felt happy. Then, after quite a while, my mind realized I was awake and started attacking me with standard thoughts. I noticed the difference, I was surprised by the emotional jump from happy to depressed. Was it like this every day and I didn't notice it? Or maybe I didn't have very nice moments in my life and I didn't wake up happy, but immediately with such a critical or full of fear and doubt look at everyday life? Amazing. I wonder what that meant, why was that? What happened?

A large group had gathered in front of the boarding house. Mixed company, everyone had an exercise mat with them. I said hello.

"Natalie, take a mat from the reception, you will need it" the overweight blonde instructed me, she was sitting next to me at yesterday's party, I already knew her name was Halina.

"Okay, thanks," I went back to the front desk. An old lady, very well-groomed, nice, took a mat from a small room and handed it to me with a smile.

"Have fun," she said.

A moment later we set off as a group to the end of the area belonging to the guesthouse. We found ourselves on a perfectly mowed lawn, near an orchard. Even the sneakers didn't get wet from the morning dew. We spread the mats and sat on them. I chose a seat in the back, it was my first time attending such an event and I didn't really know what to expect. It certainly wasn't meant to look like on TV shows or pictures of Buddhist monks.

Olivia sat facing us, took off her shoes and settled back with her legs crossed in the lotus flower.

"Welcome to you very warmly," she began. "I am very pleased that there is such a large group, I congratulate you on your stubbornness and willingness to get up and come here after yesterday's very interesting evening. All right, dear ones, sit comfortably so that your spine is straight. Check if everything is fine, if it is as comfortable as possible. Today in meditation we will deal with letting go. Letting go of everything that holds us so firmly in place and does not allow us to move on, letting go of what has not served us for a long time. We will clean ourselves up a bit, we will feel light and pleasant. Some of you will feel as if a huge weight has been lifted off your shoulders, those of you who are doing this for the first time may feel nothing at all. That's okay too. Everything takes time. We don't tense up, it's not a race, just a moment of respite for yourself. All right. Are you ready? This is what we do, a deep breath, she presented, taking a deep breath through her nose."

"And exhale."

She exhaled very slowly through her mouth. "Again, inhale and exhale. Inhale through the nose, deeply, let the air flow down to the belly, and exhale very slowly through the mouth. Concentrate all your attention on the airflow, how your chest rises when you inhale and falls when you exhale. Check what happens to the whole body when you inhale and exhale. Watch it. Again, inhale and exhale. Slowly. If any thoughts arise, and they certainly will, go back to breathing. Don't worry about the thoughts, let them come and let them go.

Olivia 's voice was slow, monotonous, but loud and clear enough for everyone to hear.

I followed all orders. At first I actually focused on my breathing, but soon I was thinking about something else. About Evelyn - which made me nervous. I calmed down, pushed my thoughts away, and focused on Olivia's words. It wasn't that easy, but I tried my best.

"Continuing to breathe at the same rate, bring your attention to your left foot. Relax your foot. Let it get heavy. Relax calf, relax knee, thigh, let the whole leg feel heavy. Now relax your right foot. Let it get heavy. Relax calf, relax knee, thigh, let the whole leg feel heavy. Now hips, buttocks, relax the stomach, intestines, stomach, relax the entire back and chest. Now my left hand is getting heavy. Let the fingers rest, now the forearm, elbow, shoulder and the right hand are relaxed: first the fingers of the right hand, wrist, forearm, elbow and the entire shoulder. Now relax your neck, jaw, mouth, let your jaw drop slightly, relax your nose, cheeks, eyes, forehead, the whole head is heavy and relaxed. Some of you may not be able to feel your body parts, which is very good. We breathe in, with the inhale we accept peace and harmony, and with the exhale we give away everything that limits us. Inhale - peace and harmony, exhale - letting go of everything that is no longer good for us."

A moment of silence.

"Now take a deep breath and hold your breath." Imagine that you have inhaled a white light that dissolves all your problems and sorrows. See that light, feel it. And slowly exhale through your mouth, see how the remnants of worries leave your body as you exhale and disappear. Take another very slow breath in through your nose and hold the air for three seconds. Now the light dissolves guilt. Watch the guilt disappear. Feel the light fill you from head to toe. And exhale. You feel relieved. Inhale... We hold the air - now let go of the anger. Anger at yourself and at others. This light has great power, imagine that it easily removes all the anger from your life... And exhale... Let the rest of the anger come out through your mouth and disappear into the air. And now inhale… Light dissolves fear. You can feel this fear for a while. Look at it, imagine how now it disappears as you exhale. There is no fear in you anymore. You feel free. Breathe easy. Slowly. You feel completely at peace. Breathe this peace and harmony. You are safe here. Focus all your attention on your breath. If unwanted thoughts arise, let them go. Let them flow away... Peace and harmony, you rest... Bliss, relaxation... Inhale... and exhale.

If you still need to clear an emotion, then take another very slow breath, hold your breath and let the light cleanse you of any negative emotions, give away all the grief, the need to control, the need to be the best, you are good enough, you are focusing on yourself right now ... Exhale... You rest... You feel harmony and peace... Everything around you is good and right... You are good and right... Inhale... and exhale... We give ourselves space and time. Inhale... and then exhale. We can slow down a bit.

There was silence. Olivia stopped talking for a moment. I felt weird. As if I looked inside myself. I always focused on everything around me, and that was the first time I listened to myself. I couldn't quite relax and relax my body, I felt the tension, but it didn't bother me. I watched with interest what was happening to me at that moment. I breathed calmly - that's it and that's it. In silence, peace. I felt the gentle warmth of the sun on my face, a light breeze caressing my skin. Somewhere in the distance came the barking of a dog and very close by the buzzing of a bee. I went back to breathing. I opened my eyes for a moment and glanced at the others, everyone sitting still, lost in their own world.

Olivia spoke again. She paused between sentences.

"In this moment, nothing limits you, you feel freedom and joy. Let the past be left far behind, the past no longer affects you... You leave everything that hurt you, you let go because you can do it... Feel how wonderful it is to be free and happy. Feel good emotions, feel joy, self-satisfaction, wrap yourself in love ... And stay with this feeling for the whole day ... And now, dear ones, we return our attention to our body. Feel your toes, calves, knees, legs, arms, belly, head. Take a deep breath and slowly open your eyes. Don't move yet. just watch."

I opened my eyes and smiled with delight at the sight of colorful butterflies flying around us.

"How do you feel?" asked Olivia.

"Look, a moment of silence, letting go, staying in the bosom of nature, how did it affect you? Even butterflies come and land on your shoulders. If you had come here under any other circumstances, you would have had to catch these butterflies to see them, and now they came of their own accord. It is exactly like happiness in life. If you're tensing up, chasing after something you want, it keeps slipping out of your hands. Sit down, calm down, wait, and what you want will come. Open yourself to the flow of good and happiness in your life. That's right, by stopping for a moment. Through gratitude, through admiration for what is and how it is. Even a twenty-minute meditation can do wonders in life. Even if you have to return to difficult duties after meditation, your approach to problems and to the reality around you will change a lot. Through meditation, you open yourself to the flow of goodness and joy. For abundance. Remember that each of us has access to the unlimited wealth that the world offers us. We have an unlimited source of love within us. This source of love is in each of us, without exception. Only in some of us is it hidden under a thick layer that we put on every day by complaining, unforgiveness, anger, fear, greed, criticism, following only material goods. To get back to this source of love, we must forgive ourselves and others, cleanse ourselves of greed, reject criticism and fear. We have to trust. Learn to be good to others. Because it is also true that what we give to others comes back to us with double strength. Help someone - it comes back to you, criticize someone - it comes back to you double. Thank you very much for today's lessons. Before lunch, I encourage you to take a short walk and internal dialogue with yourself."

Olivia stood up and each of the participants slowly straightened their bodies. Some stretched, others delightedly tried to catch the butterflies, but now they failed.

We returned to the guest house in a fairly stretched group. Olivia started to say something and I quickened my pace to hear it.

"If any of you want to meditate, it's best to do it in the morning or in the evening, then we have less responsibilities, things to do and it's easier to quiet our thoughts. And here a little note for beginners, there is nothing to be discouraged. At first your mind will rebel, you'll hear thoughts like: this doesn't make sense, it doesn't work, it's too long, I'm uncomfortable, I forgot to brush my teeth, I need to drink water and all kinds of excuses just to discourage you. This is how it works if you want to make any changes to your everyday life. The first two days the mind will observe, and then it will start making excuses for you. In such a situation, one must be stronger and more resolute than the mind. Really worth it.

I listened surprised. How is it to be stronger and more resolute than our mind? I didn't understand it.

"Tomorrow we're going to have a little chat about that, specifically how the mind works and how it affects us," continued Olivia. "I think tomorrow around 10:00 will be a good time." I invite everyone. There will also be an announcement on the board by the reception.

Incredibly interesting, I thought. I was planning to go to that meeting and find out more. Right after breakfast, I sat on the terrace with my phone in my hand and started reading about meditation. I completely immersed myself in the virtual world in search of information. There was a lot of it, people described their feelings, how it affected their everyday life. So many delights that it was hard to believe. Of course, I'd heard a bit about it before, but I never really cared, I thought meditators were freaks. However, looking at Olivia, her optimism, charisma, joy of life, it made me want to follow this path. I was so absorbed in reading that I didn't notice Anthony approaching me.

"How's Sad Eyes?" he asked, leaning against the vertical wooden beam supporting the roof the terrace. - Isn't it better to look at the blue of the sky than at this tiny screen?

"Good morning," I said, surprised. I put the phone down on the bench. - You are right. Everything looks better live.

"Oh, and I like that. And I'll like it best when your sad eyes show at least a bit of joy. You're too young to be sad.

I smiled.

"And you're right again," I admitted. "I'm going to the forest right now. Which way will you suggest?

"My dear, straight ahead, past the orchard, and then there are paths, very well marked, and they will all lead you back." There's no chance you'll get lost, and if you do, don't worry, I'll find you,' he said with a theatrical gesture. He placed a hand on his chest and bowed slightly. "Sad Eyes, you can always count on me.

"My name is Natalie," I said, because I didn't like the nickname he came up with.

"And I know that, I remember it perfectly well. And I also remember what we agreed on - in the "Bella Vita" area only in short skirts. Have a nice trip to the forest - with these words he went away, singing happily.

I put my phone in my pants pocket and slowly walked towards the forest. I passed the orchard and found myself on a fairly frequented broad path. I noticed the footprints of horses' hooves and bicycle tires reflected in the ground. I thought that I would like to ride a bike, I wonder if they have such equipment for guests here. I looked around, it was very nice here, I walked slowly, passing magnificent rocks, bushes and tall trees. On some of the larger boulders, I walked from one to the other, keeping my balance. After this short game, I decided to ask myself a few questions that Olivia was talking about. The first thing I like. What I like? I thought for a long time, but somehow nothing specific came to mind, complete emptiness. There must be something, you just need to concentrate more. I like peace, meeting friends too, I mean it used to be like that, now it turned out that I have no friends.

The depression came suddenly. I like watching movies, having order around me, tidy even deep in the wardrobes. I like reading books on various topics. I like theater. However, there are some activities that I like. It's okay, I reassured myself a bit. I know what I don't like: being lied to, rejected, humiliated, fired from work, left when I was a nine-year-old child, because earning money in Germany is more important. I don't like feeling like I'm nothing, an insignificant pawn in a game of people I shouldn't give a shit about. I felt my nerves surge. I stopped noticing the beautiful views of the surroundings, which simply ceased to matter to me. I turned sharply, walking quickly towards the boarding house. Anger gave me strength. I just stopped in front of the door gym. It surprised me, I didn't even think about where I was going,

I was so blinded by anger at the recent events in my life. I entered the room briskly and grabbed my gloves. Yesterday's boxing helped me a lot, today it will definitely help too - I thought, pounding hard on the punching bag. I was making wild animal noises. I kicked, feeling pain in my leg. Then, completely exhausted, I threw my gloves on the floor and sat down, leaning against the wall. Out of breath, all sweaty. I just looked around now. I saw two guys staring at me. They sat motionless, one on the weightlifting bench, the other by the multi-gym, and watched me in silence.

I felt a strong embarrassment. How could I not notice them?

"Hi," I said, and stood up briskly, making my way quickly to the exit. "It's nice here, isn't it?" Have fun - and I left.

I breathed deeply. Well, it was a nice show! I thought angrily. I was furious with myself for storming into the gym believing no one was there. I didn't even look around or check. I walked briskly to my room, reproaching myself for my vacuity on the way.

During dinner, Marilyn sat down with me.

"Hi," she greeted. "How are you?"

"All right," I replied.

Were you meditating this morning? Because of course I overslept, how else. I woke up just after ten. This place is magical, I sleep here like a little baby. Silence peace. My father was supposed to wake me up, but of course Marian had already spoiled Lucy after two days of stay, and you can see for yourself - she pointed to the next table, where a couple of fifty-year-olds, content with their lives, were having a lively discussion, looking deeply into each other's eyes. "Well, I won't disturb them."

"Your father always like Casanova?"

"NO. He was always faithful and honest. It's about time he found someone else. How long can you be alone? He has been a widower for five years."

"I'm sorry," I said sincerely, and looked at Marilyn. She gave information about the family drama in a rather unusual way.

"It is how it is. We have to move on," she said. "Will you go boating with me?" It's no fun by itself.

"Sure, why not," I replied, chewing on my chicken.

"Eat well," Marlene advised. "There's going to be a barbecue tonight, the guys are having dinner tonight, so it might be different."

I smiled widely but didn't comment.

After lunch we went to the lake. The boats were tethered to the dock, so we unmoored one and carefully climbed inside. I oared us off the pier. The boat rocked gently.

"Why did you come here alone?" Marlene asked.

"And you?" I answered with the question. I swung my oars a few times and set them aside.

"I already told you I'm here with my father to catch up on relationships. My father lives in Radom and I in Krakow. We rarely see each other. I am finishing my studies in Krakow. I also work, I have friends there and I will not return to Radom. The father completely understands and accepts this. I am not permanently attached to anyone. And how is it with you?

I glanced toward the boarding house, debating whether or not to tell my story to someone I had just met.

"Don't say anything if you don't want to." It's just nice to talk, just like that, said Marilyn.

"I was supposed to change my marital status next week on Saturday," I began. I wanted it to sound light.

"Unfortunately, the fiancé did not grow up to a serious relationship, he has not yet cut the umbilical cord, and the would-be mother-in-law showed me where I belong. Our paths diverged. That's the whole story."

"Ho, ho, not so fast," Marlene asked. "I will ask for details, because it is a very interesting story.

I told her briefly the whole event, trying to speak without much emotion, although it cost me a lot. I already made a fool of myself in the gym, venting my worst emotions. I couldn't forget it."

"I admire you, it took courage," Marilyn commented seriously. - Really. You gave her a hard time. Such a grandmother is probably not used to any refusal. And now she had to cancel her youngest son's wedding. It's a strong nose punch.

I didn't think of it that way. It would not have occurred to me that my behavior affected Evelyn's reputation. And she always wanted a flawless image. I felt a bit of malicious satisfaction, but only a bit.

She quickly got back at me by getting me fired from my job with a wolf ticket to any job in town.

"You can do it. If you don't succeed in school, try other places, in sales, in the office - there are many possibilities, you just have to look around. A little more faith in yourself and your abilities. You've already shown you have balls and courage."

I didn't see myself that way. I saw myself as a victim in the whole situation, only Olivia made me a little bit aware, and now Marilyn. It was very revealing. They both introduced me to mine role in the event in a similar way, maybe they were right. The more I thought about it, the easier it was for me to look at the whole thing from the sidelines, as an outside observer. From that moment, my despair was much less, it turned into anger. It's still much better than the bottomless apathy I've been in for the last two weeks.

We sailed the boat for over two hours, it was a very nice time. Marilyn turned out to be a very bright and intelligent person. Lively and direct. She taught me life wisdom in a rather unique way.

"Because, you know," she explained. "A woman is supposed to be like a woman. When she's pissed off, she's supposed to be pissed off, when she's scared, she's supposed to scream in fear. There is no suppression of emotion or smiling pleasantly as it boils inside. We have a whole range of emotions that need to be shown. We are real! Only, unfortunately, men are afraid of such women. When we were little girls, we were told that it was not appropriate, behave yourself, be polite. How does it relate to today? All these good girls are suffering now because they can't say no. They can't fight for themselves. They sit in failed relationships and pretend that everything is ok. You, Natalie, were really lucky that your eyes were opened at the last moment. I'm afraid to think that you were crushed there

"I wouldn't let that happen," I said.

"Of course not, but how much you would suffer ... You should be glad that it turned out this way.

"Right now, I'm pissed off," I said sadly.

"Somehow you don't show it." Marilyn looked at me angrily and I laughed.

"Come on," she said expectantly.

"What's next?"

"Let your emotions out. shout out."

"Are you crazy?"

"But it's good. All piss off, it'll come off of you."

"Now? Here?"

"Well, who will hear you here?" She stood up and waved her hand in the air. The boat rocked dangerously.

"Everyone," I said, holding on to the wooden sides of the boat.

I glanced briefly at the groups of boarding house guests strolling near-by.

"And what about this? Will you offend them? You're not going to yell at them" she said, then screamed loudly."Greg is a jerk!!!"

"Stop!" I laughed.

"Well, that's true," she shrugged. "Now you shout, it's very liberating."

"I can't," I said. Under other circumstances I would have been very upset, I was enjoying the situation then.

"The sooner you get over this, the easier it will be." If you don't try, you won't know. Treat it like fun.

I collected myself for a moment, then screamed, but not very convincingly.

"Greg is a jerk!"

"Harder."

"Evelyn, I hate you!!!" I screamed, closing my eyes.

"Oh, that's better. You can see that Evelyn got under your skin more than Greg.

"Because with Greg I have nice memories, but not with his mum."

"Better?"

"Better," I sighed and looked around. People obviously weren't interested in our screaming, didn't seem to notice us at all. Marlene followed my gaze.

"Ninety percent of people are self-centered. Even when they pass you by and look at you, they are still thinking about their own business. There's nothing to worry about."

Amazingly, I came there with a great need to isolate myself from people, and after just a few days I made new, very interesting friendships. In the afternoon, as part of dinner, a barbecue was organized. Appropriate equipment was set up near the lake, two cooks in white aprons invited all the men to join them. On the wooden tables there were huge bowls with sliced, previously marinated pork neck. The task of the male part of the guests of the guesthouse was to prepare dinner for everyone. With the support of professional chefs, they eagerly set about making masterful dishes. It took a long time to grill the meat and make the garlic bread, plus several kinds of salads. They obviously had a lot of fun with it. Olivia laughed as she listened to the comments of the female part of the audience.

"My dear, don't be like that, give them a chance. Dorothy, you chased your husband out of the kitchen, where should he practice? Now he has a chance to prove himself, she said. "Maybe it will surprise you?"

"Mine can only boil water for tea," one of the crowd laughed.

"And my potatoes will peel and put, that's already a lot."

"More faith, my dear," Olivia said. "Look at your men with pride. They try for you. Maybe instead of criticism, some kind words towards them? Someone will learn, someone will show culinary talent. Don't judge hastily.

"I'm already afraid of what will come of it," one of the women said cheerfully.

"I'm going to invite you, my darlings, for a little trip to my neighbor's." You'll like it for sure. His name is Luke and he is a car mechanic.

The whole group went to the neighboring yard. There was plenty of room there. We passed a two-story house and headed for a long brick building set along the fence. It was a car repair shop. I saw a black Volkswagen parked on the ramp. However, this place was not our goal. Olivia led us a little further, to cars parked under a spreading pear tree.

A well-built, medium height, bearded man with hair tied in a ponytail was waiting for us there. He looked calm, composed. He was not impressed at all by the large group of amused women of all ages. He was only smiling.

"It's on me. I have a task for you, ladies and gentlemen. Divide into several groups. I have three cars here. Your task is to check the level of oil, washer fluid and fluid in the cooling and braking systems. Let's go." He pointed to three old Mercedes.

"Relax, the cars are mine, they serve more as a passion and decoration."

There was perfect silence. Women looked surprised at Luke, then almost simultaneously moved their eyes to Olivia.

"Each of you has a car at home, you even came here in these cars. I'm sure most of them have a driver's license as well. For safety, all fluids in the car must be checked at least once a month" said Olivia.

"Well, but that's what my husband does," said one of the ladies.

"That's right, it's a man's job," said the other.

"I think that every woman should do it without problems" said Olivia, pretending to be surprised that no one moved. "Please, impress your husbands."

I watched everything from the sidelines. Of course I was able to do it without any problem. However, I gave a chance to prove myself to others. I suspected that Olivia wanted to convey a certain truth with this task to some of the most critical women.

The first four people approached the Mercedes. As it turned out, the ladies couldn't even open the hood of the car, let alone everything else. Olivia and Luke stood aside and watched curiously. More people approached the other two cars. The first managed to lift the hood up. Discussions, debates, even arguments of women bent over the engine, made an impression.

"I like it here more and more," a female voice said next to me, and I turned around.

I saw a short brunette with short hair. Her hair was neatly arranged, and she looked very pretty. Dark skin and light makeup. Dressed in loose linen trousers and a sports shirt.

"You think they'll make it?" I asked.

"Shall we help them?" she asked amused.

"Not yet, let's not spoil the fun," I replied.

"Daria," she extended her hand in greeting.

I did the same.

"Natalie."

"It's a pity that my Fred can't see it," she said. "What an amazing idea."

"You will tell him everything."

"It's impossible to tell," she laughed. We received comments from women. What they came up with exceeded all limits. One of them came up with the idea to look for information on You Tube on how to check the oil in the engine.

We moved closer to see and hear everything better.

There were other ideas and problems among the ladies:

"Oh dear, and which of these liquids is oil?"

"Ask the handsome Mr. Luke."

"We'll be fine on our own. I already have a video. Oh, see, here they show, it's easy."

"What's easy? Where should I look for this wire? There it is. Oh crap, I got dirty."

"And what's that for?" What's that fluid? And where to pour it?

Marlene came over to me. It just showed up now, I didn't notice it at the grill.

"What have I missed?" What are you doing? she asked curiously. - Any action? I'm a little late.

"We're supposed to check all the fluids in the car," I explained.

"Alright then," Marlene said, leaning forward.

"Wait," Daria called after her. - Come on, look.

Marilyn came back to us, not understanding any of it. After a moment, she smiled and went to work anyway.

"Stand back, I'll show you everything," she said loudly, pulling up her sleeves. And she took care of explaining which liquid for what, what amount in the tank is correct and how to refill the liquids. At the end, she received thunderous applause.

Don't you smell these smells? she called, pointing to the grill far beyond the fence.

"Shall we invite the handsome Mr. Luke to dinner?" Halina suggested.

"Luke, you have no choice," Olivia said, spreading her hands.

On the way back, one of the women said loudly to Olivia:

"You gave us a good punch in the nose, my dear.

"Exactly. Everyone is great at something else. That's why let's appreciate each other, let's not criticize" commented Olivia.

Dinner was very good, passed in a nice atmosphere. I met Daria's husband, Fred. Very positive and kind people my age, full of passion and personal charm. They loved cars, participated in various rallies in the deserts. They talked about it a lot. In all the crowds circulating from the table to the lake, I ran into a guy who had been watching me at the gym.

"Hi," he greeted.

"Hi," I replied, feeling a bit awkward. I smiled and mingled with the crowd of people. I didn't want to talk to him. I went to the wooden pier. Dusk has already fallen, the lanterns have been lit some time ago, giving a pleasant glow of warm light. I leaned against the wooden railing of the jetty railing and stared at the depths of the lake. I felt a gentle breeze of cool air. Every now and then I glanced at the large group of guests enjoying themselves at the barbecue. Someone had lit a large bonfire in the exact same spot as yesterday. It was nice to see all these happy people. I couldn't integrate with them yet, I needed to calm down. Deep inside, I still felt immense pain and sadness.

I took a few deep breaths and closed my eyes. A few minutes of stillness. I remembered Olivia's morning words to look inside myself.

Now was the right time to do it. I focused on my legs, hips, then my stomach, then my chest. I felt my own heart beating. I put my hand in the middle of the chest to feel it better. I imagined that every heartbeat sent essential nutrients, such as oxygen, to my entire body. Could it also spread joy so quickly? Would do well to. And was it even possible? And then I turned my attention to my head. Jaws clenched tightly, mouth in a straight line, no hint of a smile. I noticed that my whole body was tense. I've never paid attention to it before. I sighed, discouraged. I noticed this change of mood. I didn't want that! She didn't want to feel like this anymore! That was not me. I wanted to be happy like all those people around the fire. Why couldn't I? Why couldn't I do that?

I looked up at the starry sky with resignation. A white light flickered high above, and I focused all my attention on the flying plane, though it distracted me from my depressing thoughts for a moment.

Suddenly, I felt my phone vibrate in my sweatshirt pocket. I glanced at the screen and froze. Greg called. I stared at the phone, not believing my eyes. I didn't pick up because I wasn't prepared to talk to him. I felt a rapid rise in blood pressure. I looked around me, then quickly walked away. What did he want? Why did he call?

I didn't have to wait long for an answer. He called again a few minutes later. I was literally a few steps from the entrance to the hotel building. I stayed where I was and answered the call.

"Natalie," I heard his voice in the receiver.

"Why are you calling?" I asked in a strained voice.

"When will you be back?"

"You're joking, right?"

"Natalie, we're getting married on Saturday. come back. Don't be silly."

It choked me. I took the phone away from my ear and checked again if it was really Greg who was calling. I put the phone back to my ear.

"It's all canceled," I said.

"Nothing is cancelled. Come back finally. I shouldn't have let you go. You must have thought it through, I totally get it. come back. Until we finish renovating our floor, we'll live somewhere together like you wanted. Maybe even in a hotel. I'll take care of you, I'll be a good husband, you'll see, just give me a chance..."

"No, you won't be a good husband," I interrupted him.

Give me a chance, I've changed. Come back and see for yourself, he said.

"Why are you calling now?" After four weeks?

"I was convinced that you would reconsider everything, understand that you made a mistake and come back.

"Not after the way your mother treated me." Emotions took over. I raised my voice.

"My mother won't interfere." I promise you this.

"I don't believe it… Let's not kid ourselves. I'm not coming back, Greg."

"You can't just disappear without a word." We've done so much for you, me and my parents, and this is how you repay me? – I had the impression that I was listening to Evelyn's words, not Greg's. "Tell me where are you?" I will pick you up.

"NO. This is already a closed chapter. You had your chance. You've wasted it forever. Don't call me anymore," I said in a pained voice full of suppressed emotions.

"What about the wedding?" With us? With our house?

"This is your mother's house," I reminded her.

"It'll be ours." You will see. They are finishing the renovation now, it looks beautiful. All you have to do is pay for everything, the money from your apartment was supposed to be used for this, you promised ...

"Goodbye, Greg" after these words I rejected the call and blocked the number so that it would never call again. I put my phone in my pocket, sat on the bench and cried. Tears seeped into the sleeve of the sweatshirt. Moments later, someone sat next to me and hugged me gently.

"Cry baby, cry, it'll cleanse you, and I'll drink you here." – I heard the voice of Mrs. Helen, our receptionist. She sat so close to me, and I let her. I let my head be stroked and hugged. When the tears stopped flowing, I straightened up.

"Thank you, Mrs Helen," I said with a smile, looking at her. I was immensely grateful to her.

I wasn't ashamed of my swollen, tearful face.

"Are you okay?" she asked gently.

"Yes. Better."

"Sometimes life throws us various obstacles, problems, to show us that this is not the way. You made a mistake, it hurt, now cry it out and move on. Now you know what you don't want. Take a lesson from this situation and get up stronger" she said.

"It's so hard. I know I did the right thing, but I still can't deal with it,"

I whispered, wiping my nose on a handkerchief.

Everyone has their hard times, all of us without exception. Your sadness today will pass, like everything else that surrounds us. Before you know it, the sun will shine for you again. You will see.

"I hope. Thank you again."

"If you ever need to talk, I'm here for you." Olivia is too. And Anthony. And all these people around. Remember, you're not alone here, baby.

Tears welled up in my eyes again, but this time I smiled gratefully.

CHAPTER 4

I woke up very early in the morning. I got dressed and went outside. I was calm, calm. I walked slowly towards the lake - it was my favorite place from the entire surroundings of the guest house. I stepped onto the dock and pulled my woolen sweater tighter around me. I looked ahead - at the light morning mist, at the sun barely emerging from behind the clouds in the east. I felt pleasantly cool. I smiled. It dawned on me that I never had time for such mornings. I have never experienced such a lazy start to the day. I had as much time to myself as I wanted.

I realized that I could stand there even into the evening and observe the changes taking place throughout the whole good. The night before was completely different, and yet I was standing in the same place. Amazing. I took off my shoes and walked barefoot, feeling the wooden planks under my feet.

I walked on to the dew-covered lawn. I felt cold, but that's okay. The cold touched something in me. It woke me up. I was reminded of a quote I heard or read: "if you want to experience something fascinating, get out of your comfort zone." So I walked barefoot on the cold grass and was happy as a child. Those little things were so important to me at that moment. My well-ordered world fell apart and I had to put it back together. Every bit of joy was like a plaster on my tortured soul.

I went back to the pier and sat cross-legged at the very end, as close to the water as possible. I watched the light waves on the lake. I also saw large specimens of swimming fish. I was delighted to be so close to nature. I wasn't thinking about myself, I was focusing on what was around me. I felt the crisp air, took deep breaths to fill myself with it and everything around me. I closed my eyes and sat like that for over two hours.

I was interrupted by the sound of footsteps. I turned my head curiously. He's the guy at the gym I was fooling around with. It's hard, I tho-ught. I found it hard to move, having sat in one position with my legs crossed for so long. My body went numb.

"Hello," the man greeted. "I brought you coffee." If you want coffee of course.

He handed me a cup.

"Thank you," I replied. I took the cup in my hand. - I'm surprised.

The man sat next to me cross-legged.

"My name is Damien," he offered his hand in greeting.

"Natalie." I hugged her.

"Olivia keeps saying that we are all one, we are all connected, so I decided to join you as one, however it sounded, and have coffee with you on the pier" he said jokingly.

"I haven't gotten to those lessons yet, but if that's what she said, che-ers." I tapped my mug against his as a toast and took a long gulp of hot, bitter coffee. "How did you know I don't sweeten?"

"I didn't know." And he pulled small disposable sugar packets from his pocket.

I raised an eyebrow in appreciation.

"You're here for the first time?" - I asked.

"NO. I come here every summer."

"Aren't you bored yet?"

"Olivia is my friend since elementary school. But as you can see, she's always busy and we don't have much time to talk. Now she is also preparing for yoga classes."

"Yoga. Exactly! What time is it?" I cried emotionally.

"Ten past seven."

"Oh, I can't miss this. I'm sorry, but I really wanted to practice yoga. I have to go."

I quickly got up and put on my sneakers.

"Thanks for the coffee." I held up the mug. "Aren't you going to yoga?"

"I prefer the gym," he smiled.

I rushed to get ready for class. I decided that since I am here, I will take advantage of all possible attractions. Also to divert my thoughts from my somewhat hopeless life situation.

After half an hour of practice, I decided that it was something abso-lutely for me. Stretching your muscles without getting tired. I listened calmly and slowly to my body. We practiced on mats spread out on the lawn. There weren't too many people, just over twenty. I did all the routines not very carefully, because it was my first time with this type of body movement, but Olivia would sometimes approach the participants and gently correct the posture. She explained how important it is to breathe in yoga, what it is for, how it calms down, calms down and restores the body and soul to balance. Yoga eliminates tension in the body, strengthens, relieves stress. I enjoyed this. I felt every muscle, every part of me. I've learned to breathe properly by putting my body in the right positions, I didn't know it was so important.

After class, I went to my room and lay on my back on the bed. I closed my eyes and allowed myself to be completely relaxed. I wasn't thinking about anything. I was resting. It was a great feeling. It made me late for breakfast, but it was really worth it. I promised myself that yoga would be a permanent part of my daily routine.

Around 10:00 am, there were quite a lot of volunteers who sat down in the largest training room. I found a free spot somewhere in the back and waited with everyone for Olivia to arrive. She came smiling as usual, colorfully dressed, her hair tied up in a careless bun, but she still looked beautiful.

"So, dears, let's talk a little bit about how to be happier in life?" she began, taking a seat in the chair across from us." Each of us wants to be happier and I will tell you how to achieve it. It is very easy. What you give to others, what you send out into the world, it comes back. You get what you give. But from the beginning" she fell silent for a moment, giving the meeting participants time to calm down and focus. The whispered conversations stopped mid-word. Olivia looked at the assembled audience with a kind look, and then continued her speech - our world is created by our thoughts and beliefs. What we think about comes into our lives, whether they are good thoughts or not. We act a bit like a magnet, that is, we attract to ourselves what we think about, what we believe in. Every day is a constant race: for money, for meeting the expectations of others, for pursuing a goal, for success. We collect material goods to feel better, to be more valuable in the eyes of others and ourselves. We have more and more. We can afford more and more expensive gadgets, and yet we feel empty inside. Anxiety. Why is this happening? After all, we work, buy, change partners, and satisfaction and happiness are temporary. What is it about? It's about our beliefs. If we are convinced that work is the most important thing in life, then everything will revolve around work - we will neglect family, ourselves, time to rest. We do not give ourselves permission to stop, because we are afraid that a moment of respite will be a catastrophe, dismissal or a promotion will pass us by. Through such actions and thoughts, we attract more of what we have, what we believe in, what we fear. We are tense, alert, always ready to control, to act.

She took a sip of water from a tall glass with a slice of lemon and mint leaves floating in it.

"We are afraid of finances, because there is not enough ... And I'm not talking about you, my dears, because you had to fork out a lot of money to stay in my guesthouse" she winked her right eye knowingly, and the whole audience laughed. "But I wanted to show this diagram. Focusing on the lack, in this case of money, we get more and more bills, unplanned expenses, as if the world wants to give us what we think about. What we believe about our lives. I don't have it, so I think I attract such situations that I don't actually have it. The universe will do anything to give us what we think about. We don't have this money, we feel worse and worse, we lose our sense of security, we worry. We try to do something about it - extra overtime, some jobs after work - but it doesn't solve the problem, it's still there, and we focus more and more on it, we deepen it ... It doesn't happen right away, of course, like a snap of your fingers, but you get it It's a process: what you focus your attention on grows. From one innocent thought, sometimes even an opinion heard somewhere from someone, we create beliefs in our mind. Let me give you an example: a young girl heard a friend tell her that her legs were too skinny, that they looked like sticks. The girl constantly thinks about her legs, exercises to gain a little weight, eats more, is constantly preoccupied with the problem and begins to believe that her legs are too thin. It doesn't matter that several other people have told her she looks great. She doesn't hear it, because these persistent thoughts have given her a strong conviction that her legs are too skinny. The years go by. She starts to be unhappy, she has complexes, she doesn't wear dresses, she only wears wide trousers. see? This is a process, constantly thinking about those too skinny legs led the girl to believe it. How did it affect her? She didn't feel attractive, she couldn't find a husband. Now look… What if that opinion wasn't true? What if your friend just said that out of jealousy? Our thoughts create our beliefs, and our beliefs create our lives. Whether we agree with it or not, that's the way it is.

She glanced at the crowd, pausing for a moment. There was silence in the hall.

I tried to assimilate the collected knowledge. I immediately thought of my slim body and long legs. Was the fact that I didn't like wearing dresses related to some childhood trauma? What could it be? I couldn't remember anything like that.

Yet another very real example. How is it that one man at work tries very hard, gives the most of himself, and earns the least? And his colleague works less, is happy, sometimes even leaves work earlier and collects the best bonuses? How is it? Exactly. Beliefs. The first knows that you have to work hard to pay for bills and food, and the second is convinced that he is the best and deserves high salaries. We now know that beliefs shape our lives. And we know how thoughts affect us. What if you swap them now? Do it differently than before? Start thinking about abundance, not about what we lack. Start thinking that we deserve what we want, that we are worth the best wages? That we can have a happy life? It only depends on us. Only from us, dear. These are our thoughts. No one else but ours. We create our own future. Nobody else but us. We were not aware of the power that lies within us. You have to awaken it now and use it to your advantage, to attract to yourself what you want. Consciously. In conclusion, everything that happened in our lives came about because of the thoughts and beliefs we had. And here's the good news - we can change our thoughts and beliefs. We can start anytime. I will tell you how to do it, but first I will explain how the mind works.

She walked over to the easel on which were hung large white sheets of paper. She grabbed a blue felt-tip pen and began to draw.

Our brain can be compared to a computer. Let's say an old computer. We work on what we put into this computer. Our operating system, or belief system, is formed in childhood. Back then, we, as little children, were just getting to know the world. At first, we had adults around us and our exploration of the world looked like this: leave it, don't go there or you'll fall over, it's dangerous, it's not allowed there, I have to be ashamed of you again, stay put, don't be interested. No because no. Go away, I don't have time, you're stupid, be quiet, I'm taking care of your brother now, people are bad, they cheat, what the neighbors will think. Then there were peers in the yard. We heard the texts: you can't, we don't play with you, you're not suitable, I'll tell your dad, you'll get a spanking ... Then school and teachers: you don't know anything as usual, you can't learn, it's so easy, you have to learn you have to do what you're told, you're hopeless, it didn't work out again, you messed it up again, take an example from Matt, he's so smart... We may not remember it, but over ninety percent of people in the world feel this way got to know the world. Let's not blame the adults who were around us at that time, they too were brought up this way, they only passed on what they learned. In this way, all the information collected in childhood was stored in our mind, i.e. on the hard drive of our computer.

She tapped the drawing with a felt-tip pen to emphasize the importance of what she had said.

This is how our beliefs about ourselves were formed. And on the basis of these beliefs acquired in childhood, we create our lives until now. We are usually unaware of the beliefs that guide us. From childhood to the present time, there were various situations, problems, traumas that further confirmed these thought patterns in us. And let me remind you that what we thought about, we attracted. That's how we've built our lives over the years. Is it understandable for everyone? she asked.

She was in eye contact with the entire group at all times. She spoke slowly, loud enough to reach the last rows of listeners. The audience was calm, no one interrupted with unnecessary comments. Only after the question was asked, there were confirmations about the meaning of the message. After a small sip of water, she continued.

"And how do you think such an old computer functions these days?" With that outdated data uploaded a long, long time ago? Think about it, imagine it. And another very important question: was what we uploaded to the computer's hard drive, i.e. to our mind, several dozen years ago, real? Was it right? We were taught by people who did not understand how the mind works. They lived in fear themselves, so they taught us to be afraid. They taught us that something cannot be done, that we are wrong, that we are not what we should be, that we lack something, that others are better than us. Is it really so? What we were told, what we believed, became our truth. I will repeat again: what we were told, what we believed, became our truth. I'll tell you what's the truth. We came into the world as little happiness, as pure love. We are all right, we lack nothing, we are complete and perfect as we are. Right now. We just look at the world through these old, outdated, long-loaded programs in our minds. It's time to change them. This is the way to happiness and fulfillment - to see yourself for real, without judgment, without criticism, without complaining, without a bad attitude, without looking for imperfections. Without all those ego-imposed false beliefs about yourself. Sounds beautiful, right? I assure you that each of us can do it. At the beginning, all you need to do is decide that you want to change something in your life for the better, to feel better. We want to see ourselves, this wonderful, true being that we are.

Let's look inside ourselves, let's remove all limitations and beliefs that don't serve us. Let's remember the important point: we can do anything. We can achieve anything, make even the biggest dream come true. The only limit is our thoughts and beliefs. So let's change them!

There were several comments in the room, people were talking among themselves, they were agitated, some of the regulars already knew the topic and just nodded, nodding fervently.

I was surprised by the information I had just absorbed. I wanted to know more. I wanted to change my beliefs immediately! Just as? What was I supposed to do? I felt relieved, hopeful. Something in me twitched. Olivia continued her speech, so I focused on her words.

"Before I tell you how to change thought patterns, I will give you a few examples so that you understand exactly what caused them to exist, and so that it will be easier for you to see them in yourself. Here we go. First example: no money - belief: I don't deserve to have money. Where did it come from? Maybe my parents always said at home: we don't have it, we can't afford it, you have to do without it, I won't buy it for you, the rich are crooks. Maybe they showed contempt for people who are well off. Another example: no friends - belief: nobody likes me, nobody loves me, I'm not important, I don't have anything important to say. Where did it come from? Maybe my parents said: I don't have time, leave me alone, you are always in trouble, don't talk so much. Maybe we were overlooked, maybe we felt rejected, unnoticed? Another very real life example: problems at work - the belief: I'm not good enough, I'm not good for anything. Where did it come from? Maybe your parents or guardians criticized everything you did, maybe they said: you're an idiot, you're causing problems again, they were ashamed of you, they criticized you. One can talk about such examples for hours. The most important thing is that we are no longer victims of unconscious beliefs acquired in childhood. And most importantly: don't blame your parents and guardians. They wanted the best for you, they tried, they did what they could at that moment. They just didn't know. Plus, they had their own problems, their own limiting thought patterns. Now we understand what motivated them, so let's have no regrets. Now I will tell you how to change all these beliefs. A moment of break? Do you want, need a break?"

"No no. Carry on, I blurted out. I was afraid that after the break Olivia might forget something important, and I needed to find out as much as possible."

"Okay, so let's move on with the topic." First of all, if we decide to change our way of thinking, anything in life, our mind, i.e. a computer with outdated beliefs from childhood uploaded, will rebel. This may sound a little strange, but he will realize that we want to change something and will do everything to discourage us. That's his role. The mind is there to protect us. He is comfortable with what he already knows. He doesn't want changes. He already has a lot of work to do, dragging us in the pursuit of prosperity, for buying new things, for climbing the career ladder, for checking on the neighbor and may the neighbor have no better life than me. You laugh, but it is. The mind is busy all the time. Check how you are attacked by thoughts. There is no respite. Even in the evening, before falling asleep, it is sometimes difficult to calm down.

Acknowledgments, whispered comments, jokes echoed through the room.

"And now, if I suggest some little, innocent exercise to do, the mind will watch, watch, give us a chance to try, two, three times, and then block us." When we want to do the exercise the next day, the mind will do everything to prevent us from doing that exercise. Suddenly we'll remember that we didn't call a friend, or we were supposed to put on soup for dinner, or we really need to pee, or we need to drink tea. During this time, we are not aware of what the mind is doing and why. And he knows perfectly well. We can approach this consciously - notice this pattern and be stronger than the mind. Research shows, unfortunately, opinions here are very divided, but let's assume that just over 21 days is enough to convince the mind that something is good for us and we want to change something. We just have to be more stubborn than our own mind. Every thought, every belief can be changed. I will give you some other effective methods.

She picked up the felt-tip pen again and began writing out the methods.

"Watch your own thoughts. At first, let it be for two minutes several times a day when you remember. It will get easier over time. And if we see a thought that doesn't serve us, let's change it. Without criticism, without anger, say to yourself: today I choose differently. I'm not inept at all, I'm just learning. Now I know not to do it this way, next time I will do it differently. Or we can say to ourselves a little shorter: I have the right to be wrong, I respect myself, I support myself. You can repeat an affirmation like: I am important, needed, I have the right to happiness and peace, I deserve a great job, I am surrounded by love. Or another affirmation: I attract love, wealth, and fulfillment to myself."

She walked over to the desk and sat on it.

"At first, these words will strongly contradict our beliefs, they will sound senseless, strange, untrue, but let's try, what's the harm? Less than a month separates us from the first signs of success. After that time, the mind accepts a new message, a new belief, but we have to keep reaffirming it over and over again, sometimes for months, for it to become permanent. Let's spend a few minutes a day doing this. First, let's find one belief and work with it, and wait for the results. These weeks will pass anyway, and it's up to us whether we do something with the knowledge gained here today and try to work on improving our quality of life, or whether we stay where we are and continue to whine about how bad we are. Just remember - we must be smarter than our mind. Get to work, darlings! The topic is very broad. I don't want to tell you too much in one day, because it all needs to be done slowly, give yourself time, think about it and start acting. We'll meet again soon, and I'm going to give you some other very effective ways to change your beliefs. So get to work. Believe in yourself. Any questions?"

The buzz of conversations, everyone wanted to comment, say something smart, there was a commotion.

"Yes, I do" said forty-year-old, elegant Irena. You said it was easy and simple. It doesn't look like that at all.

"You think so?" Olivia smiled widely.

"Yes, because you have to work on yourself for several weeks."

"Look, at first all you have to do is sit in a comfortable chair and observe your thoughts, what and how your mind is saying to you for five minutes. And then tell yourself: I am valuable, important, I have a wonderful life. That's all. You can focus on it while walking or emptying the dishwasher."

"But how is it that we're supposed to watch our mind?" – began thirty-year-old Fred, a car rallies enthusiast. "Aren't we the mind?" After all, our life is based on thinking. Can you explain it somehow?

"Good question, Fred. I should have said that at the very beginning. We humans are multidimensional. We are made up of body, soul and mind. Then there is the division into the subconscious and the conscious. There is also the superconscious. The subconscious is our computer with uploaded beliefs. Beliefs create thoughts, and thoughts create our lives. According to research, the subconscious mind works about 95% of the time, and the conscious mind only 5%, which means that we are on autopilot for most of the day. It is easy to know whether we are being guided by the conscious or subconscious mind at any given moment. The subconscious is usually in the past or future. So we think about what was or about what will be. And the conscious mind is about the present – being here and now, and that is our greatest potential. And this is where the magic happens. You can see it "here and now", focus on it, but after a while you will start to be bombarded with thoughts and drift into the past or the future. So the control is taken over by the subconscious with our beliefs that do not necessarily serve us. And this is where meditation works very well. Meditation puts us in the "here and now", calms our thoughts and, allows you to observe the creations of the mind, as if looking at them from the side. As you can see, Fred, you can see yourself as an observer of yourself. And such a long-term goal is to be in consciousness as long as possible, to consciously choose what serves us, to consciously build our lives on the right, supporting beliefs. It takes work on yourself, patience and stubbornness, but it's really worth it. I have walked this path myself. Beloved, this is a river topic, we will talk more about it. Today I just showed you an outline so that you understand the general, superficial way of how the mind works, because that will be the basis for further conversations. I'm glad you've gathered here in such a large group. If you want, I invite you to the next meeting. So to sum up, my dears - it's all about unlearning self-criticism, blaming, punishing, taking away permission for something good. To throw out of your mind all the ballast of anger, grief, anger, hatred, jealousy. Why carry it? Why drag these difficult, energy-consuming emotions with you and use them unnecessarily every day? It will be easier without it. try it.

"Is it really so?" Questions and comments poured in. Discussions among themselves.

I sat motionless in my chair and processed the information I heard. It was a revolutionary discovery. I believed Olivia that what she said was true. It's amazing how little we know about life and the world. For so long we allow the information hammered into our heads in childhood to have such a huge impact on an adult. And so I wasted my time, I remained ignorant for so many years. I wanted to know as much as possible.

I left the room thoughtful. I headed straight for the exit of the building and without even looking back, I went towards the forest. I took a few deep breaths. An acacia tree was blooming nearby. I slowed my pace, calmed down a bit, and looked around. There were many rough rock formations around me. A river flowed nearby. Well-trodden, often traveled paths - I felt safe there.

I decided to watch my thoughts a bit. What were they saying to me? To me, or to whom? To what part of me? I didn't know that yet. I focused for a moment, but I didn't think about anything. Then, when I heard rustling in the roadside bushes, a flood of memories flooded my mind. I remembered trips to the forest that we organized together with Greg. Thoughts immediately went to his mother, Evelyn, and stopped there. I replayed our last conversation in my head, how she treated me, humiliated me, how much dislike, even hatred, towards me, where did it come from? I haven't done anything wrong.

And suddenly, after half an hour of emotional and regretful consideration, I realized what I was thinking about. I stopped in awe. I remembered everything that had been going on in my mind a moment earlier. This hurricane caused an avalanche of emotions. I saw it! I noticed. eureka! I need to do this more often. Incredible. How long it took me to wake up. Unfortunately, after a moment of euphoria, I drifted into unconsciousness again. I got busy planning the next day, referring to what happened yesterday.

In the afternoon I went to learn horse riding. Lena, as always in a great mood, was very talkative.

"Tonight I'm going with my friends to celebrate graduation," she said, leading the horse by the bridle. I sat in the saddle and enjoyed the leisurely ride. Tina lazily walked forward. "I'm so glad that all my exams are behind me." Now only holidays.

"Congratulations. This is an important life event."

"Thanks. Learning comes easily to me, so it wasn't stressful."

"And next? Any studies?"

"Krakow Academy. English in Business. I would like to travel around the world, work in a freelance profession, for example as a translator. I know two languages well, I want to learn two more."

"Beautiful, great plans."

"Maybe I can help my dad in business...?" We'll see what the future brings.

"And holidays? Will you spend here with the horses?" I asked. "Are you going somewhere?"

"I want to spend as much time as possible with my mother, because from October I will be living in Krakow. Only at the beginning of August I fly with my grandfather to Tuscany, to my uncle. For three weeks. It's great there. I love Italy. Uncle is old now, but he has a fantastic daughter and grandchildren. We like each other very much. And I will practice Italian by the way. I can not wait."

"Great perspective. It's nice to have a family in Italy", I said.

"Yes. Grandpa is also happy, he misses his home country a bit."

"Your grandfather is from there?" – I was surprised, at the same time I understood where Lena's dark complexion came from.

"Yes. He was born and raised near Florence. My grandfather's brother has a small vineyard there and produces wine. Sometimes he sends us a few cases of wine, a few kilos of good coffee, Olivia oil, spices, so we have a solid supply."

I drank red wine with dinner here recently and it was fantastic, I couldn't get over the subtlety of flavor. Now I know that I will not buy one in the store.

"If you want, I can bring you some bottles," she said enthusiastically.

"Yeah, you'll be back in mid-August, and then I won't be here. I'll be somewhere ... Somewhere in Poland ... for sure - I saddened. My future prospects did not look bright. I sighed.

"Oh, there are couriers, parcel lockers. Everything can be arranged, Lena said, then offered." This is your fourth lesson, I suggest a slight gallop, what do you say?

"I don't know, let's try, in the event of a fall, I won't fly far" I looked at how far to the ground.

"Don't worry," she smiled and attached the rope to the bridle. Holding the end of it, she stepped back and called something to the mare. Tina moved faster and I tensed up. I tried to stay in the saddle. After a while it turned out that it wasn't so scary at all, in fact it was quite cool.

When I finished the lesson, Anthony appeared next to the stable. He looked at me meaningfully and said:

"Good morning, Sad Eyes." How are you?

"Good morning, Mr. Anthony, I'm doing great" I replied, glancing at the relaxed old man.

"I will believe that it's great when I see a beautiful colorful dress instead of these pants, because only such a dress fits a beautiful woman."

"Grandpa!" Lena admonished him with a laugh.

"Am I not telling the truth?" he scowled.

I looked at Lena and Anthony, surprised. Who would have thought. Anthony father of Olivia? Lena's grandfather? Hmm, that would be fine.

"Thank you very much for today's lesson. Take care, see you! Mr Anthony, it was nice to see you again" after these words I left, leaving them arguing about whether it is possible to tell others in such a direct way how they should dress. I'm afraid Lena lost this verbal battle. I went to my room with a smile on my face and took a bath.

That evening, after dinner, Marilyn came to my room. She had a large colorful bag with her.

"Hey, there's some romantic movie downstairs, all the couples are embracing and watching. They show off one another. And I'm not going to sit with them, so I went to do some scouting, looked in the hot tub, and there's no one there. Free. So get into your bathing suit and let's go." She rubbed her hands together in satisfaction. "Come on, get going before someone occupies our spot."

"Now?" I asked. I didn't want to go anywhere. I planned to sit alone. I even felt a little melancholy.

"Yeah. When? It's early, are you going to bed? Well, put yourself together yourself."

Without a word of objection, I went to the bathroom and prepared myself accordingly.

As soon as I plunged into the warm water and felt the bubbles massaging my body, I immediately relaxed and decided that Marilyn had a great idea. We sat in the hot tub and talked.

– What would you like to do in the future? What dreams do you have? Marlene asked.

- I don't know. Not so long ago I had dreams, and now I don't know. Some job, some apartment, small.

"Oh, don't be so mundane. Let your imagination run wild. Holidays in Mallorca, on a fancy yacht, or a villa in the Alps, I don't know, maybe a balloon flight over Greece, or participation in the carnival parade in Rio de Janeiro? Or being an influential grandma that all the guys bow to almost to the ground…

"I never dreamed of anything like this," I admitted with a smile. But yours are great.

- You have to dream. And believe that at least some of them will come true. Without dreams, life would be gray and boring. You have to have a goal and work towards it.

Suddenly we turned towards the entrance. In a long, sports sweatshirt and flip-flops, a woman in her thirties entered, a blonde woman with fancifully styled short blonde hair. She had glasses on.

"Hi girls, can I join you? Do you mind?" she asked with a happy look.

"Yeah, come on, there's plenty of room," Marlene called eagerly. "Sylvia, I remember well, right?"

"Yes, you remember Marlene well."

"I'm Natalie" I introduced myself when the emaciated Sylvia sat next to us in the water.

"Hi. Nice to meet you," she said, squeezing my hand. "This movie is boring. I don't like romance novels, far from reality."

"Have you had a failed relationship too?" I asked about her comment.

She waved her right hand in front of her, showing the mark of her wedding ring.

"I had a husband once. He sat and languished at home. He did not want to go anywhere, his most faithful friend after work was the TV and beer. Nothing else interested him. Our marriage ended quickly. No regrets, no pretensions. You only live once, you don't know how long you have left, so you have to take what you have and do everything to make it fun. So I guess I can pin it down to a failed relationship.

"And where's your girlfriend?" - I asked.

"He talks to children via Skype. He has a great family. Martha's husband took the kids and they went to his parents in the countryside for a few days so that Martha could come here with me and relax. They are my wonderful friends. What about you girls?"

And discussions began, jokes, telling interesting stories. It was a very nice evening. I felt great with these girls I had just met. No one was judging anyone there, it was honest and fun. How far it was from my recent meetings with friends.

ROZDZIAŁ 5

The morning was a bit cloudy. I got up early and went outside. Wrapped in a warm sweater, I went to the lake. This time I didn't sit on the wooden boards, but walked along the shore and looked at the water. I walked slowly through the grassy area around the lake. Here and there were small coves covered with sand, like tiny beaches. Someone really went to great lengths to create such a unique place. In the distance, I saw two people jogging. One of them was Olivia, I recognized her by her colorful tracksuit. A man was running beside her. Once they got to the property, they slowed to a walk. They started talking. Finally they stopped completely. Olivia explained something, sometimes she put her hand on her companion's shoulder. I thought it was Damien, but wasn't quite sure.

I turned and looked back at the lake. I went a bit further. On the grass-covered shore, a fifty-year-old man sat in a tourist chair. He had two fishing rods in his hand. He threw one away, prepared the other. I watched him struggle with his tackle, but he obviously knew what he was doing. He was doing very well.

"Good morning," he called to me.

"Good morning," I replied and walked closer. – Do they take fish? Did you manage to catch something? I asked.

"I just started today, but I catch something every day.

"I've always wondered what it is about fishing that you can sit there for hours, sometimes even get up very early."

"Relax, my dear. Peace and quiet. This is the only place my wife won't go. I have time here to think, to be with nature, to look at the water. I'm resting. And by the way, it's good when you catch something."

"I've never fished," I said.

"Do you want to try? I have two fishing rods, please." He stood up and pointed to the tackle in his hand."

"Really? I will not disturb?" I asked contentedly.

"Are you kidding? I invite you"

"Will you show me how to handle it?" I asked, taking the fishing rod in my hand.

"My name is Zbigniew, I will be glad if you call me by my name. According to the rules here. And I feel a little younger."

"I am Natalie. So what should I do?" a fishing rod "like a simple stick with a fishing line and a reel, but you still need to know what to do with it."

Zbigniew patiently explained everything. He is a very nice, warm man. Slightly round, not tall. With a great sense of humor. I spent a pleasant morning with him. I was glad that I managed to catch one. But I asked him to put her back in the water. What's this fish for? What would I do with her? Let it flow better. I found out that Zbigniew came here with his wife, Dorothy. I deduced from the conversation that she must be quite a domineering and temperamental person. I had the impression that Zbyszek felt overwhelmed, underestimated and simply misunderstood in his marriage. It was his wife, Dorothy, who ruled, and he agreed to everything, for peace of mind.

There was no yoga or meditation scheduled for that day. It was supposed to be a surprise in the afternoon. I decided to use the time after breakfast to practice meditation on my own. First, I checked on the Internet how to go about it. I remember exactly the session that Olivia conducted with us. I figured I could handle it. At least I'll try. I sat in my room, cross-legged on the floor. I relaxed my whole body and focused on my breathing. There were noises coming from the street, distracting me. So I got up and closed the balcony window. I sat back on the floor. I relaxed my whole body as Olivia had told me. I carefully scanned my feet, legs, hips, and up to the top of my head. I don't even know when I forgot about conscious breathing, and my attention wandered somewhere far behind my thoughts.

I woke up some time later that this is not the way, I got lost, so I got back on the right track. Inhale and exhale. I felt my whole body expand when I inhaled and contract when I exhale, it was as if I was breathing all over me. Interesting feeling. Again my thoughts wandered to the past. I caught on to it pretty quickly. I went back to breathing. I focused on being inside myself, I read that it is good to put your hand in the center of your chest and focus all your attention there. Be in the field of the heart. The heart supposedly has its own neural connections and communicates with the brain. The heart generates a strong electromagnetic field, much stronger than the brain, and entering the state of coherence through slow breaths, i.e. consistency at the level of the brain and heart rhythm, has a very positive effect on a person. It has the power of healing, regeneration, full harmony.

I tried to calmly focus on myself, on proper breathing, while giving myself space to make mistakes. I studied and my practice was far from ideal. I didn't give up, I cared, I felt that I should go in this direction.

When I opened my eyes, I was still sitting still, a delight taking in silence. I was relaxed, calm, I felt good. My body was a little numb from being still in one position, but I didn't mind. I got up and took a deep breath. Nothing special happened during the meditation. I know that there is more to it, that it takes practice, more concentration, and most of all, I couldn't expect anything to happen at the very beginning. It calmed me down, and I appreciated that I was able to stay focused for a while. It's still a big success.

With a slightly better attitude towards the world, I went to dinner.

Around three o'clock, all willing women were to gather upstairs in a smaller conference room. The male part of the guests of the guesthouse, led by Anthony, went to the forest to build a hut. As the group of men retreated, one clear conclusion came to mind: all these guys, without exception, could learn a lot from the perky and charismatic guide of seventy. They followed him like little boys, devoid of any imaginativeness.

In the conference room, on a long table, a row of mirrors were waiting for us, one next to the other. Several baskets filled with cotton pads and cotton buds. We were greeted by a beautiful middle-aged woman who was slightly overweight. She was wearing perfect make-up and amazing joy in her eyes. It literally glowed from a distance.

"Come, come, come, my dear. Take your seats, please. You have mirrors in front of you. I am a consultant of a well-known cosmetic brand and today I will teach you professional make-up. Surely each of you can paint well. Today I will tell you some secrets. We will perform a skin examination and assessment, select cosmetics and with these cosmetics selected for you, you will do your own makeup using our tips. My name is Eve, and these are my assistants: Gosia and Elvira – she said at the beginning.

I sat at one of the mirrors. And I looked at my own reflection. No makeup. Gray complexion, serious look. I tried to smile, but somehow it came out artificially. So I focused on Eve.

"My dear, I will invite each of you for a skin examination in turn. There's three of us, so it'll be quick. You will also get catalogs and you will mark the numbers of creams, foundations, shadows and lipsticks that will be best for you. Elvira, hand out the catalogs, and I'm already inviting the first people to do the research. I just ask that you remove your makeup before the examination. Here's some cotton pads and some lotions. Let's get to work.

I picked up the catalog and started looking. Nicely published, encouraging to buy, but the prices are quite high. However, nothing at first glance appealed to me. I bought good cosmetics and never had any problems with my skin. I set the catalog down on the table and watched the confusion that developed in the examination line. All the women wanted to be at the beginning, as if it was of some great importance. One of them, a very young woman, well-groomed, refused to remove her make-up. Eve encouraged her gently, but Aileen, almost in tears, refused. In the end, she had to give up the study. She sat at the end of the table and stared at her reflection in the mirror. She checked that everything was in order, then went through the catalog.

I went at the very end. I sat down and let myself place the metal analyzer head on several places on my face.

"Good, skin hydration level 55%, oil triple. Very good. You could use a good scrub, I'm writing it down, we'll definitely pick something up. There are no inflammations on the skin, they are single, few under the skin, but there is nothing to worry about. No redness, slight discoloration. Very good. I invite you to the table" Elvira handed me a test card with circled results.

Moments later, makeup lessons began. We were divided into three groups, each of the consultants took care of their charges. They advised, chose serums for each of us, then creams. We put layers on the face one by one. We could only pick up the cream with a disposable cotton bud, so everything was done in full hygienic respect. I enjoyed this. The problem arose with Aileen, a beautiful girl who did not want to remove her make-up for the examination. Now she would not allow herself to be touched, nor would she apply the cream herself. Her foundation was carefully applied and she resented the thought of tapping on anything that might ruin her perfect image. But she was still sitting in front of the mirror.

"All right, Aileen, if you don't want to, that's fine. We don't force. Maybe you will choose something from powders or shadows, you will surely be interested in something" said Elvira patiently, and then she began to provide information on how to apply creams, how often, what amount, what to pay attention to when choosing foundations. She chose the cosmetics for each of us perfectly. She squeezed foundation from the tube onto our hands and we rubbed it on our face ourselves. Then there were eyeshadows, eyeliners, mascaras, powders, bronzers and lipsticks. We recorded all our choices in catalogs.

"You can join our club and buy all cosmetics at good prices. You have already selected what is best for you and marked the codes. I encourage you to buy, you can see that the cosmetics are of the best quality. You can also become consultants. People who order from us today will receive an attractive gift" said Ela convincingly.

After these words, Olivia came out into the middle of the room.

"My darling, look in the mirror. You look beautiful. And you did it yourself. You did this professional makeup yourself. If anyone wants to place an order, please go ahead. I just have an announcement: I will give you another half an hour for questions, conversations with girls, use this time because they are specialists, the show was free. And then I invite you to a larger conference room, there's the rest of the surprise. The surprise will have a charity aspect. I'm sure you'll like it and if you want to support a worthy cause financially, it's on me. I'm waiting for you, my dear."

Olivia left, and after a while there was an incredible racket. Three consultants were even surrounded by women. Each of them wanted to ask a question and get a comprehensive answer. Elvira gave us a small hand cream as a gift. I had a good time at this show. I received some important tips that I will certainly use in the future. But I left the room. It was too noisy here. At Olivia's suggestion, I headed to the other conference room. There I stood surprised. A graphite cloth was draped over a large easel, and two lamps stood right in front of it. Olivia was accompanied by a young, slim woman in loose, slightly extravagant clothes. She held a large camera in her hand.

"Natalie, welcome!" cried Olivia. We have a little photoshoot for you here. If you want, we will be glad. Agatha is a photographer by passion, and by profession she is the director of the local children's home and collects money for her charges, so we ask for donations in the can. Not obligatory, only for volunteers. This is a charity event.

I was surprised.

"I will take a few photos, develop the best three in 15x21 format and deliver them in a few days – explained Agatha." You are ready? Would you like a session?

"Yes, of course," I agreed, stunned.

"I have a suggestion. We can do a session in what you are in or I have a white or light gray raw material here - you can wrap yourself in it like a towel. I mean the effect will be amazing. If you can strip down to your underwear, here behind the screen..."

"Okay, maybe," I replied and let myself be led behind the screen. Agatha first moved the fabrics to my face, then definitely chose white.

"Okay, this will be better," she handed me the fabric. "Wrap it around you so your bare shoulders are visible." Here on the table you have bracelets, put a few on one wrist and invite you to the stage.

I felt weird. I did what she asked. I stood in front of the camera, holding down the rough, linen material that fell down to the floor. Agatha came over and adjusted my hair a bit, brushed back my hair and, touching my chin gently, set my head in the right position.

She asked me to extend my knee so that part of my leg would stick out from under this strange dress that I had pinned up on me. She improved the positioning at the chest a bit.

Olivia came from the other side and spoke to me in a warm voice full of delight.

"You look beautiful. Agatha is a true artist. trust her. Feel this beauty within yourself. You know you have incredible power, show it here to the camera. Show what you have the best in yourself, all your sensitivity, this uniqueness, what no one else has but you. Show your true self. You're beautiful. Come on! I believe in you. Now you believe in yourself."

I glanced at Olivia, her eyes glowing with sympathy, and looked straight at the camera.

"It's good. Now tilt your head slightly down, not too much, it's good" said Agatha, she was focused. I heard the rustling of the shutter, looked ahead, tried to summon all the sensitivity and joy at the same time. I wanted these photos to turn out well.

"Wonderful," said Agatha. "Now turn slightly to the right. Yes, it's great. Beautifully! We have it! Thank you."

"Thank you," I said, and went behind the screen to change into my clothes.

When I came out from behind the screen, Olivia asked me not to remove my make-up.

"It's not over yet. Don't take off your makeup, we'll all do it together after dinner. All right? It is very important. Great photos, you really did a great job."

"Of course. Thank you. Tell me, here in town, how big is this orphanage?" I asked, moved. "Is it far?"

"About twenty kilometers from here. There are several kids of different ages. Agatha tries to make sure that they don't miss anything, that they feel as little as possible in your situation. I support her as much as I can."

"Approx. thanks" I left after that. I quickly found myself in my room. I found my wallet in my backpack and pulled out four hundred. I put it in my pocket. I was sorry those kids didn't have parents. It should not be like that. I understood them a bit. At least I had mine until I was nine. I knew that they were somewhere in a distant world and I could call them at any time, and sometimes they even appeared for a moment, I was grateful for that, even though they left behind a great sadness each time. Agatha's charges did not have such an opportunity.

I ran to the second floor. Several women had already gathered in the conference room. Olivia explained what the purpose of this project is. The first of the ladies had already had a photo session, and the rest watched with delight and anticipation when it would be their turn. I discreetly walked over to the box and put in the money. Then I stood by the wall and watched Agatha's work and women's emotions. It was great, exciting. I was a bit tense during the session, now I'm relaxed. It was nice to see the already familiar faces of the friends from the boarding house pry with the camera, how much joy it gives them. How much fun they have and how generously they throw huge donations into the tin.

It's amazing how in a very short time of staying at the guest house the women made friends with each other. Some of them had only just met and were showing so much kindness and sympathy. They opened up to each other and talked a lot. I noticed these intimacies. They certainly arose from girl meetings organized by Olivia and common challenges, such as swimming in the lake in only underwear after dark, a great action of checking fluids in cars and now this. A beautiful initiative. I felt good in this place, very good indeed. And to think that just a few days ago, I shunned everyone, wanted to be alone with my own grief. And here please! Beautiful place, beautiful energy.

Dinner went very happily. All the ladies were in great spirits, there was no end to the discussions about the photo session.

Only one, Dorothy, was dissatisfied because after long discussions with cosmetic consultants, she was late for the session and took part in it as the last participant. It was almost unthinkable.

Damien sat next to me that day.

"Hi. Can I sit down?" He asked.

"You're welcome," I replied. I still remembered that situation in the training room where Damien and another guy had witnessed me venting my anger on a punching bag. I still felt embarrassed.

"I hear you had a very successful afternoon."

"As you can see, women are easy to make happy."

"Well, not necessarily. Sometimes you get older and it just gets worse" he said. I gave him a curious look to keep him busy with his plate and not continue.

"Did you manage to build a hut?" I asked.

"Of course. As we had most prepared in the woods, this was not a great philosophy. Appreciate the idea. Olivia and Anthony are amazing. It's different here every year. Getting better. Constant development. I admire their willingness to organize it all. It's a lot of work every day. And it's good work."

I absolutely agree with that. There's no chance of getting bored here. Before, I didn't even know that there could be such a guesthouse in the mountains, amazing.

"And how did you get here?" - He asked.

"By accident. Long story."

"Tell me," he encouraged.

"Unfortunately, that's not a cool one."

"It doesn't matter. Come on, you got me interested."

"My sister gave me a paid voucher to stay here. She couldn't come herself, so she sent me. I just got in the car, punched the address in the navigation and here I am."

"A great gesture."

"Not necessarily. I stayed with her for two weeks, maybe she just wanted to get rid of me for a while," I said, trying to make it sound like a joke.

"Seriously?"

"Of course."

At that moment my phone in my pocket rang. I glanced at the screen and frowned.

"We're talking about the wolf," I said, tensing. "Excuse me, I have to pick up."

I got up and went out into the corridor. I answered the call.

"Hi Eve," I greeted my sister over the phone. I know she didn't call for no reason.

"Natalie! How are you? How are you there? Nice hotel? Are you comfortable there?"

"It is fine. And with you? How to prepare for the show?"

We're almost done, lots of emotions. I'm so excited that I don't sleep at night. I meet fantastic people. Lots of famous personalities from the world of fashion. I'm very screwed up. Listen, I'm calling because my friend has an apartment to rent. In the center of Warsaw, maybe you would be interested? After knowing him, he will count a little cheaper. Very nice, comfortable, personally checked. What do you think?

I held my breath, then let it out slowly through my mouth.

"I will rent an apartment wherever I can find a job. I don't know where it will be yet. There are currently no vacancies for an English teacher."

"I'm sure you'll find something, keep your head up," Eve said enthusiastically.

"I understand that I cannot stay with you until I find a job?" It was more of a statement than a question.

"You know, you can, you can, of course. Only in a week Marcin will move in with me. He proposed to me! I agreed, but you know, I prefer to observe him and live with him before we take any further steps. It's just to make you feel comfortable when the three of us live together. That's why I'm calling to warn you."

"Congratulations. Somehow you've known this Marcin for a long time" I reminded him.

"We've been dating for half a year. He's a great guy, you'll meet him, you'll see.

"Great, I'm happy for you." congratulations. And get along with your friend. I will rent this apartment from her.

"I'm sure you will be satisfied" Eve's voice was full of energy and enthusiasm. "Oh dear, they're calling me, I have to go." Take care.

"Sure, bye."

I put my phone in my pocket and went out onto the terrace. I leaned against the wooden beam and sighed. I lost my appetite. I heard the clatter of cutlery and the sound of conversation coming from the dining room. I didn't even want to think. I just stared at the slightly cloudy sky and my mind went blank. I felt alone like a finger in a big world full of people. Damien was waiting in the dining room, but I didn't feel like talking further.

I left the terrace and headed towards the lake. I just focused on what was around me. Trees, bushes, fragrant flowers, birds flying low. I was just walking ahead. I've shed so many tears in the last three weeks that the tank is empty. I preferred to focus my attention on something more pleasant than analyzing the conversation with Eve. I was walking through the meadows towards the forest. I touched the ears of tall grass with my hand, I looked at the vegetation around me.

I got back to the guest house late. Calm, serious, reconciled with what I have and where I am. I had the impression that my life was going on as if without my participation, as if I had no influence on anything. Other people made the decisions, and I was just a puppet. And the more I rebelled, the more unhappy I became. I've come to terms with it. I was going to stay at the boarding house for two more weeks and then go back to worrying about my future.

After dinner, Olivia invited all the women to the conference room, where until noon we learned the art of make-up, applying it on our own faces. The mirrors were still lined up on the long table. In the center were several containers of cotton balls and makeup remover.

We sat on chairs, each of us had a mirror standing on a leg in front of us.

"How are you, my dear?" Olivia asked enthusiastically.

"All right!"

"Great!"

"This photo session was great, thank you."

There were a few comments and assurances that it was great. I was silent, of course.

"I'm very happy about that," Olivia said happily. "You were great at the session, what energy and emotions it was, I am impressed! listen. We are gathered here for a specific, very important purpose. In the morning you painted yourself, perfect make-up with your own hands, some of you are masters at it, but some of you have jumped, you could say, to a higher level in this field. Now look in the mirrors. How do you feel? How have you been feeling all day? Better? More cheerful? A well-groomed woman, in a beautiful dress and good make-up, usually feels fantastic."

Compliments, praise, acceptance poured in.

"Look in the mirrors. what do you see?" asked Olivia, carefully watching all her charges.

The women took turns answering, shouting over each other.

"Better skin!"

"Eyes look better with thickened eyelashes. It could be even better. Overall it's ok."

"My cheeks are pink, I'm not so pale after all!"

"And my facial features were softened, I couldn't get over it."

"It didn't cover all my pimples, they are still visible. Poor foundation."

"I look younger."

Olivia listened to everyone carefully, then asked a question:

Do you like that reflection in the mirror? Are you happy looking in the mirror every day? Just sincerely please.

Women willingly shared their observations.

"No, rather not."

"I can look in the mirror in the morning only after I wash my face and apply cream."

"It's not without make-up."

"For example, even though the make-up is perfect, I still focus on imperfections. Because the nose is too big, because the eyes are too wide apart. Now I am happy because I look prettier, but I would like to be prettier" said Martha. "But today I'm happy."

Olivia said seriously:

"It's easy to look at yourself with acceptance when you have nice make-up and a nice hairstyle, isn't it? And the most important thing is to look at yourself with admiration always, no matter where we are, what we are doing and in what shape we are. Look at yourself again, straight in the eye. We abandon criticism, judgments and opinions. Right now, what other people think of us is completely irrelevant. Look each other straight in the eye, deeply. What do you see there? What do you see there? No criticism, no evaluation. I know it's very difficult. Who do you see there? Take your time. In silence."

I looked in the mirror and saw my face. I wasn't a beauty, but I didn't really have anything to reproach myself for either. I usually looked in the mirror to see if I had got toothpaste on me or if the cream was applied properly. I also checked my hairstyle, usually after washing my hair, holding the hair dryer in my hand. It never occurred to me to stand in front of a mirror and stare at myself. What for? I couldn't change the way I looked anyway.

I trusted Olivia, she knew what she was doing, so as she instructed,

I looked in the mirror further, deeper into my own eyes. I saw the pupil, the iris. For a moment, I even thought that the structure of the eye resembled a cluster of galaxies in space. The day before, I saw a photo of such a phenomenon on the Internet, which delighted me.

"The eyes are the mirror of the soul" Olivia continued after a short moment of silence. – There is a lot of truth in this saying. If someone is sad, you can see it in their eyes and, regardless of assurances that everything is ok, they feel great, they even smile widely. The eyes will show everything. If someone is really pissed off and pretends to be calm, that's also easy to oh notice. True? So let's learn to look deeper. What do you see? What's playing in your soul?

I saw a lot of sadness and resignation, a serious look. The sadness was so intense that I held my breath. My eyes widened in disbelief. That's why Anthony used to call me "sad eyes" and recently a woman came over to ask if I was okay. I'd noticed that serious look before, briefly looking in the mirror, but it was only now that it caught my eye with such force. I saw the real me. And what's next? Even deeper? Do I want to visit there? Will I be able to? What if the truth I find there is too much for me? What if I don't accept it?

I took a deep breath, held it too long. I felt strong emotions inside me.

I looked at this depth of sadness and pain in my own eyes. What was I supposed to do with it now? Have I always been like this, or just because of recent events?

"Remember, we do not judge, we do not criticize, we are looking for the pure truth" Olivia's voice was heard, then silence fell again.

I paid no attention to anyone, completely forgot that I was sitting at a table with more than fifty women. I was completely focused on myself. I put the mirror down for a moment to distance myself, but grabbed it again. What I saw and experienced was very revealing. Surprising.

Olivia broke the silence again with words.

"Now look at your beautiful makeup." Is he so important after what you just saw in the mirror? It's beautiful here - she placed a hand on her chest - from the inside, from who we really are. And I assure you, each of you is unique, unique, beautiful, you just haven't discovered it in yourself yet. It's not perfect make-up that makes a woman attractive - it's self-confidence, a sense of her uniqueness. A woman who feels attractive is attractive no matter what she is wearing. A woman who feels valuable has other intentions to take care of herself. I don't paint to please someone else, I paint for myself. He doesn't have to look at himself in the mirror or in the eyes of other people, because he knows that he looks good. She's sure of it. She puts on nice, colorful dresses not to make her office colleagues jealous, but it results from the need to ensure comfort and well-being. Because it deserves it. Just. Can you see the difference? Yes? So, my darlings, you have cosmetic pads and micellar waters on the table - now take off your makeup. Slowly, carefully. Take your time. Give yourself as much time as you need.

"How do you remove makeup?" Aileen was outraged."Now? In front of everyone?"

"Yes, right now" Olivia explained gently and moved towards Aileen. She suspected she might be in trouble.

"I'm not going to show up here without makeup." "No way!" – Aileen was unpleasantly moved.

"Of course you don't have to," Olivia assured her. "If you're not comfortable with that, that's fine."

"Hey, why not?" Dorothy replied. She was the type of woman you notice immediately when you enter a room filled with people. Energetic, well built, with oxidized, perfectly styled hair. She always had a lot to say about anything and she said it very loudly so that everyone could hear it clearly. "What's so terrible about that?" We all do it already.

"Absolutely not! Aileen got up. She was getting more and more pissed off." How can you even appear in public without makeup? It's unthinkable! she screamed.

"Aileen, you are a beautiful woman. Who, like who, but you don't have to worry about it, really" said Marilyn from the other end of the table.

"What can you know? You don't know anything" after these words she ran out of the room crying.

A lively discussion ensued among the group of women. No one could understand Aileen's behavior. Such a woman, like a model, and she had a problem with removing her makeup in public? How is this possible? There was no end to speculation.

Olivia at that time went out for a moment, probably to console Aileen.

I did not comment on Aileen's behavior. She certainly had her reasons for reacting this way. It's so easy to judge others without knowing exactly what the real reason is. I listened to the women's discussions and was clearly surprised by their ideas and conjectures.

Only the appearance of Olivia interrupted the discussion.

"What stage are we at?" she asked loudly, over the buzz of conversation "Shall we take off the make-up? Remember, it's only for volunteers, I'm not forcing you to do anything."

Conversations died down, each of the ladies took care of herself and careful makeup removal.

"Remember, my dear, you are doing this for yourself, for that wonderful woman you saw in the mirror. You already know that it's not makeup that makes you beautiful.

"Only our own awesomeness! Sorry, I got distracted! I didn't want to interrupt" said smiling Marilyn, clasping her hands as if in prayer.

"Very well said. I couldn't have put it better," Olivia said.

There was laughter in the hall.

"And now see yourself in the mirror. This is the same person you saw fifteen minutes earlier", said Olivia.

"Well, not anymore," came the comment. "I preferred the version of myself I was fifteen minutes ago."

"Exactly. Everyone prefers that" Olivia agreed. "Now look deep into each other's eyes again." Very deep. Has anything changed deep down? Has who you really are changed?

There was silence. Nobody said anything for several minutes.

"It's about accepting yourself just as much, no matter what shape you're in. Now I'm going to tell you about a very powerful and effective tool that we can help ourselves to build self-acceptance. This exercise seems simple and pleasant, but I assure you that it is not that simple. However, I think it's worth taking up the challenge. I cordially encourage you to do so. This is the mirror method. It consists in standing in front of the mirror, looking at yourself, preferably deep into your eyes, and saying to yourself: "I love you. You are wonderful. I'm so proud of you. I really love you". This should be done every day, as often as possible, on every possible occasion. Entering the bathroom in the morning, when the eyes are still sleepy, the eyelids are swollen, the hair is untied. Stand in front of the mirror, smile at your reflection and say "I love you". That's all, dear. And so much. A lot of people can't do that. They do not like to look at themselves, they run away when they see their own reflection. They get angry, they get angry. They look in the mirror and immediately judge and criticize. What does this mean? Does this person even like themselves? What do you think? Does this person accept themselves?

There was a murmur of conversation in the room, but no one said anything aloud.

"Well…" continued Olivia. – We look for everything we need outside, in the world around us, and the point is to find it all inside ourselves. Look inside, look at your soul, see the truth about yourself and come to terms with it. We want acceptance? Of course, everyone wants it - so let's give it to ourselves. We expect love? Let's love ourselves first, and if we love ourselves, others will love us automatically. This is the correct order. Whatever we change in ourselves, whatever we give to ourselves, or take care of ourselves, the effect of this will be the change we will see on the outside. Not the other way around. It is very important to have contact with yourself, to understand yourself, to support yourself. Know what I want, who I am and what I am. If we want to change our lives for the best, we must start with ourselves, with our thoughts and beliefs. It's the only way. And such a seemingly innocent word to the mirror for good morning does a great job. Check how it works for you. Pay attention to the thoughts that arise on the first day of working with the mirror, then in two weeks, in three weeks. You can write down your feelings daily. You will see what a huge difference there will be in how you see yourself. After a month, you will be smiling happily at yourself in the mirror, even if you see your reflection in a shop window, anywhere. Smile and joy. And you say "I love you" to yourself a hundred times a day, and if possible, a thousand times a day. And you will see how your life will change. For the better, of course. Self-confidence, faith, inner strength and conviction that you deserve the best will appear. There will be great opportunities, cooler people, fantastic experiences. And if there is a problem or sadness, you can deal with it more easily. And that's just for two words: "I love you." That's it from my side for today. I consider this day very successful and fruitful. Thank you very much and have a peaceful night.

The next day, right after waking up, I went to the bathroom and, remembering Olivia's extremely valuable lessons, I put my hands on the sink and looked in the mirror. I was asleep, half awake.

"I love you. You are super. You are wonderful. I really love you." I said to my reflection. I saw that the same serious face was still looking at me, without a trace of a smile. I stretched my lips into something that might have been him, but within seconds she was wearing the same grim expression again.

I washed my face with cold water. I thought maybe it would be better now.

"I love you. I love you so much. I love you very, very much." My voice faltered. It finally disappeared. I looked at my reflection and felt sad.

It felt weird saying those words as if they weren't about me. They were empty, meaningless. I just sighed and did my morning routine.

After a yoga class on mats on the orchard lawn, and a hearty breakfast, I strolled around the guesthouse. In one conference room, through the open door, I saw Olivia spreading sheets of paper on the tables. She had a lot of it.

"What interesting are you doing? Can help you?" I suggested.

"If you want, feel free to join." I prepared classes for couples for the afternoon. It's supposed to rain in the evening, I decided to come up with something so that the guests wouldn't get bored, I planned a little entertainment.

"What do I should do?"

"Place two pens on each desk. Right next to these cards."

"Promises to be interesting."

"It's going to happen."

"Do you organize any conventions or external trainings here?" I asked, bearing in mind such a well-prepared place for such activities.

"Bright. November, February, March. These are the months when I have a bit less guests and I reserve places and rooms for companies. These are usually two or three day sessions."

"Where do you get so much strength and ideas to organize entertainment practically every day? I asked, walking between the tables."

"I like this. I enjoy it. Besides, it's my job," she replied.

"You're lucky to be able to do whatever you want, to have a job you're passionate about.

" So can you"

"Are you kidding?" I smiled bitterly. This life is only for the chosen ones.

"And why do you think you can't have the job you want or the life you want?" What stops you? Olivia asked, looking at me seriously, attentively.

"What's stopping me?" Everything.

"Everything, so what exactly?"

I fell silent. I didn't know what to say to that question, nothing made sense to me.

"I don't have a job or a home because of my would-be mother-in-law. I'm alone. I'm in a hopeless situation. So how am I affecting my life? No. What prospects for the future? Rather lousy, I said, still unfolding my pens.

"First of all, you've already done a lot. You freed yourself from a toxic mother-in-law and from a guy who didn't grow up in a relationship. It was your decision, notice.

"It was Evelyn who made me do it."

"But you chose it." You do not see it? You could have stayed and let yourself be pushed around, and you chose otherwise. You made the best decision you could under the circumstances. As for the future… You're at a point where you can do anything right now, let's say zero, from where you can go either way. So choose what you really want, not what you have to.

"Sounds nice, but it's not that easy," I sighed heavily.

"Depends on how you look at it… If you want to see problems, you see problems. You want to see solutions, you see solutions. The only limits are in your head" said Olivia and sat down on the table top. She put her work aside and focused her full attention on me. I didn't feel very comfortable with it, but I went on with the subject.

"But I can't do otherwise," I said.

"I understand perfectly. I just want to make you realize that looking at everything negatively, with fear, you close yourself off to certain favorable circumstances. You may not even notice them. Sometimes there are, let's say, coincidences, you have to accept them and use what they bring. And don't be afraid. You will find that even from the most difficult situation you can find a way out if you want. All it takes is a little faith and focus on the positives."

"What if you don't see the positives? If they don't exist?"

"They always exist. Look - if Evelyn hadn't pissed you off, you wouldn't be here. We wouldn't be sitting in this room and talking. You wouldn't learn yoga, meditation, the fact that you can jump into a lake at night with a bunch of almost strangers and have a great time. Natalie, first of all, there are no people who do not have problems or do not suffer for one reason or another. People just don't talk about it out loud. They complain and criticize, but no one will admit that they feel weak or lonely. Second, everything that happens to you in life is for a reason. Certain unwanted events are there to show you that you may not be on the right path. Sometimes it has to be bad for a while to get better later.

Third, your life depends only on you. You create them."

"It sounds so beautiful in theory," I said honestly.

"In practice too, but you have to be willing to take responsibility for yourself" replied Olivia.

I looked at her carefully. What she said touched me.

She continued speaking.

People always blame others for their failures. Everyone is to blame but them. This is the easiest, the simplest. Will something fail? Here you go - you can immediately name at least a few people who can be blamed. And the truth is that if something does not work out around you, you have to look for a solution within yourself. This is what taking responsibility for yourself is all about. It is worth considering why mistakes are made? Why is everything around me collapsing? What are our beliefs? What thoughts attract these events. What can we do about it? This is the key. Finding your misconceptions, those childhood programs I was talking about, and healing them. You will change something in yourself, even a little bit - the world around you will change too. It requires hard work, patience and willingness. Yes, it is not easy, but it gives a sense of peace and trust.

How do I find these misconceptions in myself?

I have one very effective method. In the morning, when you get up, immediately after waking up, take a piece of paper, a pen and write. About whatever comes to you mind. It may be without composition and order. No dots, commas. Everything you can think of. Even if you don't know what to write. Make it three pages each day. No less. These three pages are very important. There, in this saved notebook, you will find everything. You will see, you will be surprised. Another way, also related to writing - if you want to know the reason for an action, write it on a piece of paper, one sentence, and then ask yourself "why?" When you get an answer, ask "why" and write. Until you see the truth. I recommend this method because it takes your shoes off. Literally.

"Interesting..." I said, listening carefully.

"Another way: sit down in the evening, as if to meditate, calm down and observe what thoughts come to you. Ask yourself what hurts you the most, what bothers you, what you can't forgive yourself and others? Let the emotions flow. There may be a lot of tears, but it means you're going in the right direction. It's very cleansing. After each such session you are stronger, calmer, with more self-confidence. This is being with you, no matter what, discovering who you are, what our soul wants, what it wants and give it to it. Give yourself what you need."

"How do you know all this?" You say it with such confidence...

"From my own experience," she replied shortly.

"So you're not a philosopher or a psychologist?" These are amazing wisdoms, the knowledge you give me turns the concept of life upside down.

"I was lost once in my life. I was stuck in something that wasn't good for me. I got warnings but ignored them. Finally, life knocked me to my knees and crawled so that I was forced to take responsibility for myself. Two years of searching for the truth, searching for myself, brave decisions, sometimes even great losses, but I made it. Strong, in harmony with each other. Happy. Was it worth it? Yes, of course. What I teach you, I first tested on myself. All.

"I thought you were lucky to just make it."

"I am lucky because I went through a difficult path, from being a constantly busy robot, meeting the expectations of others, to a happy, strong woman. And you can too, Natalie. You can do anything."

I smiled gratefully and went back to arranging the pens on the tables. I sighed happily, feeling a little lighter in my heart.

It was raining hard before lunch. I ran across the yard and got wet to the gym. I was pleased to see that no one was there. I looked around carefully before I started training. I put on my boxing gloves and focused on my punching bag exercises. I imagined all of my anger pooling in my hands and bursting out the moment I hit it. He is forcibly thrown away from me. I punched and kicked with power, sometimes I was out of breath, but I didn't give up. Sweat ran down his body. I lasted half an hour. Finally, I sat down on the floor, leaned against the wall and, breathing heavily, put my gloves aside. I felt fatigue in my body and incredible lightness in my soul. I smiled. I started noticing my thoughts and feelings, it was amazing. There were fractions of minutes when I focused on being aware, on observing myself. Big progress. What Olivia told me in the last conversation was a topic for many hours of thought and consideration. I wanted to be strong and happy. I decided that I would learn everything necessary to achieve my goal. I still have a week and a half left to stay at this guest house. I will use it to learn as much as possible. How good that I got there.

A large group of people gathered in the conference room. Couples eager for an entertaining quiz sat at the tables. The buzz of conversations, the shuffling of chairs, laughter. I walked in at the moment when Olivia started talking about what awaits us at the meeting.

"I have a lot of fun for you." Before we begin, I wanted to say a few words about relationships, not just marriage. Remember that the basis of healthy relationships is respect for the other person. It doesn't matter how old you are and how long your seniority is - this rule applies to everyone. In addition, if you are happy with yourself, accept and re-spect yourself, then your other half will be happy and joyful too. Be-cause somehow I can't imagine that satisfaction in a relationship can be created by an eternally nagging, whining and criticizing person. I personally would run far away from that. Or such extortion, emotio-nal blackmail, mutual clipping of each other's wings - this is unaccep-table, it will never bring anything good, it will tire even the most in love. Instead of focusing on your partner's flaws and mistakes, let's fo-cus on what he is good at, what he impresses us with. A simple exam-ple: when a woman or a man realizes himself, has his passions, he au-tomatically has a lot of positive energy, can support the other person, makes him feel better, motivates him to act well, generally the quality of such a relationship is much better more valuable. So let's take care of our well-being, and also respect and understanding. And now you have the papers in front of you, I asked you not to look at what is writ-ten there yet. You will answer the questions asked so as not to offend your partner. It should be positive, nice, with humor. The questions are simple, please be honest. There is no time limit. I will add that at the end you will exchange these cards with each other. You will read what your partner wrote. what? Ready? we start? The first question is: what do you value most about your partner?

Sitting in a chair to the side, I watched the blush-faced women write. The men were less optimistic.

"Oh, I forgot the most important thing" - Olivia said. - "A commis-sion consisting of people who are not in a relationship, because we have many of them here, will choose the most nice and cool couple. And for this couple there will be a prize - a relaxing massage perfor-med by our master, Monica. So it's worth the effort.

There were jokes, questions, anecdotes. The fun has begun.

I felt a bit out of place here, so I left the room. I went outside the bu-ilding and stopped on the covered terrace. I sat on a wooden bench and watched calmly as the rain fell. Dark gray clouds slid heavily across the sky. The rain was getting stronger, and the sound of a thunderstorm could be heard in the distance.

I sensed a presence behind me, so I turned around. Damien was standing in the entrance door to the guesthouse, his hands shoved into his jeans pockets. He looked up at the sky as the rain fell. When I looked at him, he noticed me. He took a few steps towards me.

"Not interested in tonight's party?" I asked.

"Not really."

"No fun for singles" - I said, shrugging.

"Exactly"

Damien sat next to me on the bench and we just listened to the intense sound of the rain.

"Do you think it is possible to create such a healthy relationship where you trust the other person? Is it possible at all?" I asked. Damien was at least a decade older than me, he certainly had a bit more to say about it.

"I don't know, I failed."

"How long have you been together?"

'Thirteen years. I have a divorce case in court in three weeks."

"Can't there be anything else to do?" I looked at him carefully.

"Nothing. I screwed up everything, I woke up too late."

"What do you mean?"

"Magda is a great woman, we met in college. We got married in our fifth year, and twin girls were born a short time later. I have two daughters. I was finishing my studies, working, making a career, and Magda stayed at home with the children. The beginnings were not easy, the girls gave us a hard time - he smiled for a moment. – Magda did everything, just everything, including getting me to sleep at night when the girls were teething or were sick. I worked more and more, stayed overtime, went to business meetings, and I never had time for her. Like the last donkey, I thought that if she was mine, she would stay mine. I don't have to try or strive for it anymore. Sometimes she asked us to go out together, without the children, to have fun, as in the past. And I didn't want to, because I missed being at home, I preferred to fool around with the kids in the living room. Magda never complained, even when it was hard for her, and I paid little attention to her. Four years ago she found a job. She broke out of the house. She changed, she started taking care of herself, wearing nice dresses and high heels to work. She started going out with friends on Friday nights. Then she stopped paying attention to me, she told me directly that she was tired of waiting. I didn't do anything smart then. I was just offended. Quiet days at home, avoiding each other, I couldn't talk to her. And there was someone who gave her what I couldn't give. Is happy. We meet often, we share responsibilities over the girls. I realized my mistakes too late. Now at least I can see it and I can talk about it. At that time, it seemed to me that I had nothing to reproach myself for, I blamed Magda for the entire breakdown of our marriage. We had a very frank conversation not long ago, and I realized this and that. I understood everything. I had a great wife and I screwed it all up."

We were silent for a moment.

"Are you thinking of getting involved with anyone else? Give yourself a chance?"I asked.

"Maybe..."

"Living alone isn't so scary," I said, thinking about my situation.

"It's not scary, but it's tiring. It's nice to walk into a house where someone is waiting for you."

I didn't answer. I just sighed heavily. After a while I asked.

"Will you tell me about your daughters?" What are the?

In the evening, after a bath, I sat on the bed, crossed my legs and leaned against the wall. I turned on relaxing music, very gentle, with elements of sounds straight from nature, such as birds singing, falling raindrops or the sound of the ocean. I listened to these tones for a long time, I was relaxed, that's what I meant. I focused on my breathing, counted slowly, first to four, then to six, inhaling and exhaling. At one point I stopped counting and sank into the center of my head. I waited for thoughts to come. Meaningless nonsense flew through my mind. I kept waiting. I asked myself directly how I felt, was there anything I should be aware of? Was there something that hurt me? touched? What in the past made me such a sad person? I sat focused and waited for something to come up. I didn't know what to expect. I resolved to endure whatever, whatever, even the most painful thing that came my way. If this is the only way to peace, strength and joy, then I will go this way.

I took a few deep, slow breaths. I felt my chest rise and fall. I started dozing off. I woke up, straightened up, and focused again on my breathing. The race of thoughts was incredible, it was hard to keep up with them. I smiled slightly. I took a deep breath and held my breath, imagining that I now had all my unwanted and tiring thoughts in my lungs. I exhaled very slowly. I heard air whistling out of my mouth. And again, I repeated the whole procedure all over again. And once more. And another. I got dizzy, so I went back to my normal breathing, a bit scared.

A long time later, I realized that my thoughts had stopped, were gone, flowed away, and I felt empty in my head. I smiled happily, a great discovery, every little step in this matter made me very happy. I stayed still like that, slightly sleepy, focused on my body, I couldn't feel my arms or legs - I knew they were there, but I couldn't feel them. I stayed in this state with curiosity, watched, and then, I don't even know when, I fell asleep. I woke up as my chin touched my chest. My neck hurt. I got into bed and covered myself with a duvet. Time to sleep.

The windows of the room faced south-east, so the sun peeked into me quite early in the morning, waking up pleasantly. Peace and quiet surrounded me. After waking up, I was still lying in bed and savoring that state. A few minutes later, I entered the bathroom. I looked at my face, a half-awaited look - immediately reminded me of the mirror exercise.

"Natalie," I said seriously to my reflection. "I want to let you know that I am going to learn to accept myself whether you like it or not. I'll do it. That's why I'll tell you, I love you. Yes, I love you." I paused for a moment to see how my mind would react. Apparently he was a little surprised, because I saw a grimace on his face. "I declare to you that I will speak to you like this every day. I'm trying, so don't make it hard for me. Just accept it without any objections, because I really don't want to force you, or myself, into anything. So I love you, I love you, I love you. I love you. It sounds weird, it looks weird. I know, but I still love you.

I went back to the room. I got dressed, took a notebook and a pencil and went out onto the balcony, sat in a comfortable armchair, leaned my feet against the railing and looked at the notebook. I already knew why he was on the TV. For several days I wondered what he was doing there. As you can see, everything had a purpose. The sun was shining in my eyes, but it didn't bother me too much, so I concentrated on what I had to write in my notebook. Olivia said anything I could think of, but no less than three pages. I grabbed a pencil in my hand and started writing.

I'm here in this boarding house, sitting on the balcony, I'm in a pretty good mood, nothing has pissed me off yet, of course, for a while. I get annoyed here sometimes, but it's better than this hopeless apathy. There are a lot of people here, it annoys me how they sometimes make noise at night. I go to bed early because I have nothing to do in the evening. During the day it's ok, but the evenings overwhelm me. So as not to be sad and not to fall into depression - I go to sleep. How do you fall asleep with those roaring fifties walking down the hall in high heels or giggling like teenagers? Are they too old for this behavior? Yes, it pisses me off. It annoys me that I don't know what will happen tomorrow, or next week, or next month.

It pisses me off that I've been here for a week and Eve only called once. It annoys me that Greg turned out to be such a weak boy. It pisses me off that I fell for it, I was so naive, I trusted him and he let me down. How could I let this happen? I'm pissed at myself, about everything, about this whole situation, about not knowing who I am or what I'm doing, not knowing what to do, where to go. I would like to hibernate like a bear in the winter and wake up in better times, if they ever come. I have a lot of this pissing off. And cool. I always tried, I always tried to make others happy with me. I helped my friends, where are they now? Did any of them take an interest in me after I left my job? Or maybe they were just acquaintances from work, not friends? Maybe I don't even know what friendship is, or maybe I'm weird? Or maybe abnormal? Something wrong with me? Maybe I want too much and hence all these problems? I want to scream out loud!!!!!

I woke up. I found myself breathing deeply, nervous, and the pencil broke from pressing too hard.

"Whew." I sighed and stood up. I was heavily agitated. I glanced at my watch: six twelve. I put on my tracksuit and ran out of the room. I didn't slow down even for a moment on my way to the gym. I was able to let my emotions out there. I knew it had a very good effect on me. Never before coming to this place had I given myself a chance or permission to vent my anger because it didn't feel right, because it looked bad, I had to be polite and obedient. And now I didn't have to. I put on my gloves and boxed as long as I could.

CHAPTER 6

In the morning I sat on a bench by a huge flower bed and read articles on the Internet on my phone about the workings of the mind, quantum physics, visualization and meditation. General information, whatever appeared in the search engine. I was extremely absorbed in it.

I didn't even notice when Anthony sat next to me and looked at me from under bushy eyebrows.

"Good morning, Sad Eyes," he said as I glanced at him in surprise.

"Good morning, Mr. Anthony" I put the phone in my pocket and straightened up slowly.

"You're not following the rules again." Such a pretty young girl in gray baggy pants. How are you going to find a husband? Dear child, you have to show your legs. It's me, a mature man, who should tell you how to expose your femininity?" he said seriously. "How to attract admirers? And you have a child of potential. And what a!"

"Mr Anthony..."

"Call me Anthony, by name, I still feel very young."

"I don't doubt it." I smiled widely. I remembered the sight from a few days ago when Anthony, full of strength and spirit, was leading a group of men into the forest to show them how to build a hut. I will never forget this view. This strength, charisma, self-confidence compared to much younger, even three decades younger colleagues. - Only, Mr. Anthony, I have to worry you - I'm not looking for a husband, so I don't need to show my legs.

"Oh, baby, you don't know what you're talking about." Just because you've dated a loser once or twice doesn't mean there aren't real men out there.

"I know they are. One is sitting right next to me," I said with a smile.

He looked at me with keen eyes and nodded his head amused.

"I still feel young, but my heart belongs to Helen. Oh, and there's my beauty." He pointed to the boarding house's front door, where the older receptionist's familiar face lit up at the sight of a small dog wagging its tail at her feet. She leaned over and stroked the dog. She called him and allowed him to enter the building.

"Lucky of you," I said.

"Oh yes. Helen is my great love. We met in Italy. She came to her cousin for a while. She lived in a beautiful house next to our vineyard. I saw her walking in the meadows, picking grapes, helping her cousin at work. I was so delighted with her. I was head over heels in love. How much did I go after my Helen, but she didn't want me. She brushed me off, kept telling me I wasn't serious enough. When she left, my life lost its meaning, I missed her terribly. I lasted two months and then followed her to Poland. Times weren't as easy then as they are now, my dear. I overcame all difficulties just to be with her. Believe me, it wasn't easy. I had to try to please her for a long time. Oh, I remember when she let me kiss her for the first time... He sighed dreamily. "It was something. I felt like the richest man in the world. It was worth the wait, oh well. I swore to her that I would take care of her, that she would be happy. Every day I tried and still try to live in such a way that she would not regret marrying me even for a moment."

"Beautiful story," I said dreamily.

"You're going to bring someone to their knees, too." Maybe not today, but who knows what tomorrow will bring... Look out, keep your heart and eyes wide open. You are young, beautiful, all the best is yet to come.

Thanks for the kind words, I'll stick to it.

"Well, then smile and uncover your legs, let them see some sun. And enjoy, enjoy every moment. And now, my dear, I'm going to my Helen's to check on her. See you."

"See you later" I watched with pleasure as Anthony briskly walked away towards the guesthouse building.

I pulled out my phone again and started reading articles on a topic that interested me.

A few minutes later Marlene came over. Dressed in shorts and a sports shirt."Hey, we are going with the girls for a walk in the forest, join us" she said.

"To the forest?" I looked at her surprised.

"There will also be Martha and Sylvia. It'll be fun, come on..."

"Maybe I can go," I agreed without much enthusiasm. It's better than sitting around trying to force things to do. "Just now?"

"Now. The girls are on their way, she waved to them."

I got up and we set off on our journey. At first we had light conversations, then things got much more serious. I found out that Sylvia, just a few months ago, was very ill, the doctors did not give her much chance, and yet, full of strength and the will to survive, she managed to overcome the disease. I was surprised. There was so much joy and optimism in Sylvia's eyes, in her behavior, that it was simply unbelievable. Only her emaciated body could indicate serious health transitions. I asked her about it.

How did you manage, where did you get your strength from? You have so much energy and such happiness.

"The beginnings were hard, I was devastated when I heard the diagnosis. I couldn't believe it, I was convinced that it was a mistake, that it didn't concern me. Then I broke down for two days. Finally, I decided not to despair. Since these are my last weeks, or maybe months, I will live them as best as I can, make all my dreams come true, go to the places I wanted to. I did not focus on the disease, but on what else I can do for myself, how to use this time. I laughed, danced, parachuted, visited Spain, Portugal and France. I was focused on the present moment, on what I was doing. I screamed loudly somewhere on the rocks or hills that I was alive and no one and nothing could defeat me. Only then did I really start living. Material things ceased to have any meaning, I squandered almost all my savings collected over the years. I needed nothing more than to experience joy. Absorb emotions, admire everything around you. I was so grateful that I am, it's hard to describe. It was a space trip. And I have this high to this day, a bit smaller, but it is there. And most importantly, a miracle happened, my disease regressed until it completely disappeared."

"How is it?" I was full of disbelief and emotion.

"I have all the before and after tests. X-rays show everything clearly. You know, I was surprised too, I started looking for information on how this was possible. I got to great publications, books on the subject. Man can heal himself. Look, after all, when you cut yourself, the body regenerates itself, it knows what to do. You just stick the plaster on. And the body does the rest. And so it is! Through the mind, through what you believe, you can attract disease and you can be cured of it."

"Sounds unbelievable," I said, stunned.

"I am the truest example of that. If you ever feel like it, read Louise L. Hay's books, she describes everything there very well. Every unexpressed emotion stays in the body and creates various ailments, and if you let go of everything that I unconsciously did then, miracles happen. There is power. In addition, breathing exercises, meditation, my life is simply beautiful now. Ask Martha. She was always with me. Let him tell you what I was a year ago and what I am today. My beloved Martha... She has two sweet children and a wonderful, wonderful husband, and despite everything, she was by my side in difficult times. And now she also got away for a week to come here with me" Sylvia hugged Martha happily and kissed her on the cheek.

"All this is true, I confirm" Martha agreed.

"Oh, I haven't told you Natalie yet, but the way we see the world is only a small, really tiny fraction of what it really is" continued Sylvia. "Man has such strength, potential and power that he cannot even imagine it. And he doesn't use it! This force, which sets the whole universe in motion, makes a huge tree grow from a tiny seed. The same strength is in each of us, I already know. It's great to be able to experience it.

"And your family? What do they make of this situation?" Marlene asked.

"I don't have a husband or children. And my parents and brother were devastated. I didn't want them to pity me, they didn't understand that I wanted to experience something more wonderful, they thought I was crazy.

"You have the power within you. Someone in your place would break down and lock themselves in the house" commented Marilyn.

"I had a plan, too, but I found it pointless. Now I look at everything differently. I see a beautiful world, I appreciate every moment, even autumn rain is cool. I'm telling you. And I look at people, I see them worrying about trifles, making problems out of anything, arguing, teasing, jealousy, I want to shake everyone and say: "hey, wake up! Start living, not vegetate!"

"You can shake me like that," I said with a sigh. I wish I was as optimistic as Sylvia. I looked at her as if she were some otherworldly phenomenon.

"Natalie, whatever's bothering you right now, just let it go." Think let it happen what is going to happen. Skip everything and focus on what's going on here right now. Seek every moment for something good, positive, and that's how you'll learn. Treat every problem as, for example, an opportunity to learn something. First of all, let go of the people who limit you and drag you down.

"ABOUT! I've had one success here. My only company is you and the people from the boarding house" I said jokingly, but I wasn't laughing at all. "Oh, and also my sister Eve and my friend Simon. Closed list."

"Then find more nice people." What problem? They will come to you, just those who will suit you. Sylvia stated. "Just want it." It's enough.

We walked along a wide path through the forest. The sky was slightly cloudy, and there was a pleasant smell in the air. We talked for a long time, telling each other our life stories, partly jokingly, partly seriously, it was really nice. We have completely lost track of time. At some point, the forest ended and we saw the road. The asphalt was not in the best condition, it looked like a shortcut, and not much traveled at that. We took this road south towards the mountains, we had a beautiful view of the Tatra Mountains, they seemed so close.

"Do you see it?" Marilyn asked, pointing to a gray Toyota parked on the side of the road. The windows were ajar.

"Shall we check?" Sylvia asked.

We walked over to the car. There was a man sitting in the driver's seat that was tilted back quite a bit. Head turned to the right. He didn't move. His eyes were closed.

We stared at him amazed.

"Maybe he's fainted, we need to check," I said worriedly. I grabbed the door handle, yanked, but the car was locked.

"And what about the corpse lying here for two days?" Marlene wondered. "I will not check."

"It doesn't smell" Sylvia put her nose to the window, which was opened three centimeters. "It's been warm lately, so it would have smelled of something."

"So, what's now?" A green tint appeared on Martha's face. She was breathing too loud and fast, I noticed. But I had to focus on the man locked in a car.

"Maybe he just collapsed and needs help," I said, walking around the car. I grabbed the passenger door.

"Are you going to give him artificial respiration just in case?" Marlene asked me.

"As it will be necessary…." I can do it," I said and pulled the door handle. Closed. I went back to the girls. "We have no way to get to him."

"Let's just call an ambulance," Marilyn suggested excitedly.

"Or the fire department," added Sylvia.

"Yes, we can also break the glass with a stone. There should be some big ones here, said Sylvia matter-of-factly."

We discussed fiercely, filled with emotions, it was quite an unusual phenomenon for us, we wanted to do the right thing. We were a bit scared and nervous.

"Okay, I'm calling," Marilyn said and pulled out her cell phone. "But where the hell are we?"

"Check the coordinates on Google maps" Sylvia suggested the idea.

Being euphoric, we stared at the phone. No sounds from the surroundings reached us.

"Okay, you check the coordinates, and I call" said Martha.

Suddenly, a loud, masculine voice was heard right next to us.

"Can I help you ladies in any way?"

We turned to the car at the same time and fell silent in amazement.

The window of the car was fully rolled down, and a slightly sleepy but conscious man was sitting behind the wheel.

"If you want to borrow my car, I warn you, it's not a very good idea." But I can give you a lift wherever you want," he said, looking at us curiously.

"Um, that won't be necessary," I said, embarrassed.

Martha realized that there was a woman on the other end of the phone. She put the phone to her ear and said.

"It's outdated, it's all right now." Goodbye." She hung up.

"We thought something had happened," Marilyn began to explain. "Car parked in the bushes, a guy looking unconscious behind the wheel, we just wanted to help.

"All right. I'm sorry to scare you." He glanced around the inside of the car briefly, then got out. He stood next to us and blinked his eyes to regain consciousness.

"Are you sure you're okay?" Marlene asked.

"Yes, absolutely. I'm coming back from the Netherlands, I drove a long way, I took this shortcut to get to my destination faster, but I was too tired. I had to stop and take a nap for a while. he explained. He was tall, thin, dark brown, with a two-day stubble and short-cropped hair in a slight mess. Dressed in a navy blue T-shirt with a tiny company logo on the chest, and knee-length white linen shorts. For this sport shoes in a gray and black shade."

"Okay then, you have to be responsible and take care of your own safety. And others - said Marilyn. "And my friend," she pointed to me. She was ready to give artificial respiration.

The man looked at me and smiled widely.

"Well, if everything is fine, then we'll go" said Sylvia, catching Marilyn by the arm. "have a nice trip."

"Thank you." The man got into the car and started the engine.

"Just be careful on the road," Marilyn admonished.

"No worries. I'll be there in just over thirty kilometers. Goodbye," and he left.

I felt a bit weird. It only lasted a moment. I frowned as the car drove away and I had the distinct impression that I knew this guy from somewhere. We've met somewhere before. But then I focused on the girl's conversation and that thought faded away.

"He must have been pretty pissed if he slept in the car," commented Marlene.

"After all, it's not that far from the Netherlands" said Martha, who had the opportunity to visit this beautiful country by car.

"It was not easier for him to fly by plane ..."

"Maybe he couldn't...."

"He didn't seem to be afraid of flying...."

Through these light discussions, we slowly cooled down from this surprising event. Emotions subsided, and we wandered on ahead.

It was late afternoon. I was tired after a few kilometers walk into the forest. I was satisfied. I was sitting on a small terrace upstairs, at the end of the corridor. I liked going there, even though there were only four armchairs and one tiny table.

My phone rang. It was Eve.

I answered the call.

"Hi dear. How are you?" she asked.

"All right."

"Ha, are you just saying that or is it true?" No shaming please.

"It's ok. Really."

"That's good. I knew you could do it. You'll recover quickly. You are a strong woman, it's a pity you don't see that, a little more self-confidence."

"We've always been able to do it, and we'll continue to do so."

"Exactly. Keep your head up and keep moving forward."

"And how are you?"

"One big chaos and momentum. I'm in my element. Show soon, I'm very excited. You'll come, huh? You'll see what I've created," she said cheerfully.

"Of course I will," I nodded. "With a lot of champagne. We will celebrate, you truly deserve success."

"Thanks. I hear peace in your voice" she noticed. "You're not taking any sedatives there, I hope . . . "

"NO. How did you come up with that?" I was outraged. "I just have peace, relaxation and nice people here.

"And how are you getting on with this asshole, my fortunately would-be brother-in-law?"

"Amazingly good. I put him out of my mind and heart once and for all.

"A good girl. Oh boy, they're calling me, I gotta go. Remember, you'll always be fine. Take care. Bye" after these words she hung up.

I sighed with a slight smile and put my phone back in my pocket. I leaned back in the armchair and stared at the treetops swaying in the light breeze, in the neighbor's yard. The blue sky stretched above them.

A ringing phone pulled me out of my blissful relaxation. I glanced at the display. Unknown number. I declined the call. The phone rang again. After the sixth time, very pissed off, I answered the call.

"Hello."

"Natalie," I heard a familiar voice. It choked me for a moment.

"Greg, don't call me.

"I need to talk to you." I can't make calls from my mobile...

Because I blocked the number.

"Natalie, your wedding dress…"

"What about her?"

"It's still hanging in the closet."

"Do you want to send it back to me?"

"NO. I want you to put it on. Tomorrow. For our wedding," he said softly, regretfully.

I was silent. I wondered if he was serious. It occurred to me that maybe Greg wasn't a bad guy at all, but a weak boy, dominated by a despotic mother. Maybe he was also trying to find himself in that rather difficult situation, understood his mistake and tried to become independent, to lead his life responsibly. I didn't know that, but I took the opportunity. I wasn't mad at him anymore. We just didn't fit together. I wish I could forgive him and forget about him, about what we had in common.

"I wish you good luck. Don't call me again." I turned my phone off completely. I took a very deep breath and went back to admiring the sights before me.

"Thoughts are false, absurd delusions that obscure the truth" said Olivia.

We went for an evening walk around the lake. Apparently she liked being here too.

"How should I understand that?" I asked.

"David Hawkins once wrote such a wise text. Very smart and life… I noticed that you think a lot. I wanted to talk to you about this."

"I know I think too much, I've heard it more than once," I sighed. "I don't need to worry, but I can't help it."

"Maybe if you understood where it comes from, it would be easier for you.

"If there's a way to let go of my overflowing emotions, I'd love to hear it," I said hopefully.

Emotions are hard to deal with, especially when they're negative. When a great wave of feelings floods us, we don't really know what to do with them. We suppress them in ourselves, push them deep into the subconscious, put them aside for later, so that it doesn't hurt now. And when we accumulate over the years a lot of these anchored emotions that had no way to flow out, how to free themselves, they start to make themselves felt in the form of headaches, irritability, health problems, emotional blockades arise.

"How do I know that… Suppression is my specialty."

"Everybody does. Each and every. It's a matter of knowing how to deal with it."

"Every little suggestion is worth its weight in gold."

"Trust me, not everyone wants to hear about it. But to the point. There is a lot of fear and guilt in our negative feelings, because that's all we're talking about. Sometimes there's so much we can't handle. Then the mind, in order to keep painful feelings away from us, represses them from our consciousness, uses the denial method, i.e. pretends that the problem does not exist, or uses the mechanism of projection, i.e. blaming everyone around. We direct all our anger and failures onto other people, hence aggression and violence. We also build self-esteem at the expense of others. And so unconsciously..."

- Exactly. This is how the mind deals with emotions. Some express their dissatisfaction loudly and emphatically. This is also not the right way, because you lose friends quickly because of it. Others run away from feelings, avoid them by distracting, focusing on something else: TV, alcohol, drugs, sex, parties. People are very afraid to look inside themselves, they are afraid to confront their own pain and fear. And that's what it's all about - to release all the accumulated emotions - we need to notice them and let them come to us.

"It could end up in a mental breakdown," I said.

"Do you think it's better to keep these emotions inside yourself and suffocate from their excess? Until they finally cause some major health disaster?"

"Oh no…"

"I'll tell you how it works." There's a feeling, a negative one. You don't do anything, no dodges, no escapes, no denials, just observe. You realize that you have been overcome by, for example, anger. Sit down somewhere in a quiet place and let that anger be inside of you. Don't resist, ignore all thoughts that come to you. If you think about that anger, you give it energy and it will grow. That's why it's so important to do nothing but watch and observe. Am I saying this clearly?

"Yes. For now, yes."

"So if we sit with that emotion and do nothing, it loses energy and just disappears." This method really works. I've been using it for years.

"I'll try. It seems quite easy."

"With time, once you've mastered this skill, it'll be hard to piss you off." There will be no need for your ego, your mind, to use all its tricks to push unwanted emotions into the subconscious. As soon as they appear, you will immediately deal with them wisely.

"How will I know that I have managed to release an emotion?"

"After the fact that she will not return soon, and besides, you will feel lightness and happiness" said Olivia optimistically.

"But what if I do everything according to this method, and yet the anger returns in a moment?"

"In that case, you have either allowed your thoughts to fuel your emotions and not just focused on observing, or there is something even deeper to be discovered and released. Then you have to look for that feeling within yourself and release it."

"It is a kind of purification of the mind and body from all the accumulated garbage ... " I said and looked up at the sky full of stars.

"Exactly."

"There's a lot of work ahead of me."

"You will make it. Think about the rEverd that awaits you for this."

"Lightness and happiness. It's unbelievable that this is the way to happiness."

"You will discover many more such curiosities."

It was Saturday morning. A few minutes after seven, dressed in a warm tracksuit, I was sitting on the mat and waiting for the meditation to start. On that day, classes were held in the backyard, on a specially prepared place near the fenced orchard. The orchard was the only place where hotel guests were not allowed. A lot of people gathered, mostly women. Everyone was relaxed, calm, some were still yawning freely. My friends were not there, they liked to sleep longer. Damien came instead, I saw him out of the corner of my eye as he was walking towards us. And he chose the seat right next to me.

"Hi," he greeted, sitting cross-legged on the mat he had just laid out.

"Hi."

"You weren't at the after-dinner party last night," he whispered, leaning slightly in my direction. "Don't you like to dance?"

"Dancing is not my favorite pastime."

"Better boxing?"

"For now, yes," I replied with a smile. However, I soon realized. That day was extremely difficult for me. I was supposed to wear a wedding dress and start building a future with Greg. At that moment, I would probably be at the hairdresser or beautician, then I would be running excitedly around the house, getting ready for this very important event. And here I was, away from all of them, away from what I thought was important, from illusions and lies. I've come to terms with my decision, but I still feel sad. I had to deal with my emotions somehow. I dreamed that the next day would only be better.

Olivia sat across from us and greeted us with a smile.

"Hi guys, it's nice to see so many of you here. We have beautiful weather, clean air, so let's enjoy the benefits of nature. What… We take a deep breath and slowly exhale. And again - after a few deep relaxing breaths she continued - In today's meditation we will go back in time a bit. Let's start. Recall an event five years ago, something important, something that made it vivid in your memory. Recall what emotions and feelings accompanied you. Hug yourself tight, imagine it, give yourself acceptance. You did everything you could at that moment. Forgive yourself if you need to... Now take a deep breath, breathe out slowly and go back five more years. And the same situation - Olivia fell silent for a moment. She gave us time to calmly carry out the order. - How do you feel with it? What you see? What happened then? Look at it from the sidelines, without emotion… Now go back to the day when you were seven years old. What was the world like around you? What was important to you? There was another long silence, followed by the voice of the leader. "And now we're going back even further." Imagine you are a two-year-old child. See that little child in you. Defenseless, learning the world and life, accepting everything that is as truth. A child who runs, cries, is happy, is also full of joy. A child who falls but gets up, dusts off his knees and keeps going. A child who tries to climb a ladder on a playground is difficult, but he does not give up, he does not pay attention to what is happening around, he wants to climb the ladder and he does it. She is brave, brave and wants to learn. You may not remember it, you were only two years old, but imagine a cheerful kid running around the yard after a colorful butterfly. How much joy there is at the moment. Then there is nothing more precious than this indescribable euphoria. You are this kid, this child is still inside you, feel it, feel this carefree joy ... Feel what it's like to learn life from the perspective of such a small, full of delight and love, little person. Imagine it, feel it...

I didn't know why, but I was moved, I felt tears running down my cheeks. I didn't wipe them away so as not to break the connection I had established with myself in such a remote time. I had so much tenderness for that creature that I saw with the eyes of my imagination. I saw myself happy, content, a little rebel in checkered trousers. I wanted to touch and hug that little girl. Then I heard Olivia's voice.

This is you, your inner child, say hello to him. It is with you all the time, in you, waiting for you to get to know it, notice it, take care of it. You meet them when they are happy and content, but this child can also be sad, afraid, confused. I feel unloved. Now you see them, you already know them. Will you take care of him? Will you give him care, attention? Love? Interest? Everything it needs and deserves?

Again, prolonged silence. I felt great emotions inside me. I focused my imagination on myself from more than twenty-seven years ago, it was an extraordinary feeling. I smiled and felt my eyelids wet with tears. I wasn't happy when Olivia asked for deep breaths and a slow return to reality. I wiped my cheeks with my hands and sniffled. I felt a bit silly showing emotion, but when I discreetly looked around, I noticed that I wasn't the only one who had such an emotional approach to that meditation.

"How do you feel?" Olivia asked happily. "I'll explain it to you." The inner beliefs that we gathered in early childhood, when we were learning about life, gaining experience, when our mind was programming, everything we learned was recorded in our subconscious and guides our lives to this day. As a child, sometimes we had to deal with great challenges, too burdensome for a two-, three-year-old. We could feel misunderstood, unloved, disregarded, even if we had wonderful parents. Such a wronged child, with these unprocessed, unconscious emotions, is with us all our lives. It has a huge impact on all of us. He interprets the situation in his childish way and triggers various unwanted reactions in us. Sometimes we wonder why we did what we did. This has happened to you sometimes, hasn't it? The inner child in us does not want unpleasant situations, avoids them and triggers emotions and behaviors in us that are very harmful to us. He wants to feel safe, loved, taken care of, which is what we lacked as a child.

"It's the alien in us, isn't it?" Like the eighth passenger of the Nostromo, someone asked from the back of those sitting on the mats.

Everyone burst out laughing.

"Well, not exactly," said Olivia, amused. "The inner child is rather a metaphor for the emotional "I". Any questions?"

"I understand that if I take care of my inner child, it will become happier and my problems will disappear?" asked Aileen, a beautiful woman in full make-up and tight clothes. She sat perfectly upright, her long blond hair falling lightly over one shoulder.

"The quality of life will definitely improve. There will come a greater understanding of yourself and a greater awareness of what you do and how you live. This is a process. It takes some time and patience, but it's totally worth it. Remember, that child in you has been clamoring for attention for years and you didn't know it, so now you have to approach him like a scared, distrustful kid. Problems will not completely disappear, but you will approach them consciously and with more strength and acceptance."

"I understand," Aileen was obviously satisfied with the answer.

"This bond with ourselves is the most important bond we build. It's the basis. If we want to build a good relationship with others, let's first build the best, most beautiful relationship with ourselves. It is very important. If we haven't already, that's okay, we can start today. I encourage you to do so. Let's stand on your side. Let's do it for ourselves.

There was a moment of silence. We had time to think and digest the wisdom we heard.

"So what, darlings?"

"I invite you for breakfast "said Olivia and got up. The others followed her.

I got up and rolled up the mat. I was a bit thoughtful."

"What are your plans after breakfast?" Damien asked.

"I don't know."

"Maybe you would like to go on a trip to Zakopane? Such a walk to the Valley of Five Ponds?"

"Interesting idea."

"I have two more seats left in the car, I thought of you."

"What time are you leaving?"

"After breakfast. So how?"

"Very willingly."

We traveled in two cars. More volunteers gathered. Damien, Daria with Fred, Marilyn, Martha, Sylvia and Hubert - Aileen's husband. Unfortunately or fortunately, Aileen went for beauty treatments to a nearby town and she didn't mind her handsome husband going with us for mountain hiking.

The day was clear, warm, we left the cars in the parking lot and, with the guidance of Damien, set off along the trail leading to the valley. We were properly dressed, provided with food and water, and our moods were high. The air was clean, crisp, giving energy and strength. We walked without feeling tired. We joked, we talked, we got to know each other. I felt very good in that company. Only after some time did I realize that I was smiling all the time, and my mood had not been so great for a long time.

By the end of the hike, I felt tired, but also a great joy looking at the mountains. I willingly climbed the rocks, because the road was difficult at times, I did not complain, I enjoyed the moment. When we reached our destination, I looked around me in awe. The sight before my eyes was a great rEverd. I sat on a rock and stared ahead. I felt as if I had overcome something powerful within myself, had done something important, something that changed my life. I felt empowered and willing to act. Despite my exhaustion, I had so much energy and contentment in me, as if I had been forcibly yanked out of years of numbness. I didn't know where this feeling came from at that moment, in this beautiful place in nature, among these people I had just met. What a surprising life. I didn't know where it would lead me, but I closed my eyes, put my face up in the sun and mentally, straight from my heart, sent the word "thank you" into space.

I loved the mountains. I decided that no matter what the circumstances, I would go back there. To catch balance, stay in that place, breathe clean air, get tired and delight again.

We returned to the guesthouse for dinner. We were all in good spirits. We sat down at one table, talked about stories and recommending other interesting trails and mountain ranges. Damien, Daria and Fred had the most to say. I listened and carefully noted down their suggestions. In the past, I most often chose the Baltic Sea or Masuria for my holiday trips, so I was very eager to hear about mountain attractions.

After dinner, I went to my room to take a bath. I was extremely tired, yet energized at the same time. It's too early to go to bed yet. I wanted this day to last. I put on clean jeans, a hoodie, white sneakers and left the room. I walked for an hour along the lake. I watched the setting sun. I realized that I looked at this phenomenon very often, even every day, but only on that day did I see the really beautiful color of the sky, where orange mixed with navy blue, where the last rays were still illuminating the tops of trees, creating a warm glow when the first stars. I looked at it with amazement, as if I had discovered something completely different, a new, more beautiful world. And yet he was the same, only I saw him for the first time really and consciously. Something amazing. I went to the pier with a smile. I sat cross-legged at the very end and stared into the depths of the lake.

After a long time, I heard the sound of muffled conversation behind me. Someone was coming. I turned and glanced over my shoulder.

"There you are," Marlene called upon seeing me. "But you hid."

"Are you looking for me?" – I was surprised, looking at the people behind Marilyn: Sylvia, Martha, Daria, Fred and Damien.

– We have something to drink here – Sylvia and Martha waved bottles of champagne.

- And what's that? - I asked. I got up and faced them.

"The first day of the rest of your wonderful, happy life," Sylvia exclaimed.

I stared at them, not understanding anything.

"I'm sorry," Marlene began with feigned contrition. "But I told them you were supposed to get married today and it didn't work out. So we came up with the idea to cheer you up, to be exact, celebrate your freedom and drink to your happiness. I don't know what it sounded like, but we're just with you." She pressed a glass into my hand and poured champagne into it.

Shocked, she didn't know what to say. I didn't expect this. It was… I was lost for words. I was moved and smiled widely.

"Here we drink," I said, and waited until everyone had their glasses full.

Marlene made a toast.

"My dears, today we drink to Natalie's freedom. Let your life, woman, be arranged in the best, happiest way, let only valuable men surround you. We drink to the courage you have shown, to the power you have within you. Cheers!" she said loudly.

We clinked glasses. I drank half a glass of sparkling champagne all at once.

Damien came over to me and gave me a tight hug. He whispered in my ear:

"I didn't know you were going through such a difficult time, I'm so sorry.

"It's better now," I replied with a smile.

They all hugged me one by one. Good thing it was dark and they couldn't see my emotion. All day I tried not to think about the fact that I was getting married today. The trip to the mountains was a blessing for me because it completely absorbed my mind with positive feelings. If I had stayed at the boarding house, who knows what my emotional state would be. I turned off the phone yesterday, wanting to have complete peace, to cut myself off from the situation and memories and regrets.

"Was the wedding supposed to be big?" Sylvia asked.

"Do you even want to talk about it?" Martina interrupted her. She was extremely tactful and always considered the comfort of the interlocutor.

"Yeah, I've kept it inside for so long, so it's okay if I let off some steam…" I said.

We sat down on jetty, Damien poured more champagne.

The wedding was supposed to be for one hundred and twenty people. The would-be mother-in-law is the mayor of the town, so as an influential person, she invited some important people. For my part, I invited less than thirty people. It was going to be a big event. She planned everything perfectly.

"You gave her a hard time pulling out of the wedding," Daria said. "It took a lot of courage for you, really.

"I didn't see it that way," I admitted. I spoke calmly, without emotion, as if the topic concerned a completely different person, not me. "She put me in an impossible situation, so I packed up and left.

"And your fiancé?" Damien asked.

He stood there watching me pack. I asked if she would come with me...

There was a moment of silence.

"Exactly. Let's drink," said Marlene.

"But somehow you got along with him before, it was ok, right?" Damien asked.

"I thought so." Maybe some things I didn't see or didn't want to see. It wasn't until I moved into the house where we were to eventually live that the whole truth began to dawn on me. Greg was completely subordinated to his mother. I remember one time we were making dinner and an egg fell on the floor. Greg started cleaning, then Evelyn entered the kitchen and saw her youngest, beloved son, kneeling on the floor and rubbing an egg - I laughed. "No, I can't go on about it.

"Well, what did she do?" Marlene asked.

"Well, it wasn't fun.

"You blame her, don't you?" Daria asked. "You say little about him, and much about his mother."

"It was fine until she stepped in. Or maybe she was the reason I avoided my biggest mistake."

"I think so, but do you know what you've done?" For a grandmother like that, it's a mega slap. A town-wide scandal. But she deserved it" said Sylvia.

"It's not my concern anymore," I said.

"Aren't you afraid of revenge?" Daria asked. "People like that don't give up.

"I know," I smiled. "I found out about it very quickly. In less than half an hour she got me a leave of absence from work and a wolf ticket in the entire province.

"What?!" they all exclaimed simultaneously.

"So here I am, gathering my strength to build the rest of my wonderful, happy life," I said lightly

"No, what a babe! We need a drink. It's good that you freed yourself from them" said Marilyn. "Thank you for your courage."

"I fucked up, how can that be?" Fred was annoyed. "Listen, we will find you a job there in Silesia. We have some acquaintance."

"You can count on me too. Within two weeks, something can definitely be arranged," Damien suggested."Because there is no problem with moving to another city?"

"As Olivia put it nicely, I am now at the zero point from which I can go in any direction" I said. "Thank you very much for your support."

"You can also count on us" declared Sylvia and Martha.

"Let's drink then." For a new beginning! cried Marlene.

Two hours later we were all lying on the wooden dock and laughing out loud. Empty champagne bottles were lined up with glasses. We had great moods. We discussed various topics, told each other funny anecdotes. My stomach hurt from laughing, but I was happy and content. At some point, Damien sat down, took his phone out of his pocket and turned on the music.

"Look, today was supposed to be a wedding, dancing and partying. And will be. The champagne was already, now it's fun."

He put the phone down on the pier next to the bottles and walked over to me.

"May I ask the beautiful lady to dance?"

"Sure." I took his outstretched hand and stood up.

Damien pulled me to him and we started dancing on the pier. I had drunk quite a lot of champagne and was a little dizzy. I glanced over my shoulder a couple of times to see how far it was from the water, because the pier wasn't wide enough. Damien, however, gave strong support and controlled the situation. He held me tight in his arms, sometimes whispering a compliment in my ear. He also danced well. Fred stepped in and stole me from a friend. The girls joined in too and after a while we had a dance party. Our laughter echoed all over the place.

The next day I woke up around noon. Before I opened my eyes, I smiled blissfully. I had a really fantastic day, maybe one of the best of my life. I stretched lazily in bed, then went to the bathroom. I put my hands on the sink and stared at my reflection in the mirror. Her dark hair was messy and tied in a bun on top of her head. I looked into my eyes, finally saw a spark of joy in them, so small, tiny, but it was there. I smiled to myself and said the affirmation:

"I love you, I love you very much, you deserve a wonderful life, Natalie, wonderful friends. And I will learn to love my inner child," I said to my reflection in the mirror. Subconsciously, I found this embarrassing and inappropriate, but I persisted, even if I felt uncomfortable saying the words out loud. "My dear, little Natalie, I am glad to have met you. I didn't see that you were here and that you needed my support. I really didn't know about you. I'm sorry, forgive me, please, I'll fix everything, I promise. I'll take care of you." I looked at my eyes in the mirror and saw their expression change, full of regret and suffering. I placed my hand on the mirror as if to touch myself, to console myself. I looked at myself, wanting to look deep into my soul. Get to know yourself, see yourself. For now, all I knew was that I was. But who? I had to discover that. - I love you.

A trip to the Valley of Five Ponds and the evening party brought us closer together. Damien, me, Marilyn, Martha, Sylvia, Daria and Fred. From that day on, we ate breakfasts, lunches together, spent a lot of time on walks and conversations. We thought up different activities for evening meetings. I continued to go horseback riding, where I got used to Tina and wasn't as scared as the first time. I was excited when Lena got on her horse and took me for a little ride in the woods. I had to grab the bridle and steer Tina myself, though she certainly knew exactly where to go.

I went to the gym every day. I gave vent to the anger that had accumulated over the years. The workouts also made my body stronger. That day I was boxing fiercely when Damien appeared in the room. He was dressed appropriately for the planned physical activity. He was going to work out on the equipment, but seeing me at the punching bag, he changed his mind. He went to the window, picked up his gloves from the floor, and offered.

"Will you fight me a little?" It will be harder for sure.

"You convinced me." I turned to him and waited for him to propose.

"Okay, let's do some evasive practice." Two blows to the gloves and dodge. And then swap.

"It suits. Start" I was already a bit tired, but with Damien I wanted to practice.

I took the blows in my gloves, of course I held my guard high, and the third time I crouched down and tilted my head to the side.

"Very good," he praised. Then I hit it back and forth. He knew I was just learning and didn't goof off. Training was exhausting, so we took a break. We sat on the floor against the wall.

"Why don't we go tomorrow with the whole team to the thermal baths in Białka Tatrzańska? I think we'll be there in an hour," he said, sipping his water.

"Great idea, but I can't tomorrow," I replied.

"What important plans? What does the prospect of rolling your ass in warm thermal water lose to?"

"With Warsaw. With a fashion show."

"Are you kidding me?" He frowned and looked at me curiously. My style of dress was far from any elegant taste and had nothing to do with fashion.

"Sister has a show of her own collection. It's very important to her. It's her to be or not to be in this whole fashion world. We always support each other, so I'll be there with her tomorrow.

"It's a long way..."

"And?"

"You could use some company."

"Are you suggesting something?" I asked, looking at him intrigued.

"I've never been to any fashion show, it's worth catching up."

"You're kidding?"

"Why, it could be interesting."

"That's not what I'm asking. Do you want to go to Warsaw and come back on the same day far into the night?"

"Sure. It will be interesting."

"I start at five in the morning."

"Perfect. Then come on, I'll tire you out a bit more." He took the gloves and slapped one against the other, signaling that he was ready for training.

Returning from the gym, I was asked by Helen for a moment of conversation. She was standing behind the half-round counter and smiling warmly at me.

"Natalie, can I have a word with you?"

"Of course," I replied and walked over to her.

"Come and see," she led me deep into the reception hall, right up to the windows, where there was a seating area with armchairs and small tables. There were pictures on the tables. Evenly arranged, large formats. I was speechless. These are photos from a session we had a few days ago. I couldn't believe they were so beautiful, like masterpieces. I simply did not recognize the women in these photos, a perfectly captured twinkle in the eye, a fleeting moment captured, exposing what is most precious in each of us. In that look you could read everything, the whole truth. Makeshift dresses made of white or gray fabric worked perfectly, showing that a person is a value, not his clothes or trinkets on the wrist.

"You're the first to see it," Helen said.

"Thank you for showing me this."

I walked from one table to the next and looked at the photos in awe. Suddenly I stopped and looked at one of them, where I saw myself. I was surprised by the depth of his serious gaze, like a bottomless pit. Peace and wisdom written on his face. Fist tightly clenched on the white material, I remember that moment, I held the dress tight so it wouldn't fall too low. Beautiful, large bracelets on the wrist. I grabbed the photo and held it up. It turned out that there are three more under it, in different poses. I smiled at them.

"Do you like them?" asked Miss Helen. "Agatha just brought them. He's talking to Olivia now.

"Do I like them?" I am delighted! Agatha is a true artist. There are no words to express my admiration. can i take them

"Of course, darling, they're for you."

"Thank you again."

"In a moment, all the women will probably fly here, and there will be one big racket."

"You are lovely, thank you."

I took my photos and happily went to my room.

The next day, a few minutes before five, I was sitting behind the wheel of my car and waiting for Damien. I didn't know whether to enjoy his company on the trip to Warsaw or not. I dressed elegantly in black formal pants and a slightly extravagant blouse. I also did my makeup. I knew Eva would notice it. Today was an important day for her, and I didn't want to upset her by wearing the wrong clothes. I even brought silver high heel sandals. I put them in my bag, intending to wear them just before entering the show.

Damien came to the parking lot, also dressed appropriately. I got out of my car to greet him.

"Hi. Come in."

"Oh, you look beautiful, so different," he said appreciatively, his eyes roving over my form. "Listen, will it be okay if we drive in my car?"

"Why is that?" I was outraged. I didn't know what he drove, but I didn't have to be ashamed of my four-year-old Opel. "Not comfortable enough?"

"No, none of those things. I just like driving."

"I am a good driver. Don't worry" not only did he force himself into this trip, he also dictated the conditions. I got angry.

"It's six hours away." I wanted you to arrive rested. This is an important and exciting day for you and your sister. You'll just be tired. And if we go in my car, you can take a nap, if only for an hour.

"Okay," I agreed after a moment's thought. I took a large bag and closed the Opel door.

The trip to Warsaw passed in a very friendly atmosphere. I leaned back in the plush passenger seat and watched the road ahead. Damien drove confidently and quite quickly. We talked a lot, and I found out that he runs a training company focused on sales and marketing together with two colleagues. They are doing quite well, there are still more and more customers, they get great satisfaction from it, but sometimes they are also tired.

"I spend a lot of time away from home, mainly in hotels. I meet a lot of people every day", he said. "There's always something going on.

"Do you also conduct on-site training in Wrocław?" I asked.

"Sometimes yes, but rarely. My colleagues have small children, more responsibilities, so I go on longer routes. They're rather close."

"Doesn't it bother you?"

"I got used to. You know, if you want a good job as a trader, I can train you properly" he offered. "I'll handle it personally."

"Me as a trader? No, it can't work."

"Do you doubt my abilities?" he laughed.

"More like yours." It's not for me.

"What's for you?"

"I don't know yet."

"However, if you chose Wrocław as your direction of life, remember that I will help you."

"Nice to hear it."

"Why did you become an English teacher?"

"Good question. I didn't quite know what to do with myself. Eve knew from elementary school that she wanted to become a fashion designer, and I did not find any talents in myself, I was interested in everything and nothing. I graduated from high school with honors, I could choose any major, and I followed my heart, which is where my friend with whom I was very much in love at the time."

"But this is not the would-be husband… Greg…"

"No, not this one. It was Philip. Our paths parted pretty quickly."

"Interesting, tell me," he encouraged to confide.

"There's nothing to talk about." Old history.

"It's hard to get anything out of you, you're mysterious," he said. "And it's still a long way to Warsaw."

"Which doesn't mean we can talk about me." Tell me, daughters didn't want to come with you to the mountains?

"Please…" he laughed. "What would they be doing here… They went with their mother to Tenerife for two weeks. A small pension in the mountains has nothing to compete with the attractions they have there. But don't change the subject. I'm asking seriously. Do you have any passions? Interests?

I took a moment to think about it.

"Until recently, I was playing with interior design, you know – furniture, accessories, playing with color, stuff like that. I like space, but orderly and harmonious. I signed up for several courses in this direction, I learned how to work with design programs, and sometimes some photo processing in Photoshop."

"Then why didn't you go that way?"

"Don't ask the hard questions," I said defiantly.

"Okay, since this was a hard question for you, what kind of pet did you have when you were little?"

I laughed out loud.

Half an hour later, Damien parked his Audi in the hotel parking lot. Before I got out, I changed my comfortable shoes for very high-heeled sandals. I took a small business card from my bag. I was ready. The show was due to take place in half an hour, and I was hoping to see my sister and we could talk.

We entered the huge hotel and headed to the hall where the show was to take place. I called Eve, but she didn't answer. I haven't seen her anywhere either. So we sat on the chairs in front of the stage and waited. Damien placed his hand on the back of the chair I was sitting on. I noticed his touch, the fact that he often looked for an opportunity to brush, as if by chance, my arm.

People were slowly gathering. There was a loud bustle, two women dressed in black were preparing to give a speech on the stage.

I was slightly nervous, while Damien sat smiling and curiously watching what was happening around.

The show began with a short speech and energetic applause. There were flashes of flashes, there were journalists, I also noticed regional television.

The event was prepared by five exceptionally talented exhibitors. Eve's creations were shown second. I recognized them immediately, smiled at the sight of them. The models presented beautiful, very feminine and colorful outfits. I kept my fingers crossed that the audience would like them, that they would delight everyone present here. Everything went smoothly, the right music, energy, beautiful costumes. I was very proud of my sister.

After the show, she went on stage for a while. She looked beautiful in a long red dress with a covered neckline. Shiny, wavy hair fell lightly over one shoulder. She said a few words of thanks, and I wanted to fly over there and hug her tight. It took a long time after the show ended when I finally managed to get to her. I was holding good quality champagne in my hand.

"You were terrific. the best! Congratulations," I said, squeezing her tightly.

"You have come! How happy I am, you don't even know how much! She squeaked happily, full of emotion in my ear. "Did you see everything?"

"Sure, everything! It was great. Really. I have champagne, we have to drink it, here, now."

"Sure," she said. "I'm going to mix the glasses right now."

"No need, I rolled it off the table," I said with a laugh, pulling two champagne glasses from my small business bag.

"Madwoman."

Suddenly I remembered Damien. I turned towards him. He was leaning against the wall and watching us amused.

"This is Damien, and this is Eve" I introduced them to myself. They shook hands.

"Nice to meet you and congratulations." Great show, he said.

"Thank you," Eve replied, and looked at me meaningfully, as if she wanted to make a question mark out of her face.

I just shrugged, no time or place to explain.

An hour later we were alone for a while. Eve was in great demand, she had to give an interview and talk to the greats of the fashion world, at that time Damien and I went to a nearby restaurant for dinner.

We sat on the table in the room where the cleanup was taking place after the show.

"Natalie, I'm glad you came" Eve said and moved closer so that we leaned against each other's shoulders.

"How could I not come… It was important to you, to me too."

"You look good. Is this Damien someone close to you?"

"He's just a friend. We met at the boarding house. I like him and that's it. In general, there are nice people there, I'm slowly coming back to balance there."

"I'm sorry I wasn't with you. I had this show..."

"I know, don't worry. You have always been with me… Everything is fine, as it should be."

"You know I'm going to have to go soon..."

"I know, it's your big day. Celebrate." I hugged her tightly.

"Thanks for coming..."

"See you soon."

I watched nostalgically as Eve quickly walked away to her group of friends. She turned for another second and blew me a kiss in the air. I got up reluctantly and went out into the corridor, where Damien was waiting for me. It's time to go back to the guest house in Kościelisko.

At six in the morning I went for a walk. The morning was a bit cloudy. I pulled my hoodie up to my chin and headed towards the lake. I walked slowly, breathing deeply. It struck me how clean and crisp the air was here, how peaceful and quiet it was. I enjoyed it. I was a bit tired. We returned from Warsaw before midnight, later I couldn't sleep, and in the morning I woke up at dawn.

I noticed Zbigniew fishing. I came over to say hello.

"Good morning," I snapped the man out of his thoughts.

"Oh, good morning Natalie, sit down, please" he moved a little on the small bench. "What are we fishing for? I have two fishing rods..."

"With pleasure." I sat down on the bench and reached for the already prepared fishing rod. Zbigniew gave me some tips. He talked passionately about fish and the way of fishing, about lures. He had said a lot of that the first time we met here, but I listened with joy.

"It's beautiful here," I sighed as he finished talking. "So calm ... A whole different world."

"People don't usually notice it."

"I didn't notice it either." Yesterday I was in Warsaw. As soon as I got there, my head started to hurt. The rush, the hustle and bustle, the noise, the adrenaline, the honking on the roads… I got tired of it right away. Only now I realized that less than two weeks in this place were enough to calm down and cut off from this rush. It's amazing to see this contrast. I'm fine here. I wish I could stay here longer - another sigh."

It's good to live somewhere close to nature. We lived with Dorothy, my wife, in a small house in the country, it was a long time ago. I was fine there, but Dorothy insisted and we moved to the outskirts of the city so that Dorothy would have closer to her friends, beauty salons and what she wants there. I used to have a pond with fish behind the fence, now I have to drive more than thirty kilometers every Sunday.

"Do you have children?" I asked.

"A daughter. Joanne. As soon as she turned eighteen, she left home. She couldn't get along with her mother. My Dorothy, I shouldn't talk badly about her, but she has a strong character and it's hard to live with her every day."

"But you're still with her."

"And what a way out," he gasped. "It's just out of habit, anyway, wherever I run, it will find me and bring me home anyway" he laughed.

"You tried?" I looked at him curiously.

"Yeah, but that was a long time ago, when I was young. And then, when Joanne was born, I stayed for her, for my daughter."

I didn't answer. We sat in silence for a long time. Another proof how difficult it is to build a normal, happy relationship, and do they even exist? I thought about it as I stared at the calm depths of the lake. Loneliness wasn't so terrible, I was almost thirty and had little prospects for a successful marriage. After what I'd been through, I didn't want to be with anyone anymore. I've come to terms with it. It was fine the way it was.

I sat there on that wooden bench and thought about the meaning of life - more sadness, problems and hopelessness in it than something good. I've always had a hard time, from an early age, with everything. I remember very well that day when my parents were leaving, leaving us in the care of a disgruntled grandmother. I remember standing on the road watching the car drive away and feeling something painfully tearing apart in my chest. They promised they would be back soon. At first I waited, then I knew it was pointless. I had to give up and accept reality. And so it has been. Then different people came into my life. Those I trusted betrayed me. Over time, I learned to function in this reality. It was only in the boarding house that I experienced what selfless friendship, support and interest can look like without any expectations.

Even before breakfast, I had the opportunity to ask Olivia about it. She was sitting on a bench by a flower bed and playing with a small puppy. I approached her.

"Nice dog," I said. Yours or someone else's?

"A stray. We kept him because where was he supposed to go... We have plenty of space and plenty of food here. He won't miss anything here" she said with satisfaction. "And how are you doing?"

"Gathering strength, regenerating" after these words I sat down on the bench next to Olivia. It was nice to look at her, her eternal joy and optimism, she had something magnetic about her that I couldn't explain.

"I'm glad of that," she replied, and petted the dog, which climbed up on her legs with its forepaws and demanded attention by wagging its short tail.

"These meditations, everything you do ... It's very positive for me. In a very short time, I rose from the feeling of hopelessness. I still have so many questions, so many doubts..."

"I'm always here to help whenever you want," she offered, looking at me kindly. "Make the most of your time here." You know, I do various talks about life, meditations, meetings - some will get a lot from it, others not at all. It depends on who is at what stage of consciousness development. If you want to know more, just ask.

I felt relieved and enthusiastically began to write my arguments.

"All my life I've had uphill" people who cheated on me or left me, it was hard for me to understand it, I always felt that I had no control over my life, that it all made no sense, every day is survival, like more, and here it is completely different with you - a different world, wonderful, selfless people. I'm already afraid that in a week they will disappear from my life and I will be alone in hopelessness again. How to stop it? How do you make it all last a little longer?

"I understand you perfectly, I know what you're talking about," Olivia began, focusing her attention on me. "The feeling of emptiness and loss comes from a lack of contact with yourself, which is exactly what I was talking about yesterday morning during meditation. You look for happiness and acceptance outside, with other people, you want them to give you what you need. You count on them, trust them, attach yourself to them, and they go about their business. In part, almost everyone feels the way you do. We all want the same thing, love, attention, interest, being important and seen by others, but this is not the way to go.

Remember what I said about childhood beliefs? They guide you now, those deficiencies from that time are still in you, undiscovered, unprocessed, unnoticed, they will go on like this for years until you do something about it. Until you take care of yourself. Until you make friends with yourself. No one from the outside will give it to you, and if you can get it from the outside, it will only be temporary and impermanent. If you find yourself in similar situations over and over again, it's because you have something to work through. I mean to face the problem face to face and face it. The worst thing is to run away, because sooner or later this problem will catch up with you and will be magnified. Stand up for life. With courage. Just like you did with your would-be mother-in-law. You've taken a very big step in your direction. It is often the case that people are afraid to take up challenges, they are afraid to take the difficult situations they are in like a bull by the horns and deal with them. Once you deal with a trauma, something important, it will never come back. What's your biggest problem?"

"I think the biggest influence on me was when my parents left."

"Will you tell me about it? It's certainly hard, but that's what it's all about for you to bring your traumas out and look at them."

"My parents left to work in Germany when I was nine years old. I was simply abandoned. They never came back permanently, they rarely visited us. They drowned out their remorse with the money and gifts they sent."

"You regret. What is your relationship with your parents now?"

"Very average, sometimes we talk on the phone, but we live in different worlds and there is simply no understanding between us. My sister, Eve, doesn't care much about it, she has her own passions and affairs and has cut herself off from what used to be. I'm too sensitive, I don't know, maybe unforgiving. Maybe weak" I decided to be completely honest, with Olivia it came surprisingly easily to me.

Would you be able to forgive your parents? Forgiveness is hard, but it is a great relief. It's not about forgetting what they did to you, but accepting that they did and that's what they did. There's no going back, it's all about letting go, for your own peace of mind.

"I do not know if I can."

"Come with me," she said, then stood up.

"Where?" I asked uncertainly.

"Trust me."

We went to Olivia's office. I was here for the first time. A pleasant place, full of harmony and peace, everything was arranged here, in its place. The entire wall to the left was filled with books. Opposite the door was a large desk, and behind it was a wide window with a balcony. To the right was a comfortable couch and armchairs. I saw many figurines, symbols, I did not understand what they meant.

"Sit down so you're comfortable. Wherever you want" said Olivia. She walked over to the laptop herself, turned on relaxing, very calm music, and came back to me. She sat down opposite.

"We're going to do a little forgiveness meditation, okay? I want you to understand something. All right?" she asked.

"Sure, absolutely."

"Then relax, just like in group classes."

Olivia, using suggestions, put me in a meditative state, deep calm. It took a long time.

"Now go back to that day when you said goodbye to your parents." Look at them. Try to reject all emotions, observe yourself in that moment as if you were standing on the side. Look at the mother. Is she happy? Or sad? Maybe this is the hardest moment for her too? You are her daughter and she must leave you. Maybe there is no other way? You were only nine years old, you didn't understand everything then. Look into her eyes. Maybe they are full of pain, worry? Your mother makes this decision because she believes she is doing the right thing. Maybe he's afraid? Maybe he wants to ensure a good future for you and your sister, and where he is, there is no such possibility? Look at your father. What do you see in his eyes? What is there, is there peace? Or maybe pain? Maybe despair? Maybe he can't look you in the eye? Notice what's going on, see all the emotions.

Olivia fell silent, giving me time to concentrate.

I breathed deeply, slowly, I can't even describe what was happening to me then. I easily recalled the image of my parents and that day when they came to say goodbye before leaving. I looked at them, I saw pain in their eyes, worry and tears. I could feel the emotions that were happening at that moment. It was very difficult for my mother, she looked at me, hugged me, kissed me on the forehead, then looked me straight in the eyes again. I stuck to that look. Then I heard Olivia's soft voice.

"If you can, understand your parents, if you can, forgive. Do it for yourself so you can move on without all the emotional baggage. To get rid of grief. Sorry. You can do it if you want."

Ten minutes later, I was still sitting on the couch with a tissue in my hand, wiping my tear-soaked face. I smiled slightly.

"It was amazing," I said with a huge sense of relief. "Thank you."

"Unfortunately, it was not my original meditation" said Olivia. "You can find such guided meditations on the Internet. There's plenty of it, find someone who does these meditations with whom you feel resonance and give it a try. There is also an old Hawaiian practice of forgiveness and reconciliation called Ho'oponopono. Think of the person you want to forgive and repeat over and over: I'm sorry, forgive me, please, thank you, I love you. Such simple words: I'm sorry, forgive me, please, thank you, I love you, and they have great power. This prayer is very effective, I use it myself until now. Sometimes, if you want, you can modify it a bit. For example, when thinking about your mother, say: I'm sorry I didn't understand you and I didn't even try to understand you, please forgive me for holding a grudge against you for so long. Thank you for being there for the first nine years of my life, I just love you because you are."

"It's amazing," I said in surprise. "You give me tips that are very simple, I did not know that such a thing and exists."

"Darling, because the simplest tips are the best. Train "Ho'oponopono", train forgiving and letting go, and see what happens in three weeks."

"How often do I have to repeat this?"

"Three times a day, five minutes is enough. Natalie, if you reject from your life what blocks you, what does not serve you, if you build a sense of security, self-love, your life will change a lot. I guarantee you that. Great people will come to you and you will have to worry about them leaving, they will want to stay with you. There will be great deals, such gifts from fate, you'll see, you'll be surprised. Just be open to the abundance that will flow to you. Open your heart and don't be afraid. Let go of your grief, resentment, forgive everyone and most of all yourself, everything that is forgivable, let go of all the past, what you were supposed to learn, what you learned, and move forward. Don't look back because you might miss something great. Open your heart to new ones.

"Thank you. Really. This meditation with my parents was amazing, very cleansing."

"That's what it was supposed to be." I wanted you to understand that sometimes people make very difficult decisions. To get something better, sometimes you have to lose something. You can't judge people without being, as the saying goes, in their shoes for a while. You have to understand, empathize with the situation, then it is easier for us to understand and forgive.

"You're right. I remembered why my parents left. Once again, thank you very much" I stood up, I was filled with gratitude and lightness.

"Take care and see you later."

I entered my room and threw myself on the bed. I was lying on my back staring at the ceiling. It was amazing, that meditation, I still couldn't shake off the sublime experience. I breathed deeply, relieved. Though their eyes were not yet well dried from the recent tears, I had the impression that they were smiling happily.

I had a completely different look at that day when my parents left me. I was aware that one meditation would not be enough for complete forgiveness, but I already knew what to do, how to deal with it.

I also remembered a very important fact from life. My father's mother, Genevieve, lived with us for a while, she was an ailing, groaning, and extremely grumpy old woman who used a wheelchair. In order for her parents to take care of her when she fell ill, they had to buy a large house on credit so that Grandma Genevieve would be comfortable. Previously, we lived on the third floor of a block of flats without an elevator. Grandma promised that she would leave all her savings and the tenement house she owned to my father, so the money would be used to pay off the loan. Unfortunately, however, that did not happen. Living with my grandma was a nightmare, and towards the end of her life, she accused my parents of neglecting her, which of course wasn't true. After Genevieve left, it turned out that she had no savings, only a lot of debts, and the tenement house had not been her property for a long time. My parents had no choice but to find a high-paying job to pay off Genevieve's debts and not lose their own home. I realized they had no choice.

I got out of bed and, full of optimism and faith, I went out into the yard, we planned to rent bikes with the girls and go on a longer trip around the area. It was a nice afternoon.

The next day, after my morning yoga class, I went to my room to change for breakfast. I was intrigued by a piece of paper lying on the table. Cream paper with the guest house logo. Every few days, such "life reminders" were left by the cleaning lady. The texts written on them were supposed to motivate you to think about the direction of your life. They gave a lot to think about. I opened the piece of paper and read what it said: "What happened the day before that you are grateful for? Give at least three reasons for gratitude. And today? What will yours look like today? What will you do, what steps will you take to feel happiness and joy within yourself?".

I smiled and put down the card. I immediately reached for the notebook with the notes I made each morning and wrote: My reasons for gratitude are being here, in this place where I have peace, quiet and can think. Where my "I" slowly clarifies, I finally begin to see myself and what is inside me, all these emotions and doubts. I am grateful for a bike trip in the company of wonderful women from whom I can learn joy and fun, for discovering that there is such a thing as carefree and trust. I am grateful to someone who pulled the right strings, somewhere in the universe, and brought me here, to this place. Everyone here says that everything in life happens for a reason, apparently it is, I don't understand it yet, but I'm going to find out. And thank you for an invention like the Internet, where I can quickly find interesting, guided meditations that teach letting go and forgiveness.

Putting the pen aside, I glanced at the previous pages out of curiosity: "...Who the hell am I, what do I want? Why am I so serious and down? Why am I so sad? How to get it out of you? Will I go fishing? I will ask Zbigniew, maybe he will help me, after all he is a specialist in fishing. oh fuck. ...'.

I smiled. Another snippet, a page earlier: "And what? And nothing. I don't feel like writing, nothing works out for me, I haven't written anything creative here yet, is there any sense in that? Is there any point in waking up before five in the morning today? That's what retirees do. I'm not thirty yet, and I feel like a pensioner in my underpants. Anthony was right, I can't even wear a skirt because I don't feel like it, because I don't give a shit what I look like. I don't want anyone to be interested in me, except maybe Marilyn, Martha, Sylvia. Well, I like Fred and Daria too. And Damien? What the hell am I supposed to think of him? He's a little cool, I hope he doesn't want anything from me. I like to train with him, I feel good in his company. And that's it. Enough".

I closed the notebook. I changed and quickly went down to breakfast. I was a bit sad because Martha was leaving us today. She missed her children and went back to her home, to her family. She was going to leave right after breakfast. Even though we only knew each other for a short time, I really liked her. Our whole team walked her to the parking lot. We hugged, thanked him for staying with us, and watched him drive away. Damien stood next to me, gently put his arm around me in a warm, friendly gesture, I hope that was his intention, and we returned to the guest house.

We sat on the terrace with cups of coffee in our hands.

"Oh, look," said Marlene, pointing to her father, accompanied by a cheerful, slightly plump woman. They walked towards the lake, embracing and laughing. – My father fell in love with me, the wedding will be like nothing.

"They make a nice couple," Sylvia remarked.

"Or at least a nice woman?" do you like each other?" I asked.

"Lucy is fine, but her father is acting like a teenager. At first, he'd sneak out on dates with Lucy as if it was inappropriate. It made me laugh to tears. He did not want to admit to these meetings."

"But you don't have a problem with that?" Daria asked.

"No, absolutely. Father has been alone for a long time, he deserves a little joy. And at least I have more time to meet you. What are we doing today?"

"I suggest thermal baths" said Damien.

"There's going to be some girl's party with Olivia tonight. We are to wear dresses or long skirts, reminded Sylvia. "It's going to be fun!" I want to take part in it.

"We'll be back in time," Damien said.

"After the thermal pools, I will be exhausted, as always, I will not have enough strength for the party" Sylvia did not give up.

"Then we'll only be going there for two hours."

"What draws you there?" I asked Damien.

"Maybe I want to see what you look like in a bathing suit," he said teasingly, looking at me with a smile.

"I'd love to watch you, too," I replied seriously, taking a sip of coffee from my cup.

We went to the thermal pools right after lunch. As soon as I immersed myself in the warm, pleasant water, I immediately felt better. It was a very good idea to spend some time here. The water washed away the remnants of my worries and I could fully relax. I sat in the jacuzzi and watched my companions have a great time on the slides and other entertainment. I preferred to sit in peace and then go for a swim. Damien, after an hour of madness, joined me in the jacuzzi. He sat back and smiled happily on his face.

"What a view, it was worth coming here," he said.

"Well, I'm not surprised, there are plenty of attractive chicks here - I stated matter-of-factly, glancing to the side towards the girls dressed in skimpy bikinis.

"But I meant you."

"Please." I shook my head incredulously.

"You're very attractive." He gave me a very telling look.

"And very inaccessible," I added to cool any further impulses.

"Oh yes. And it's a real pity…" He moved a little towards me and placed his hand behind my back. He was right there, so close. I could feel the warmth of his almost naked body.

"It's getting hot, I'll go cool off in the pool," I said and stepped out of the hot tub. I walked a dozen steps, bounced off the tile floor, and jumped into the largest pool of cool water.

"What's that supposed to be?! said Dorothy in a loud voice, looking at a young girl, dressed quite provocatively, who had just got out of the car. "Is she the one who has classes with our boys today?!"

"Yes, Dorothy, Izabela was invited for a little chat, as you put it nicely, with your peasants" confirmed Olivia.

We stood in front of the guest house entrance, waiting for a larger group to gather. It was late, the first stars appeared in the sky.

"What's she there for?" asked Dorothy indignantly.

"We have our parties, gentlemen have theirs, so that they don't get bored waiting for you. Don't worry, Izabela is a professional" explained Olivia.

"And from what?" What will she do there?

"What are you, jealous?" the woman standing next to Dorothy got angry.

"I'm jealous?!"

"Calm down, my dear," Olivia said in a raised voice. "It's on me. We go to the lake, there waiting for us a small snack and mulled wine. And don't worry about your husbands. Come on, my dear."

We set off in a large group towards the lake. A fire was already burning in the distance. Two young girls were bustling about, finishing preparations for the party. It sounded interesting.

We sat on the thick oak benches around the fire. Olivia walked over to a large table that was lined with mugs and platters of snacks and audio equipment. She played soft, soothing music.

"You look gorgeous," she said, looking at our colorful, airy gowns. "Perfect for our meeting today." It's going to happen... Ready for total madness? she asked, sitting between us on the wooden bench.

"Bright! Yes! Enthusiastic cheers rang out."

"I think we must first find out what this young girl is doing to our peasants. Who saw it, let them into the boarding house" Dorothy was angry.

"Dorothy, come on, let it go," said the woman sitting next to her.

"Aren't you worried about yours?" You just told me you gave him a second chance because he was seeing someone else. Now all of a sudden you trust him?

"Dorothy, that's enough," Olivia admonished. "We're here to have fun, have a good time." We're not forcing anyone here.

"I just want to know what they're doing there," said Dorothy indignantly.

"Nothing wrong," said Olivia. "I assure you. Tell me, has Zbyszek ever given you a reason to be jealous?"

"What envy! I'm not jealous, but the peasants have to be kept short" she snapped back offended.

"Okay, but answer the question. Has he ever given you cause for concern?"

"Not yet…"

"Did you give him cause to be jealous?"

I smiled. Dorothy flirted with whom she could. She made ambiguous proposals, not caring at all that her husband was standing next to him and could hear everything. She excelled in society, liked to show off, maybe she was just playing with words, personally I've never seen her alone with another man.

"And what does this have to do with it? She was outraged, but finally fell silent. She made herself more comfortable and with her head held high, she waited for the situation to develop."

"Okay, my dear, today I will tell you how to make your dreams come true. Or maybe you have some patents of your own and want to share them?" asked Olivia.

"You have to have those dreams first," one of the women said.

"Exactly, after so many failures in life, you don't think in such terms anymore" added one of the ladies sitting in the back. "Dreams are for dreamers, and they will never come true.

"Why do you think so? This is how you block yourself from anything good."

"If you don't expect something, then it's less of a disappointment. How many times I kept my fingers crossed that I would succeed, and then nothing came of it - said a slim brown-haired woman sitting next to Marilyn. "Then you'd better be prepared to fail." Better not to jinx it.

"And the universe listens and grants your wishes," said Olivia. "Women, a little more faith… I've told you so many times that what you think is what you attract. How are you going to succeed if you're setting yourself up to fail? Well, come on. Where is the sense and logic here?ok, i'll explain how it works. The whole world is energy, we are energy, our thoughts and feelings are energy. The point is to tune in energetically to abundance, wealth, love. To contentment, to lightness. For this to work, we need to be on the same wavelength. It's the same as with other people, with some we like each other, and with others we can't get in touch. It's like with radio waves, if you set it to RMF, you will hear RMF, not Zet. do you understand it?"

"More or less."

"Yes, that's understandable," some replied.

"You know very well how much energy is in us, when we get mad, how much of it comes out of us during an argument. It would be enough to power half a settlement with electricity. I'm joking of course. And when we're excited, we're waiting for something cool to happen. We know it from life, right? And our dreams are also a kind of energy. And to make dreams come true, let's give them space to exist in life. Let's trust that we deserve something good, that we are worth making dreams come true. Let's give them attention, let's connect with what we want, let's feel it. Imagine what it will be like when this dream comes true. what will we do? How will we behave, what will we think then? Our mind will get used to it, consider it real and will do everything to adapt, to deliver what we want. Share your dreams. Aileen, what will make you happy, what would you like to achieve?"

"Own spa or at least a beauty salon" said Aileen seriously.

"Great, spa. Who else? Marlene?"

"Own psychological clinic. I'm just finishing my studies in this field. I would like to help people"

"Great. I will invite you to weekend lectures at my place, if you find time, of course" said Olivia appreciatively.

I looked at Marlene curiously. She never said what field she was studying in Krakow.

Anyone else sharing dreams?

"I want to make an exhibition of my paintings, I want to finally have the courage to show my works to the world."

"Asia, bravo. An artist has a duty to share his abilities with others.

Think about it, if Ed Sheeran didn't dare to show his works, or Elton John or Shakira, we wouldn't have music or entertainment. It would be grey, boring. Same with actors, movies, any form of art. Asia, we are doing an exhibition at my place in three months. You have my word."

"I want to travel the world," exclaimed Sylvia.

"Very good!" Olivia praised.

"I want to be a veterinarian, but I'm too old to study."

"And who told you that you're too old" Olivia was indignant. "You can learn and develop your skills at any age. You have to do what makes you happy, what gives you joy, what you want and don't have to. Each of us has some passions. How do we feel doing what we love? Great, right? Time flows differently, we feel such a flow, a flow of energy, we have power ... And this joy? How about earning money from what we love to do? Fantastic right? We can, why not! What's stopping us?! Exactly! Our beliefs. Only our beliefs stand in our way." She paused, giving her time to think.

"What? Let's change our beliefs, our lives will change" said Marilyn.

"Exactly."

"Okay, but today we are talking about making dreams come true" continued Olivia. "Now let each of you choose a dream to fulfill. Think it over carefully because I guarantee it will come true… Already? We have it? You can close your eyes to focus better. See this dream. Aileen is the boss in her own spa, Asia watches how everyone raves about the exhibition… I, for example, want to go to the Maldives. I imagine that I am on this beautiful island, I focus on what I feel. It's warm, the sun warms me pleasantly, I feel the sun's rays on my skin, I hear the sound of the sea, the water is so clean and transparent, the views are breathtaking. I am there, I see it, I feel it with all my senses. This is real, real. Just do it. There are no restrictions. Feel the energy that flows, see what's going on ... How much joy is in you ... What do you get when you tell people about what you have, what you do ... Feel yourself deeply ...."

It was a difficult task for me, what could I want? I closed my eyes, calmed myself down and waited for something to come into my mind. I heard Olivia's words: "feel the energy that flows, see what is happening ... how much joy is in you", I imagined myself happy, content, standing on the pier by the lake. That was all I could recall. I focused on the visualization and the feelings that come from it.

The music was louder, energetic, I didn't know those songs.

"Feel grateful," Olivia continued. "Gratitude, that this dream has already come true, you are already in it. You already have it all. You are happy, satisfied. Feel the joy bursting inside you. See it, feel it. Dear women, do you feel this joy? The energy is buzzing, we have the power within us. come in roles, stay in them until the end of the day. Each of you is now a fulfilled woman. How do you feel? How do you walk, what does your voice sound like? what can you do? Now show the world how women who have made their dreams come true have fun! Butts up, we're celebrating successes!"

The music got even louder. The women jumped up from their seats and started jumping up and down happily.

Let the energy flow! We have power! Let's open ourselves to all the possibilities that the world offers us. We deserve the best!

Olivia passed between the women and asked them questions:

"Krystyna, you are a great veterinarian, how many animals have you saved today?"

"Aileen, how are you feeling in your spa?"

"My darlings, don't be ashamed, if you feel good in your new role, it will come, for sure. This is the best and shortest way to make your dreams come true. Just like that! Be in it, feel it before it comes true. Therefore, let's be, let's give ourselves a chance to experience this now and in the future as a new reality. Let's dance as much as we can. You can close your eyes."

I felt the joy of the group. Olivia was able to effectively stimulate emotions and madness.

"Let's feel like witches who have acquired secret knowledge that has been passed down for generations. We already know it, we can already recall our future and the best" cried Olivia with a laugh. She stood by the fire and danced, bending her body in different directions.

I looked at everything from the side. What was happening was amazing. Big bonfire. A bunch of energetic, shouting women, raging under the starry sky. Colorful dresses swirling around. Emotions were at the highest speed. At times I even felt tears in my eyes. What was going on there… Some magical force united us all and brought out extraordinary layers of the most beautiful emotions straight from the depths of our hearts.

All the women let themselves be carried away to an exotic dance. Only one, Dorothy, slipped sidEveys and walked briskly towards the boarding house.

The party lasted until midnight. We had snacks prepared on the table and mulled wine for those who wanted. Tired, after dancing to lively music, we sat on oak benches and talked, all the time sticking to our roles. We asked each other what it was like to be a fulfilled woman, how life changed after achieving success. It was great fun.

The next morning I spent on the balcony with a notebook in my hand. I wrote. I wanted to dig deep inside myself and find out what I wanted, what would make me happy. In which direction should you look when trying to build your future? I finally had to make a decision. I have a week left at the boarding house, now what?

"My sister rented me an apartment in Warsaw. Do I want to live there, do I want to be there? What will I do there? I want to live in a place as peaceful as where I am now. Do I still want to be a teacher? Anyone want me to work? I was not supposed to undermine my worth, well, again, this conviction spoke through me, great, I noticed it. So otherwise, do I want to work in the profession I have been doing so far? Did it give me satisfaction? A bit like that. I used to be more specific. Now I know that I know nothing. I don't even get mad at myself because it doesn't do anything. I have a total blank in my head and it's hard for me to move in any direction. If only anything came to my mind, and nothing here. I need to get a grip and think about the future. I have to. Even today. I am supposed to do what I want, not what I have to. They don't stick to each other. It's not like a man does what he wants and not what he has to. Okay, that's different. what do i need??? Move out of here in a week. I don't like this idea. I know I have to. What else? Find a job. Only what? Where? Approx. What do I want? What I want? Peace, a sense of security, a small house with a beautiful view. Friends I can trust. I don't want a partner, I've had enough of men, at least for now. Maybe someday I'll change my mind. I'll see. I still want to learn to show emotions, it's a bit uncomfortable, but I liked the atmosphere at the party last night. No one judged anyone, we all felt so connected to each other in understanding and mutual acceptance, it was special, I wish I always had such a group of people with me. Oh, I'm going to practice what it's like to have great friends."

I entered the room, put the notebook on the table and sat on the bed. I calmed down, focused my attention on imagining myself sitting in a cozy apartment on a comfortable sofa, in the company of a few kind people. I imagined them, trying to evoke feelings of gratitude and joy. I saw how we laugh together, we have unlimited trust in each other, common interests. I felt calm and fulfilled, very positive emotions.

I was in this visualized reality for a long time. I liked it and wanted it to be my real future. It was a very enjoyable exercise, and I decided to do it every day.

CHAPTER 7

I met the girls in the morning. We sat on the terrace and drank coffee.

"What do you think about forgiveness?" Daria asked.

"Why are you asking?" Marlene was interested.

Because everyone has something to forgive someone. I'm trying, but honestly, I'm not completely ready for it yet.

"And who can you not forgive, Daria?" Marlene asked.

"My father left when I was little. He left me and my mother and started a second family. It's not that I miss him, because I haven't had contact with him for a long time, but the fact that he abandoned me."

"It's difficult, but just wanting, making a decision is already a big step forward" said Sylvia. "We have to put it all behind us once and for all. Try to stand face to face with him during meditation and tell him what you think, you will definitely feel relieved. Yell at him, get angry, cry as much as you need to let out the accumulated emotions."

"I'll try it this way." And you, Natalie, have you dealt with your anger at your mother-in-law?

"I try not to think about her." I decided not to spoil my stay here - I said truthfully. Not once have I thought of my would-be husband or his mother since that evening by the lake, where my companions came with champagne to drink my freedom.

"I have an idea. Natalie, we will write a letter to the pompous mayor" said Marilyn.

"What letter?" Sylvia asked. "What are you talking about?"

"Letter. I already tell you what. On a beautiful card, it will be written: "Dear Future Mommy. I am immensely grateful to you for forcing me to leave your beautiful and refined abode. And your wonderful, manly son. Thanks to this situation you contributed to, I now lead a wonderful life. I live in a big two-story villa, I have many friends and great prospects." So far everything is true."

"Are you crazy?" I laughed.

"No why? Since grandma likes to set people up, let's put her nose in the ass, "ą", "ę", politely. I'm going to get a piece of paper" Marilyn entered the building and soon returned with a notebook and a pen.

"For now, it's dirty, Mrs. Helen will share the printer. This is what we write... Natalie, write so that you can read it later, I scribble too much."

"What should I write?" I was amused by this situation.

"What I said earlier: "Dear Evelyn. I am immensely grateful to you for forcing me to leave your beautiful and refined abode. I think marrying your son would be a mistake.""

"It will be better: "now I know" instead of "I think"" Daria noted.

"Right," Marlene admitted excitedly. "Keep writing: "Now I know that marrying your son would be a huge mistake. I've learned a lot from you and I'm stronger and wiser now. You saved me from the biggest mistake, I can't imagine having a man by my side who hasn't grown up to be a husband or a father. Thank you for showing me the whole truth before we got married. I'm leading a great life now. I live in a large two-story villa, I have many friends and great prospects. With gratitude and best wishes, Natalie."

"She's going to hit something when she reads this," I said, amused.

"That's the point," laughed Marlene. "Write on the computer, we'll print it at Helen's, address the envelope, and I'll send it from Krakow."

"You're crazy." I shook my head incredulously.

"Of course not. You will show class with this thank you. She definitely underestimated you."

"Okay," I agreed, amused. In my mind's eye, I saw Evelyn's face when she got this letter. It will surely be surprising.

Our cheerful chat was interrupted by Dorothy's familiar, loud voice. She left the boarding house in the company of her friends, greatly agitated, she discussed yesterday's men's activities with the attractive Izabela.

"It's inconceivable how you could come up with something like that." This scantily clad babe was confusing our husbands. I'm surprised Olivia allowed it.

"As far as I know, they had an hour-long lecture, some discussion, and that's it," said a friend.

But did you see how she was dressed?" Dorothy was annoyed.

"Okay, in pants and a shirt."

"Leather trousers and waist-length neckline."

"I didn't look too closely."

"Justin, you saw it, didn't you?" Dorothy did not give up.

"He was attractive, well-groomed ..."

"But it was a lecture on how to make a woman happy. What gifts to buy, how to understand a woman, how to try for her despite a long marriage. She even suggested what underwear to buy for my wife" interrupted one of the women, Agatha. "What's wrong with that?"

"And how do you know?" Dorothy attacked.

"Because my Adam told me. He even showed me on the Internet and asked if I would like him to buy me something like that" added Agatha.

"Hmmm, my Zbyszek didn't say anything."

"And it's interesting why..." Agatha sneered.

We looked at each other surprised to hear this conversation. The women moved farther into the yard, so we didn't hear the rest of the discussion.

"Interesting," Marlene commented.

"Zbyszek is a great guy," I sympathized heartily with him.

"And how do you know?"

I fish with it often. First thing in the morning,' I explained, looking after Dorothy as she walked away.

"Well, then be careful with these fish, because if the lady catches you on common mornings with Zbyszek, it can be fat" said Sylvia.

"I would not like to fish you out of the lake one fine day" Marilyn received.

We started laughing.

I saw lightning flashes in the distance, a storm was approaching. The wind died down completely. I was horseback riding with Lena and anxiously watched the billowing dark clouds drifting across the sky at the height of the mountain peaks.

Will we make it before the storm? I asked, because Lena wasn't going to turn back.

"Relax, we still have plenty of time," said the young girl. "Look at this," she gestured to the sights ahead.

"I see. And I know that clouds can go 100 miles an hour" I said.

"Now throw away your fear and look again" said Olivia's daughter, as you can see, the apple fell not far from the apple tree. She was very similar to her mother physically and intellectually.

I looked. We rode horses through some open meadows in the valley. Before us was a beautiful view of the Tatra Mountains, now they looked menacing, majestic, surrounded by dark clouds, hanging heavily just above the top of the mountain range. The sun shone from the right side, giving a phenomenal impression. It looked menacing yet incredibly beautiful.

I felt a thrill. What if we don't make it back to the guest house in time?

"Maybe we'll come back, huh?" Tina is restless, I said.

Lena looked at the mare I was riding.

"She'll be fine, but ok. If you want, we can go back."

we turned back. We trotted home. I didn't feel stable or safe in the saddle yet. Every now and then I would turn around and see if the storm was close enough that I should be afraid. The wind has broken.

"It'll go sidEveys," Lena said, looking up at the sky. "Look, the clouds are moving from east to west.

"If you say so ...."

And as I feared, we didn't make it.

The rain caught us a kilometer from the guesthouse. The storm passed by, but it still caught up with us and we got wet. At first, when it started to rain, I got very angry, and then when I was all wet, I let go and, feeling the water dripping from my hair onto my face and I can't see much in front of me, I started laughing. The mare was walking ahead, and I had to trust her. I closed my eyes, gripped the reins tight, and let Tina lead me to the stables, she knew the way best. I found the rain to be warm, not scary at all, even fun. I always ran away from the smallest drops of drizzle to the house or under an umbrella. Here I had nowhere to run and I discovered that riding a horse in a downpour can be really fun.

Satisfied, I helped Lena unsaddle her horse. By the way, I saw how it was done, and then, with my head held high, I marched across the yard. I went up the stairs and stopped suddenly. I left so much mud and the building was always so clean. Right outside the front door, I took off my shoes and soaked jeans, grabbed my clothes, and tiptoed silently to my room. On the stairs, I met a crowd of people heading for a larger conference room. Everyone looked at me amazed, I was running barefoot, in only panties and a T-shirt, wet, I presented quite an interesting view. I just sighed, smiled and kept running. Another fusion.

I took a shower, wishing I could sit in my room and wander around the boarding house in my underwear, but I knew there was another meeting in the conference room that I couldn't miss. I dressed quickly, combed my wet hair, and headed to more personal development classes.

I arrived just as Olivia was finishing her short speech. I found an empty seat in the back and sat down, trying not to be conspicuous. I felt only one gaze on me - Damien.

" ...I think you will like this film, it will open your eyes to life, to what we have, what we can have, how powerful visualization is, it will show how easily and pleasantly we can change our lives at the level of wealth, health , relationships, happiness. It is a documentary film, and a book by Rhona Byrne with the same title has also been written" Olivia told the audience. "I have seen this film several times, I encourage you to watch it very warmly, and then to discuss it. It's raining anyway, so let's use this time productively to learn something, to know the key to success. Others are already using it, myself included. You also can. This secret was understood by the greatest and most important people in history. These wisdoms are found in religions around the world, passed down from generation to generation and shrouded in mystery. Now this knowledge is also given to you. Take as much as you want from this video. I'm not prolonging this, let's start.

Olivia pressed the start button on her laptop and on the huge screen hung on the wall we saw the title: "Secret".

"The movie can be easily found on You Tube" added Olivia.

Out of curiosity, I glanced at what was written on the screen - The Secret dubbing PL 2006".

Olivia turned up the sound volume even more and we could start the movie screening.

After only fifteen minutes, I was very impressed with what was flowing to me from the screen. Statements of philosophers, quantum physicists, conveyed in such a simple way, on examples of how real miracles can be performed in life. How to get what you want, how to gain success, wealth, health, how to fight all obstacles. I was stunned at how simple, how obvious it was. It is enough to imagine our future, to feel as if we already have what we need and to believe that the Universe takes care of us and gives us what we want. However, we must first know what to ask for. Olivia gave us a bit of this knowledge last time, at a girl's evening by the fire.

There was silence in the room during the movie. Everyone was focused on the positive messages that were coming to us. All the information was very interesting and extremely valuable. I wish I had something to write with at hand, I would have taken notes so I wouldn't miss anything. I had the impression that the hour and a half movie lasted only a quarter of an hour.

"And what do you think?" – asked Olivia after the end of the movie.

"It's pretty unbelievable," said one of the men in the middle of the crowd. "I don't know if there are any scientific studies on this. In this video, they clearly say that we can have anything we want without the slightest effort. It's bullshit. I have worked hard to build my company and I know that nothing comes for free.

"Yes, Artur, but before your company was established, you had to imagine it: the building, the people, the scope of activity. You wouldn't build your empire without it, right? Olivia asked, referring to the comment. "First, everything was created in your head, in your thoughts. You believed that you could run a successful company. Thoughts become things."

"I'm not convinced of that," he replied grimly.

"And I think it's nice to know that we are a magnet attracting everything in our lives, which means that a lot depends on ourselves, we are the creators of ourselves and our own destiny" said Marilyn. "It's like you told us before, Olivia, what you focus on, it grows. Bomb movie for me. I realized that every person is important, but they don't know how much potential they have and unfortunately they can't use it."

"Exactly," said someone from behind.

"You just have to focus on positive thoughts, and it is very difficult" said Lucy.

"Yes, you have to be careful, watch your thoughts, but thanks to this we get to know ourselves better, we have contact with each other" said Olivia. "It's also like you'll never attract something into your life that isn't in harmony with you." You will attract what you believe is true for you. Why can't this truth be a new, beautiful house by the sea? You just have to believe that this house is for you, you deserve it. Just. People usually make a very big mistake in the attraction process. They want it now, and if they don't get what they want, they get tense, they get offended, they're convinced it's not working. It works, but everything takes time, the right circumstances. Dreams come true in the least expected moments, when we let go. The universe knows what it's doing and there's no need to rush it. The best comes at the right time when we are ready for it. And sometimes, if he doesn't come, it means he has something better planned for us.

The debates continued for another hour, with many skeptical but also enthusiastic supporters. A very interesting discussion.

In the evening I sat in my room and searched the Internet for books on personal development. I found many interesting items with positive opinions. It took me a very long time, as a result of which I placed a large order at the bookstore. Now all that's left to do is wait for the courier. I wanted to delve into the subject. I learned things that completely changed my worldview, were completely different from what I had believed before. I like to learn, I like to gain knowledge, I have an open mind for all inspirations and news.

I closed my laptop, glanced at my watch, and left the room. I had an appointment for an evening walk in the woods with my friends. I felt like I could say that about them. I liked them, I could be honest with them, and I wasn't afraid of being judged or misbehaving.

It was quiet in the forest. The sky after the storm became cloudless, here and there single clouds floated, tinted orange from the setting sun.

The forest roads were full of mud and slippery stones. We walked slowly, close to each other, to help each other in case of a fall. The full moon appeared in the sky, illuminating our path a bit. We could have stayed at the boarding house during that time, but that would have been boring. We preferred a walk in the woods.

The girls went ahead, and me and Damien stayed a bit behind.

"Let me know when you end your emotional mourning for Greg" he said at one point. "I hope it won't take you too long."

"Why should I have emotional mourning for Greg?" I asked surprised.

"So can I go on a date with you now?" he smiled playfully.

"I don't know if I ever want to date anyone," I replied agitated, then realized what Damien had just said. I looked at him carefully.

"It takes some time, that's understandable. You'll change your mind someday, I hope it won't be long," he explained lightly.

I didn't answer so he continued.

"There's no need to shut up, you have to give yourself a chance. It didn't work once, you have to try again."

"Certainly," I admitted. "And how are you doing?"

"Me?"

"Yeah…"

"Hmmm… Uplifting."

"Then try harder," I said, then repeated his own words. "There's no need to shut up, you have to give yourself a chance. It didn't work once, you have to try again.

He laughed out loud.

"So, can I take you on a date sometime?"

"Maybe someday…? How will the emotional mourning after Greg pass…" I said. I liked Damien, he's a nice guy, maybe if we met in different circumstances, at a different time, who knows what it would be, friendship or maybe something more. My feelings towards other guys have been heavily blocked. I wanted to be alone for a while now. Not to enter into any relationship, it was too early for that, I also lost confidence in male-female relationships.

Suddenly I slipped on a wet stone and nearly fell. Damien grabbed my hand and I avoided bruising my knee and getting my clothes dirty.

"Okay," I said, regaining my balance. It was quite dark, the road was illuminated only by one flashlight, which Sylvia was navigating, and the glow of the full moon.

"I'm holding you tight," Damien said.

He grabbed my hand again and didn't let go until we were out of the woods.

It was a very nice and pleasant evening.

"Natalie, people focus on what they lack. They don't enjoy what they already have, but focus all their attention on what they lack. That's how it is. Look, you often say that there is no future for you, you have lost everything, you have nothing, no home, no job. You focus on it, you get depressed, you feel insecure, insecure. This is perfectly normal in your situation. However, try to look at what is happening in your life a little differently, just today, this one day. See what you got today, now. So realistically, look around, think about it" said Olivia. We were sitting in her office. She invited me here when we passed each other in the hallway. Of course I accepted the invitation.

I was pondering. I felt a bit uncomfortable. I racked my brain for an answer. It was supposed to be a nice chat, I was supposed to listen, learn something, and it turned out that I had to work mentally.

"I'm sure there is something like that," Olivia encouraged.

I sighed loudly, glancing up at the ceiling as if I was going to find the answer there.

"You have a comfortable bed, right?" I tried to ensure that all mattresses in the rooms were of the best quality. You have hot meals, space to walk, time to think. See what these values are, how important it is.

Focus on this." She continued after a long silence in the office. "I see you've made new friends here..."

I smiled.

"Yes it's true. I feel great here. My favorite place is the pier by the lake. I stand there sometimes or I sit there and I feel good there. You're right, I've never had so much time to myself to stop like this, to think, to watch the sunset, to take a quiet walk. For looking at the mountains. Everything was always on the run.

So, focus all your attention on what you have today, feel grateful for what you have today. And then tomorrow will be better. Trust that the Universe is kind to you, takes care of you."

"Well, I'm not entirely sure about that," I smiled. "If he had been favorable, he would not have put me in a relationship with Greg and Evelyn."

"Not necessarily, or maybe he put you in just because the consequence of this whole situation is that you came here? Nothing happens without a reason. Under different circumstances, would you be here, now, in this place?"

"Certainly not."

"Sometimes we do not understand that difficult, painful events actually serve us in the long run, they are supposed to teach us something, change something. We notice it only after a long time, when the dust settles, emotions calm down and then we can see everything clearly. Something that was an unbearable burden for us turns out to be a blessing over time. I know that a great future awaits you, I am convinced that you will choose your life path properly. As I told you once, you can do anything, you can go in any direction and do whatever you want. Just listen to your heart, not your mind, just your heart. And then everything will be fine. Everything will work out for the best for you."

"Very refreshing," I said gratefully.

Do you know what the hardest way is? From mind to heart.

"I do not really understand…"

"The mind is limited, it only knows what it has experienced and learned. We humans only see a fraction of what is actually in the universe. There are many aspects still unexplored, incomprehensible. One thing is certain, there is something greater than we can imagine: the force that set in motion the entire Universe, the planets, everything that is. Everything is made of atoms, of energy. We too. So we have a connection with everything that has existed and exists. This is quite a difficult topic, but very important. Imagine that this force, let's call it the Universe or God, knows best what is best for everyone. We have access to this power, each of us has. We connect with it through the heart. The heart produces a much larger electromagnetic field than the brain. Looking at life, at people, at every day, from the position of the heart, i.e. what we have in ourselves, this universal truth, we see more, we understand more, we have more peace and a sense of power. We see a broader perspective. The problem is that few people let their heart speak. We live in times like these and no other, where most of us are firmly entrenched in the mind and ego. And because of this, a person feels far from happiness, from such a connection with oneself. It's a pity. As I have already mentioned, the heart is a link with the superconsciousness, our soul, thanks to which we have all the answers within us. We have the potential, we have the power. We have what we believe we deserve. Natalie, answer the question of what you deserve and just let it come to you.

"Oh, from what you said, I need to work on myself a lot," I said, leaning back and leaning back in my chair.

"It's important for you to be aware of that." You must definitely do something, or you will return to Warsaw, to your old habits, habits, surroundings and let the same problems repeat themselves over and over again in your life, or you will stand bravely and wisely towards your future and go in a new, unknown direction and you will build something that will serve you and give you joy.

"I know, I think about it every day.

"Quiet all those voices and dialogues in your head and listen to what your heart tells you."

"But how? How am I supposed to listen to my heart?"

"Be silent, remember to write whatever comes to your mind every day. As I mentioned, but I will repeat it again, with this writing, first the voice will come from the head, and then from the heart, you will notice the difference. This is why it's important to write down three pages, not less, to give yourself time for your mind to get bored and let go. Walk in the woods alone. Nothing good will come of chaotic thoughts, only when you calm down your emotions, you will get out of your head faster and easier, connect with your soul and find all the answers."

"Hearing it sound so simple," I sighed. "Harder to do."

"Maybe it's worth a little effort? Try harder? Believe in yourself and your abilities? I believe in you," said Olivia.

"Thank you." I smiled sadly. "A lot of work ahead of me, how will

I find myself in all this? It will not be easy."

"Suffering isn't any easier either."

In the evening we had a meeting with Olivia.

"I'm going to teach you something," she said, facing the group. All the tables had been moved to the side, and so were the chairs. There were yoga mats against the wall.

"It will be only for willing and completely healthy people. If someone has problems with blood pressure or frequent dizziness, I would suggest giving up these exercises. Joanne, one of our group members, is a doctor and agreed to supervise today's activities. There's nothing to be afraid of. We're not going to do anything difficult or health-threatening, it's more about improving health. We will learn to breathe properly. Wim Hof, the Dutch Iceman, developed a special breathing technique. It aims to stimulate physiological processes. Deep diaphragmatic breathing raises blood pH, stimulates the nervous and circulatory systems and stimulates metabolism. A very interesting experience. I've personally used it for years. If anyone is willing to try it, I invite you, I suggest dividing into groups, it will be easier and more convenient."

There was a buzz of conversation among the gathered. Almost everyone was interested in the experience.

I joined the first group. There was some confusion, because Olivia asked that only those currently participating in the exercise stay, the rest had to wait in the corridor.

I lay on my back on the mat. I relaxed my body.

"Okay dears, I'm sure you'll get dizzy, it's normal, there's nothing to be afraid of. The breaths will be deep and intense. On the inhale, the air should go all the way to the navel. The belly should rise as you inhale and fall as you exhale. It is very important. After thirty such breaths, I will count out loud, let out all the air and stay like that for a minute. If someone needs to take a breath during this time, that's fine. Then inhale and hold with air in the lungs for fifteen seconds. The first time is quite difficult. It will be dizzy, it will be buzzing in the ears, it is quite natural. Remember, Asia is with us. What, all clear? we start?"

"Let's go! voices rang out."

"All right. Take a deep breath in through your nose and then exhale through your mouth. Remember, the air goes down your belly. Accept that it's possible. Inhale and exhale. Inhale and exhale..."

The rate of breathing was fast. I placed my hands on my stomach to better control my body. Belly rose and fell. After a series of thirty breaths, there was an exhalation. I held my breath. I've never done it before. Weird feeling.

"Exhale all the air and hold for one minute. I will count the time. If you need to take a breath towards the end, take it, if you can stand it, great. Relax your body. Focus your attention on the body. What's going on, how is he reacting? Twenty more seconds… Five more… Great. Now take a deep breath and hold the air in for fifteen seconds. Feel dizzy? So it has to be. And exhale slowly through your mouth. You're doing great - Olivia was close to us, watching everyone closely." And now round two: inhale, exhale. Inhale Exhale…

Thirty breaths later, another stop. I felt tingling all over my body. My mind was screaming for air, but I didn't give up, I persevered. After the third round, the hold on the exhale was extended to a minute and a half. The tingling in my body intensified. There was a buzzing in the ears. But I trusted Olivia, she certainly knew what she was doing and wouldn't put anyone in danger. At Olivia's suggestion, I took a deep breath and held it for fifteen seconds.

"All right, darlings. We breathe out calmly. you were great. You are breathing normally now. Don't get up yet, the body has to come to equilibrium. A few more minutes."

Pleasant music played in the hall. Not too loud.

I felt the tingling subside. I felt like I was floating in the air, I felt light. I touched the floor with my hands to see if I was still there. Amazing feeling. After a few minutes, I got up and sat cross-legged.

"All right?" asked Olivia.

"Yes. It was extraordinary. Can I do it alone in the room?" I asked.

"Yes, but only lying down. It won't fall off the floor, so it'll be safe" she explained.

"I couldn't stand it until the end, I had to take a breath" said Aileen.

"Alright, it's not easy at all. Everyone knows themselves best," she said. "If you're feeling well enough to get up, we'll invite another group."

When I was leaving the room, I heard Hilda asking Olivia if she could do such exercises with sinus problems.

There's been a lot going on lately, frequent meetings with friends. I like to call them that, they're really great people. We met often, we took trips to the forest, to the jacuzzi, we swam on the lake, or we just sat with cups of coffee on the terrace and talked. Sometimes I caught myself thinking that in a moment, in a few days, it would be gone.

Each of us will go our own way, return to our duties and orderly life. I felt a great emptiness in those moments. I drowned it out by concentrating on the conversation or focusing my attention in another direction. But I knew that day would come and it was near.

That day we took a trip to the mountains. Exactly above Morskie Oko. A few minutes after seven in the morning we parked our cars and set off along the road towards the peaks. It was warm, pleasant, each of us was well supplied: decent shoes, light clothes and backpacks full of food and drink. Humors were good, so the long road was not boring even for a moment, and the views were simply fabulous. Damien urged me to move to Wrocław, from there it was a short drive to Karpacz or the beautiful Kłodzko Valley. He talked about the Karkonosze Mountains, about the coolest places, later he showed photos on his phone from a recent trip to Błędne Skały in the Stołowe Mountains, near Kudowa-Zdrój. It sounded appealing, an interesting prospect of living near the mountains, but I had no plans for the future yet. I was waiting for some sudden insight or anything that would show me the way I was supposed to follow. No matter how hard I tried, I couldn't come up with anything.

Despite the enormous fatigue I felt after the mountain hike, I was very happy. We got back late, around eight. We were entering the guest house when a black Mercedes drove into the yard. An expensive, perfectly maintained car. A middle-aged, slim, well-dressed man got out. He exuded calmness and self-confidence.

Damien turned on the stairs and looked at the man, then ran down the stairs and came to greet him with a smile. They shook hands like very good friends. They exchanged a few words jokingly. Finally, the man pulled a large suitcase from the trunk and entered the hotel.

"What's this guy?" I asked when Damien came to us. Of course, the whole group watched the event.

"Olivia's husband. He just got back from Dubai, had some business there."

"Oh," I looked at the man as he walked away. Then I entered the building. All I dreamed about was dinner, which the cooks had left for us to heat up at our request. And then a quick bath and a sound, healthy sleep.

More yoga classes. I felt my body stretched, every movement fluid and conscious. I quickly learned more asanas and I was very happy with these classes. After the exercises, I felt calm and focused. My form was also influenced by the gym and boxing. At first, I associated boxing only with the discharge of unwanted and painful emotions, then I was a bit calmer and focused on the punching bag technique. I liked it.

That day, right after yoga and breakfast, I had some time to myself. The girls went shopping in a nearby town, and Damien and Fred planned to play on the tennis court.

I sat comfortably on the carpet, crossed my legs and put my headphones on my ears. Calm, relaxing music played from the phone. I chose one of the guided meditations available on Youtube and got lost in it. As usual, I did not expect anything, I sat and listened to the pleasant female voice. Thoughts flew away quickly, leaving me in total limbo. I was relaxing. Suddenly I felt something unusual, something like a concentrated energy inside of me. I got scared and opened my eyes. I was breathing deeply. The feeling that suddenly appeared was gone so quickly. What was it anyway? First time I encountered something like this. I calmed down a bit. I realized that I felt my own energy, I wanted to get it back, feel it again, look at it more closely.

Excited, I closed my eyes and breathed deeply. I slowed my breathing and listened, waited, but nothing happened. I was slightly disappointed. I let it go. I looked at my watch, I still had plenty of time. In my phone, I found another piece of guided meditation, this time a man's voice was guiding me. As instructed, I relaxed my body, inhaled, and exhaled long enough. I imagined the light inside me and then it reappeared, I tried to control my emotions so as not to scare the feeling away. It was a very subtle, barely perceptible energy that filled me. She was all over the body. At first it appeared in the chest area, then spread to the arms and legs. She must have been there all the time, only I recognized her and noticed her at that moment. The feeling was gone, and yet I was still sitting on the floor and smiled contentedly.

"My darlings, today will be short, I will try to summarize in half an hour, it will be intense" said Olivia to everyone gathered in the conference room. - Each of you has a sheet of paper and a pencil. You will be planning your future soon. But before we get to that, I wanted to bring to your attention one very important point about the way to the goal. Some of you have already achieved spectacular success, others still don't know what exactly they want. I wanted to encourage you to live a more conscious life, to follow your own path, not looking at others, not comparing, because there will always be someone better than us and someone will always be worse than us. Comparing yourself to others leads nowhere. There is also no need to look into the neighbor's yard and envy. It's all about focusing on your goals and working towards them.

Olivia sat on the desk across from us and continued her speech.

"If our lives are calm, predictable, that's what we need, that's fine. It is important to live consciously, and conscious life calls for learning, for development, for taking some steps to make your dreams come true. Let's not be afraid of it, let's not be afraid to take a risk, and our gray everyday life will become colorful. Let's start by realizing that for most people, each day is a routine, unconscious set of automatic, repetitive activities. Every day, from morning to night, we do everything the same, from breakfast sandwiches to going to the same shops, cafes and even vacation trips. At work, usually the same problems, everything fixed by the hour, according to the daily rhythm, everything familiar, predictable. You know it, right?"

Several people nodded loudly.

"And how can we expect our lives to change if we do the same things over and over again, thinking the same things over and over again, holding the same beliefs?" Will something cool happen? Well, it won't change, because how? We rely only on the past, we recreate what is known, our past becomes the future. Acting in this way, we still have the same, already well-known effects. For anything to change, you have to get out of this cycle. There is no other way. You have to start doing something differently, for example, taking a different route to work, sometimes you will make up for a kilometer or two, but then we will see something on the way that will inspire or interest us, we focus more on what surrounds us at the moment, maybe we will see something new possibilities. Look, it's just one innocent change, and it can make a difference. We have been going to one bakery for years for rolls, and maybe it would be worth checking out the new one around the corner? We look, and it turns out that they have delicious, healthy sourdough bread. And we are already starting to take care of our health. These are small things, but thanks to them, we broaden our perspective, we have a broader view, we see opportunities that we have not seen before."

"Come on, come on. Or maybe some people are satisfied with their lives, just like that, and they don't want to change anything" Dorothy said haughtily.

"Of course, but if someone has a great life, they can always have an even better one" said Olivia.

"Oh, Dorothy, save your wisdom for later," said the woman sitting next to her.

Olivia waited a moment for silence and continued her speech.

"Let's do something different every day, in reverse, something unpredictable, instead of coffee and a donut, let's go for a run in the park, or at least walk the dog. You can meet new people there, with new perspectives. Understand, in order to make changes in your life, to make it more fun, we need to start acting differently than before. Let's start by finding the target. It is worth pursuing even small goals, because they will show that we can manage, that we are able to achieve what we need or want. They give us strength and motivation. Once we find our goal, we will know it, we need to focus on it. The point is not to be distracted by insignificant trifles, so that nothing distracts us from this main goal. Then you should act, consistently, do a little bit every day in the direction you have chosen and not get discouraged. And now ... how to go towards achieving the goal? You have pieces of paper in front of you, please, write on it your most important goal and two smaller ones. At the end, be sure to write the end date by which the goal is to be achieved at the latest."

Each of the gathered took care of writing goals on their own cards.

One of the men, a rather stout, unpleasant fellow, always had to make a comment, so he couldn't help himself this time as well.

"I have already done a huge business, my company is the largest and most important in the Lublin region, so I have achieved my goals with the greatest success" he said proudly in his voice.

"Congratulations, I'm glad to hear that." So, as a successful man, you know perfectly well that you don't have to develop and invest all the time in business. You cannot afford to stagnate.

"Of course I know that," he grumbled.

"Then you certainly have a goal to accomplish," Olivia said calmly.

"Well, there will be something small there. I have already achieved a lot. I know how to run a business...

"Excellent. Since you've had such an extraordinary experience, why don't you share with us here how you succeeded? Tell us about your methods, values and ideas, we'd love to hear from you, right?"

"I'll think, I'll think," he said, and went back to writing.

On my piece of paper I scrawled: "have a job that gives you satisfaction", "feel needed and fulfilled", "have great people with you". It didn't look impressive, but it had to do.

"Just the fact that you wrote them on a piece of paper increases faith and deepens the belief that they are possible to achieve. Now make a list of things you will do to get closer to your goal. Everything that comes to your mind, for example: "I will sign up for an additional course", "I will buy some books on the subject I am interested in", "I will meet people who are already working in this industry", "Find a new group of friends, clients who would gladly take advantage of my offer. This is of course in the case of business development. Each of us has different goals. Now, from this list of activities, circle the most important activity and focus on it. Around this you can add a few more comments, I'm sure something will come to your mind, the writing itself really opens the mind and shows different possibilities that we haven't considered so far, right? Now all that's left to do is put the plan into action. Every day, consistently, until you get what you want. Enjoy even small successes and don't worry about failures. Everything takes time. How's that, Vladimir? Can we count on you to share the secret of how you managed to build your empire?

"I am a businessman, not a speaker" grumbled Vladimir. Let everyone do what they're good at.

"I see. I thank you very much. I know that among the whole group there are people who successfully run a business, are successful in various fields, maybe someone would like to share some information? I encourage you to talk. You already know each other, so go ahead… I leave you now and wish you fruitful conversations."

I sat at the table and looked at my piece of paper, at what I had written.

"How you doing?" Damien asked as he sat down next to me.

"Excellent."

"Do you have written goals?"

"Of course. And a detailed action plan."

"Because, you know, I'm pretty good at my trade, I can teach you something," he joked.

"Better grab a cup of coffee."

When he went to get coffee, I took a piece of paper from my pants pocket, on nice paper with the logo of the guesthouse there was an inscription: "What area of my life do I have an impact on today? What can I do today to improve my situation?" It was another note I found in the room on the table. As usual, the text was intended to provoke, to look at yourself from a broader perspective. That card didn't bother me. I've been carrying it since morning in my pocket and trying to find the answer to this question.

In the evening there was a party, dance lessons to be precise, led by a lovely couple specializing in salsa. Dressed as if for a tournament show, they first presented their skills in two songs, after which the women's part of the gathered people was taken care of by the dancer Marietta, and the men's by Krzysztof.

Very reluctantly, I walked with the other women to the center of the room. Marietta with a smile on her face showed us the simplest movements, we were only supposed to repeat after her. The music was quite loud, it was supposed to motivate us and encourage us to shake our hips. I was tense, it didn't work out for me.

Marilyn slid nimbly over to me and stood beside me. She was having a great time, she had no hesitation in moving to the music.

"Come on, my dear, you give, you give," Marlene encouraged, glancing at me.

"I don't have much to spin," I said, pointing to my hips.

"It's not about the hips, it's about the stick up the ass." Pull it out, even if only for a moment, and loosen it.

"I haven't located the stick yet.

"Then try harder," she laughed and made an extra turn. She slapped my ass hard.

I could be offended, but what good would that do?

"And don't be afraid, you won't fall apart," Marlene added.

I shook my head in disbelief and focused on the explanation of the lecturer. I tried to make the figures as best as I could, but when I didn't succeed, I got annoyed. But I looked at the women around me, they did everything their way, they enjoyed themselves, they sang, what they did was certainly far from salsa. It dawned on me that everything I do must always be perfect and accurate, even in such casual games. Focused on the goal, I couldn't enjoy learning, all these activities carried out for the assigned task. I was surprised by this discovery. I stood uncertainly in the room for a moment longer, then let go of all limiting thoughts and began to truly enjoy what I was doing. I got better right away.

The learning lasted about an hour, it was interrupted by antics and jokes of the participants, but you learned something we did. After many, many attempts, we were able to dance one longer routine almost flawlessly. When we were joined by men, as trained as women, the real party began. Marietta and Krzysztof made every effort to ensure that no one stood against the wall, partners were changed, so that everyone danced with everyone else.

It was a special evening, I laughed a lot and discovered that I could move my hips pretty well, even in a dance like salsa.

CHAPTER 8

I was walking early in the morning by the lake. It was cool, a milky mist hovering over the water and over the meadows. I was in a sad mood. I only have two days left to finish my stay. Sylvia and Marilyn were leaving tomorrow after breakfast. How quickly the time flew by, I just couldn't believe it, I was extremely sad that everything I had experienced there was coming to an end. All these walks, meetings, yoga classes, meditations, trips to the mountains, conversations with girls in the jacuzzi, will be a beautiful memory in a moment. I felt a tightness in my chest at the thought. The funniest and saddest thing was that I wasted my first days there feeling sorry for myself. I was introverted, I didn't want to get to know anyone, and I certainly didn't want to build any relationships. I regret that I did not immediately see the potential of that place, how much good can be experienced there.

Walking and breathing clean, crisp air, I realized how quickly I recovered from the failure called Greg and Evelyn, how I learned to find myself, piece by piece, slowly discovering what was unconscious in me. I gave myself more acceptance and understanding, I learned to live again.

I wasn't as scared as I was three weeks ago. I knew I could figure something out. As Olivia said, I will follow my heart. Only my heart refused to speak to me. Maybe it wasn't time yet, maybe it was too early. I was going to wait to get ready.

I learned to trust, first Olivia - a complete stranger, who selflessly led from a sense of regret to a conscious view of my life, to power and a sense of greater value. My gratitude to Olivia knew no bounds. Then I trusted Marilyn - a very bright student, direct and open. She did not spare me the truth in my eyes, but I felt her support at every step. It was also thanks to her that I easily climbed out of the emotional hole. Sylvia - showed us how much strength and will to live we have, that we must not give up, that every day is a miracle and we should make the most of it. Daria and Fred - full of passion, empathic, it was impossible to get bored with them, they are great travelers, and Damien stayed. He also played a very important role - he restored my faith that there are still valuable guys in the world.

I walked along the lake thoughtfully, stopping only near Zbigniew fishing.

"Good morning," I greeted.

"Good morning! What are we fishing for? Ready a fishing rod?" He asked.

"No, I'm just going to sit down for a while today." I'll look at the water.

I sat down on the wooden bench and rested my chin in my hands.

"What's so sad today?" Zbyszek asked, looking at me carefully.

"So a bit melancholy, you have to say goodbye to this place."

"That's right, each of us will return to everyday life, to our own affairs" he sighed. "We will have to get back to the old tracks quickly.

"Would you like to change anything? Start from the beginning? Otherwise?" I asked, staring at the float bobbing in the water.

"And what could I change in my life, Natalie? I know only one job, I've been doing the same thing for many years. Sometimes Dorothy and I will go on vacation, where she wants. All I have left is fishing. It is enough for me. I don't need anything else."

I didn't answer, I understood him. It's sad that a guy in his prime was already so resigned. He didn't believe anything good could happen to him. I sincerely hoped he would be okay. I sat with him for a while and then went to the boarding house. My sneakers were soaked with dew. Staring at the ground, lost in thought, I did not immediately notice Anthony galloping on the horse. He came over to me and stopped.

"Good morning, Sad Eyes, why so early for a walk?"

"I like that, Anthony. Thinking better in the morning."

"And there thoughts, it's best to silence them," he said. He looked impressive sitting bareback on his horse, he didn't need a saddle at all. - What? a little ride? he suggested.

"Now?" I was surprised.

"Every time is good for a little fun and madness."

His horse was a bit vicious, he stepped restlessly on the spot, but Anthony guided him with ease.

"Okay, why not?" I agreed.

"Jump in, we'll go right now."

"The two of us on one horse?" I was surprised.

"You are skinny, the horse won't even feel it. jump in."

"Well, I don't know if that's a good idea."

"Until you try, you won't know what an idea it is, whether it's a good one or not."

I laughed and extended my hand to Mr. Anthony to help me jump onto the horse's back.

We rode slowly, I held Mr. Anthony around the waist, I didn't want to fall, because it was far from the ground, and the horse's hooves filled me with respect.

When we reached the road between the meadows, the horse galloped away. I felt excitement mixed with joy. The presence of Anthony and the awareness that he was driving the horse made me not afraid of a fast ride. I felt positive adrenaline. Wind in hair, the dock of meadows gently shrouded in mist, the morning sun sometimes breaking through heavy clouds, made an amazing impression. In moments like that, the world was just beautiful.

"Mr. Anthony, thank you very much" I said with sincere delight after the end of the ride. "It was amazing."

We stayed at the stables. The old man jumped off the horse easily.

"It was worth it, if only to finally see a spark of joy in those sad eyes" he said happily, looking at my face with appreciation. "My pleasure."

"Thank you again. Have a nice day, Mr. Anthony" I raised my hand as I was leaving in a farewell gesture.

Anthony nodded, grabbed the horse's bridle and led it to the stable.

I was happy to go to the guesthouse, I was surprised how easily and quickly you can change the mood "from gloomy, melancholy, to truly joyful, and in less than half an hour. This is power, I need to look at my own emotions more and learn to direct my thoughts consciously. Thoughts create emotions, and emotions affect my life, so let this life be better."

In the morning Mrs. Helen informed me about the package delivered by the courier. I was happy to pick up a large cardboard box from the reception. I followed him to my room and unpacked. There were books inside. I ordered them a few days ago, they were all about psychology and spiritual development. Excited, I opened the first one - Brian Tracy "Change your thinking and you will change your life". As soon as I read a small piece, I knew it was for me. I reached for the next one - Louise L. Hay "You can heal your life." There was also Camille Rowińska's bestseller "Build a life responsibly and boldly", Joe Dispenza "How to break the habit of being yourself", David R. Hawkins "The technique of releasing" and two Osho books. I wanted to read them at that moment, all at once, to gain the knowledge contained in them. The pleasure had to wait, however, because I had an appointment for a bike trip with the whole team. I put the books on the table, took the key and left the room.

There was no trace of the morning fog, the sun was shining, it was warm, but not hot. We went on bicycles for a long trip to the forest.

"Well, I don't know how we'll get out of here tomorrow," said Marlene. – Father and Lucy do not part even for a moment. He's from Radom, she's from Sandomierz, it's a long way away, and they can't live without each other.

"They will manage, they are adults" commented Damien.

"There's nothing romantic about you," Marlene grimaced.

"And what does romanticism have to do with it, there are trains, cars, video calls on Messenger. Lots of possibilities," he added. "You just have to want it."

"Yeah, they want to be together. They just can't agree on which one should come to which one. It is quite important to me where I will visit my father. Apparently, Lucy has a growing son, I would rather not let him move into my old room – continued Marilyn. "You have to keep an eye on everything. Great love love, but from practical thinking in the family is me.

"After all, you are going to stay in Krakow anyway" Damien reminded.

"And I will stay. But he's my father, sometimes you have to visit and check on him."

"At least he won't be alone," I said.

"That's it."

"Too bad you didn't meet a nice guy here," Sylvia joked.

"Everyone's busy, unfortunately," Marlene said with a theatrical sigh. "I think that the best match would be Vladimir, the king of the Lublin region."

We laughed unanimously.

"But I must admit that it would be nice if some extraordinary guy came especially for me from the other end of the world, it would be something" she dreamed.

"Everything ahead of you," said Sylvia.

But I don't travel much. I'm graduating, I don't have time. Where will I meet that?

"There is always time for everything, you just have to want it. We can agree on a shorter trip to Europe sometime" suggested Sylvia.

"Yeah, I'd love to," said Marlene.

"If anyone would like to join, we invite you," added Sylvia.

I smiled. The prospect of another meeting sometime in the future cheered me up. For the next hour we made various hypotheses regarding plans, joint trips. It was really fun.

I was sitting alone in the room. I had a notebook and a pen in my hand. I stared at the blank page. Lost in thought, I bit my lip painfully. I finally sighed and started writing. I used one of the methods Olivia told me about. I wanted to find out what emotions, what beliefs anchored in the subconscious are hiding from me.

"I don't want to leave here.

Why?

Nothing good awaits me in Warsaw.

Why?

I feel bad there, you have to tense up, people are not kind.

Why?

I don't have anyone else there besides my sister who cares about me.

Why?

Because I'm too weak. I'm not brave and I don't find it easy to make contacts, I don't trust people, maybe only outside this place.

Why don't you trust people do i trust people?

I don't trust them because they let me down, maybe I didn't stand my ground enough, I wasn't visible enough, I wasn't clear enough, I let go too quickly. I couldn't fight for myself.

Why?

Because others have always been more important.

Why do I think so?

I couldn't and still can't speak out loud about my emotions and needs, as if it were something bad, inappropriate, something to be ashamed of.

Why?

I always felt inferior to others, I was left out of everything and I let it happen.

Why?

I felt unwanted and unloved. Because I don't deserve anything good.

Why?

Because I'm hopeless. I think there's something wrong with me.

Why?

Other people can enjoy life and have fun, but I can't. I'm tense, stuck, unhappy.

Why?

I'm afraid, I'm always afraid that I won't be able to cope with life.

Why?

Because I don't believe in my abilities, I don't trust myself.

Why?

I'm afraid of life. I'm afraid of tommorow. I'm full of goddamn fear of being NOTHING. That no one will want me, that I will be alone forever.

Why?"

I looked surprised at what I wrote. Writing in this way supposedly shows the truth about what is inside us, provided that we do not think about the answer, but write immediately what comes to mind first.

Osh, whore.

I left the guest house and stopped on the terrace. In the distance I saw a large fire, not many people gathered yet. It was a warm, pleasant evening.

Suddenly, I heard a conversation next to me.

"Andrew, for God's sake, just don't swallow it. You have a handkerchief, blot it.

"It's too late," I swallowed.

I recognized them, they were a couple in their fifties - he was a simple manual worker, she ran a shop with elegant clothes.

"Andrzej, behave yourself, you are not with your employees in the carpentry shop, but in a decent hotel. What will they think of us?"

"That I have untreated sinusitis?" he replied.

"Andrew…" she rose with pretension in her voice.

"Hilda! But what do you mean. Why do you care so much what people say?"

Because it's our image.

"Who cares?"

"I care! Me! I've been working on my image for thirty years, you know how important it is in our town. You won't be sniffing at me here and swallowing this" after these words she turned on her heel and walked away full of regret towards the flower bed.

"Come on, Hilda, come on… ""Well, now, I promise, I won't do that. Hilda, I'm going to the doctor. As soon as we get home, he ran after his wife into the yard."

I sighed and walked slowly towards the fire. The music was already playing, platters of snacks were set on the table. Damien added wood to the fire. I stood next to him.

"They have mulled wine here, would you like a drink?" he suggested.

"Maybe later," I replied, staring at the high flames and sparks flying skyward. "I don't think everyone should be drinking, since most of them are leaving tomorrow."

Within two days, all hotel guests were to be replaced with a new group. I had learned earlier that Olivia deliberately organized stays, usually three weeks long, so that people could get to know each other and establish closer relationships, sometimes even friendships. She could also run a lecture program at one time for everyone to keep everyone up to date.

"The boys won't drink today." I have already witnessed how women deal with it, they are very protective of their husbands.

"It's a good thing you don't have a wife," I said.

"Maybe well, maybe not." I extended my stay by one day, so the wine will be drunk. Tomorrow we are going with Adam, Olivia's husband, to the mountains. Such a manly outing.

"Great. Have you been friends for a long time?"

"About twenty years old. I've known Olivia longer, I met Adam shortly before their wedding."

"Is he as lively as Olivia?" I asked curiously.

"No, rather the opposite. Balanced, calm. Very sensible. They are quite an unusual couple."

I looked at Damien curiously, hoping he'd say more, but he changed the subject.

An hour later, the party was in full swing. Dancing, singing, having fun. What some, already quite drunk, gave thanksgiving speeches to Olivia for her respectable, empathic attitude and creating the perfect place to relax. Everyone was applauding and cheering.

Olivia was very pleased. She talked to people, but she spent most of her time with her husband Adam and friend Damien.

Music was playing, a few people were dancing around the fire, others were sitting on comfortable benches and talking. Marilyn took two bottles of wine from the table, a few disposable cups with the logo of the guest house and suggested:

"Go boating"

We agreed gladly. We went to the pier with the whole group. Daria, Fred and Sylvia got into one of the boats, the other one was taken by me and Marilyn. We went to the middle of the lake. We were in good moods, we laughed, there was no end to the antics. We recalled the funniest events during our stay.

"Remember that car fluid test?" It was great, a great idea – Daria laughed. "These YouTube videos on how to open the hood…

They managed - Sylvia could not stand it and also laughed heartily and loudly. "Only Marlene ruined everything. Hero of the day!

"Because the food was getting cold," she said indignantly.

"But it was really strong.

"And I liked the action with this guy the most, in the forest, we thought he had tripped" recalled Marilyn.

"But he had a face when he saw us," added Sylvia.

"We had this face when it turned out that the guy was still alive" Marilyn was holding her stomach with laughter.

"Natalie, he was quite nice, it's a pity that you couldn't give him artificial respiration…" Daria giggled.

"I still don't sleep at night because of the grief," I said, wiping tears of amusement from my face.

"We also had great classes" said Fred.

"Tell me!!!" we shouted simultaneously.

"It wasn't as fun as yours, but it was fun." Once we went to the forest to build a hut. We had everything ready, all we had to do was bend down and do some work. Let me tell you that Anthony is a great guy. None of us could surprise or defeat him. I wish I was like that when I was seventy.

"Well, well, you have to work on fitness, I'll watch you in it" Daria interjected.

"I know. Relax. Of course, only experts in building the hut, everyone knew everything. The hut lasted half an hour and fell apart."

There was a loud female laugh.

"We had an archery competition" continued Fred. "Of course, no one hit the target, but in the ass of the bent Vladimir, it's sooooo ...

After this one hit, the party is over. There was also a treasure hunt with a map in the forest. It was great, teamwork was not working for the hell of us. But, as Anthony said, what is this treasure, everyone immediately to attention, one overtaking the other to reach the goal."

"And what was that treasure?" - I asked.

"Two cases of whiskey."

"Well, that's understandable."

Three hours later, empty wine bottles in hand, we swam to shore, moored our boats at the dock, and went out to play. Damien joined us. The fire was still burning, no one was going to go to sleep, it was a pity for such a fantastic evening. The dance party was in full swing. Damien grabbed me in his arms and we danced slowly to the rhythm of lively music. I felt his unshaven cheek with a day's stubble against my temple. Damien sometimes whispered something nice in my ear. I closed my eyes, my head spinning from the wine I drank. I felt relaxed and content.

And then he kissed me.

That day there was no more meditation or yoga together. Nobody went out with a mat into the yard near the orchard. No one was going for a walk in the forest. After breakfast, most people were to leave the guest house. Some people were sleeping off yesterday's party, others were already packing their luggage into their cars.

I walked along the lake and sometimes glanced towards the parking lot. The next day it was waiting for me. I sighed. I had a feeling that I would soon run out of that place. I experienced so much there, met so many wonderful people. My thoughts immediately went to Damien, to the kiss the day before. From the very morning I felt a slight discomfort because of this. I liked Damien, his sense of humor, warm smile. He listened attentively, gave a sense of security. I valued him as a friend. When he kissed me, I didn't feel anything out of the ordinary. Just the touch of warm lips, nothing else. I just realized that he wasn't the guy for me. I noticed that Damien wasn't surprised when I pulled away from him, my face serious. He just smiled understandingly. Whatever he wanted from me, all I could offer him was friendship. I didn't want that kiss to ruin our relationship. Until the end of the party, Damien acted as if nothing had happened, but I knew that kiss was important to him.

I went to the aid. I sat down at the very end of the wooden structure, took off my shoes, and dipped my feet in the cold water. This refreshed me greatly, but I did not bring my feet to the surface. I felt a peace within myself, a kind of surrender. What the future will bring, it will bring, at that moment the most important thing for me was sitting on the pier and looking ahead, into the calm depths of the lake, at the outline of the mountains visible in the distance. I just wanted a little more time to enjoy this place. I really wanted to stay here forever. I smiled at the thought. It was my only dream. Sometimes miracles happen, somewhere, to someone in the world, but unfortunately not to me, it's a pity.

After two hours, I put on my shoes and got up. I went back to the guesthouse. Right at the front door I came across Zbyszek and Dorothy.

"Don't shuffle those suitcases like that" Dorothy admonished her husband. Can't you see there are stairs here?!

Zbigniew left the building laden with luggage. His face was grim, obviously the morning had not been a pleasant one. He smiled genuinely when he saw me. He placed the suitcases and bags on the cobblestones.

"Good morning," he greeted.

"Good morning," I replied. "You're leaving… It was very nice to meet you."

"Us too, Natalie" Zbyszek smiled warmly. "I wish you luck."

"You too. Thanks for the fishing lessons" I shook Zbigniew's hand.

"It's my pleasure," he glanced cautiously at his wife as he said this, but Dorothy wasn't listening, she was busy rummaging through her purse for her car keys, and muttered something angrily under her breath.

"Oh, they're finally here. It would be enough for them to get lost. Zbyszek, let's go!" she ordered.

"Have a nice trip. And good luck," I added, watching them walk off towards the parking lot.

I went to breakfast last, I didn't eat much, I had no appetite. Then, with a cup of coffee, I sat on the terrace. In front of the entrance there is constant movement, commotion, conversations, laughter. I was looking at it from the side. Mr. Anthony all the time circulated among the guests of the guesthouse, thanked them for their stay and invited them again. He said something jokingly to everyone and wished them a nice trip.

"Just remember, you're invisible to radar!" And so it shall be. Well, then go easy, he repeated to each departing.

After some time, Marilyn and Sylvia came.

"Here you are, we've been looking for you everywhere!" cried Marlene. "Let's go, we wanted to say goodbye."

"I don't know if I want to say goodbye to you," I said seriously.

"What about you, after what we've been through here together?" Sylvia sounded disbelief.

"That's why," I explained. "You two are fantastic, and I don't want to part with you.

"Oh, we will see each other, for sure" Marilyn hugged me tightly with emotion. "We'll call each other." And meet as often as possible.

"Sure," I replied, then hugged Sylvia tightly. "I will miss you."

"We love you too"Marilyn and Sylvia added simultaneously.

"Remember, I have a letter for your lady mayor." I will send it from Krakow today - said Marilyn, patting her large bag hanging on her shoulder.

"Thanks. I'm sure she'll love it." I smiled. "I'll help you carry your luggage."

"They're already at the front desk. We left our suitcases and went looking for you," explained Sylvia.

I walked them to the parking lot. I glanced out of the corner of my eye as Marilyn's father embraced and kissed Lucy without any embarrassment. They were standing next to Lucy's little blue car.

I said good-bye to the girls and watched as they drove out into the street one by one and disappeared around the bend. I was so thoughtful for a moment.

Mr. Anthony approached me quietly. I jumped when I heard his voice.

"Sad, eh? And miss it already?"

"A bit like that."

"Dear child, you know you can't suppressing emotions is unhealthy. If you want to cry, if you want, swear properly, but don't suppress anything in yourself, let it flow through you, don't stop it" he said.

"One day I will learn it, Mr. Anthony, but it's a long way to go" I said with a sigh.

"Just allow yourself to feel."

I nodded, but I don't think I understood the message. It was too early for that.

Around noon, after dinner, I went to my room. I felt a little sad. I picked up one of my new books and started reading. At first I couldn't concentrate, then it was better, I delved into the subject of how the mind works, how it guides us, how it imposes certain filters and illusions. Why is this happening, where do our beliefs come from and how to change them. I was fascinated by it, I wanted to explore all the knowledge at once, to reach myself. Sometimes while reading I was genuinely surprised by the information I got, sometimes I smiled because certain patterns were familiar, I had noticed them earlier in myself, now I understood where they came from.

After an hour, I put the book down and went to the bathroom. As I passed the mirror, I stopped and looked at myself carefully. I looked deep into my eyes. That look was different from three weeks ago. I smiled kindly to myself. As usual, I quietly said to the reflection in the mirror "I love you". I've been doing this every morning for over a week now. I continued to look in the mirror and saw tears streaming down my cheeks. I felt a huge relief. I do not know why. I breathed deeply, happily. I looked at myself and wiped my tears with the back of my hand. I allowed myself to. I already knew that a lot of emotions must come out of me, sometimes I may not understand myself, but I'm definitely supposed to let out of me whatever I want. To clean up, to make room for something better. I felt a delicate thread of connection with myself, with my being. I stood there for a long time, afraid that I would lose this subtle impression.

Then, feeling a joyful purification, I went for a walk in the forest. A lonely walk. In the end, the most important thing is to learn to be alone with yourself, make friends, like yourself. I realized that as long as I have myself, I will never be lonely again.

In the evening I packed up. I set the suitcases against the wall, at that moment there was a knock on the door of the room. Curious, I went to open it. It was Damien. He was leaning against the wall with a slight smile on his lips.

"Hi," he greeted.

"Hi."

"I wanted to take you on a romantic walk," he said.

"It's late."

"So much the better, no one will disturb us."

"To make it more romantic, how about tea on the terrace by the cafeteria?" I suggested. I didn't want to go anywhere far. I preferred to stay where I was, go to bed earlier, be alone for a while.

"There may be a terrace, please" he extended his hand to me.

I grabbed my room key from the shelf by the door and left with Damien.

A moment later we were sitting on wooden benches at long tables on the terrace. Damien brought two teas. He sat next to me, very close, touching my shoulder.

"It's so quiet here today," I said, looking around. Only a few windows shone light in the guesthouse, there were no people walking around in the yard, so strange, sad, unnatural.

"You know that Wroclaw is beautiful…"

"I know," I sighed.

"I know every district there, every nook, if you want, I can show you everything there".

"Maybe someday…"

"We can tomorrow, one concrete decision," he said suggestively.

"I'll keep that in mind."

"We have beautiful parks, monuments, and a well-developed entertainment section.

"So everything that I also have in Warsaw" I commented, sipping my tea while it was still hot.

"Well, not everything. I am not in Warsaw" he said with a smile and funny sparkles in his eyes.

"I'm not there yet either."

"Exactly. What will we do with it?" he asked, touching my hand.

"Nothing for now. I'm not ready to make important decisions yet. It's all too early,' I said truthfully, and pulled my hand back."

"What are you waiting for? What for?"

"I need to get my life in order first. With myself."

He straightened up, leaned back slightly, but never took his eyes off me.

"It's good to have a friend's support," he continued.

"I know, I have your phone number just in case." I smiled. "Tell me how your trip to the mountains went."

"Great."

We talked for another hour. Damien didn't let go all the time and persuaded me to go with him to his hometown. I wanted to tell him directly not to get his hopes up. I didn't mean to offend him, I just brushed it off with excuses.

I started the morning with a visit to the gym. I gave vent to my emotions on a punching bag. I couldn't understand myself. On the one hand, I was strangely calm and reconciled with what I have in my life, and on the other hand, I felt anger, rebellion and clear opposition as soon as I thought about returning to Warsaw. I thought the exercise would clear my head a bit, but it didn't. I came back to my room sweaty and tired. I sat on the bed and hid my face in my hands.

After breakfast, I went for a walk by the lake, I wanted to say goodbye. I stood on the pier motionless for a long time. During the last few days, during evening meditations, I imagined that I was standing on such a platform and jumping up for joy. I held my hands up high and felt very happy. I remembered that now and smiled sadly. I sighed heavily and slowly made my way to the boarding house. Time to take your suitcases…

Mr. Anthony was walking around the yard, as soon as he noticed me, he approached me with a confident step.

"Good morning, Sad Eyes," he greeted, looking at me with concern.

"Good morning, Mr. Anthony."

"Oh, and what is this sadness in those beautiful blue eyes?"

"Because it's time to leave. Well, what I can do?" I felt a strong grip in my chest as I said those words.

"Do what you want, my dear. What the heart wants, what it calls you to. Not with the mind, remember. Follow your heart…"

"It is not that easy."

"But easy. Just ask yourself what you want, what you need and get to work. If you don't try, you're immediately at a loss, and if you make an effort, who knows what the rEverd is waiting around the corner - he said. "What, darling, what do you want?"

With that, he patted me on the shoulder and walked away, leaving me confused.

"Ask yourself and do it," he said, turning away for a moment.

What did I want? What did I want?

I wanted to stay there! Yes, I wanted to stay there longer. It's impossible.

Full of resignation, I went to the room. I reached for my suitcases. One hit the other and both fell over with a thud. I picked them up, the handle of one of them got stuck. I was nervous because tugging didn't help. I took a few deep breaths and left the room. I pushed one suitcase in front of me, the other I dragged to the side. I took the elevator to the reception.

"Mrs. Helen, it's time for me" I said, handing over the key.

"I hope, Natalie, that you have found what you needed with us" said Mrs. Helen with a nice smile.

"I will have beautiful memories from here," I said. "Thanks for everything."

"I wish you luck, dear."

"Thank you, Helen, it will come in handy. And for you too, lots of peace and some time to yourself."

She laughed at my words.

"I've been retiring for over a year, but somehow it doesn't work out, we have too much work here. But I'll let it go this fall. I don't have as much strength as I used to."

"Please take care of yourself and enjoy your retirement. Thank you again. Goodbye."

"Goodbye."

I grabbed my suitcases and headed for the exit. I felt like my legs were made of lead.

From a distance I saw Damien, he was leaning against my car. When he noticed me, he walked towards me.

"I'm waiting for you," he said, taking the suitcases from me.

"And I thought you were looking after my car."

He laughed at my words. I opened the door with the remote. Damien packed the suitcases into the trunk of the Opel.

"Did I convince you?" he asked, coming close to me. He looked me in the eye. "Will you go with me? I have a big apartment, you will have a lot of freedom."

"I can't. It's not a good time. You know it well."

He nodded understandingly. He pulled me to him and hugged me tightly.

"Let me know how you are sometimes." Does Warsaw serve you? And remember, just in case "I'm here."

"Thanks."

I waited for Damien to leave. I stood by the open car door and thought, what do I want? It gave me no peace. What did I want? stay here.

And suddenly it dawned on me. It hit me. I wanted to stay there. It was possible. I couldn't stay as a guest, but I could have been an employee. Helen wanted to retire, they had a lot of work there. There had to be a job there for me. Yes!

I felt a strong rush of adrenaline. Joy. Without thinking, I slammed the Opel door and ran to the boarding house. Feverish, I rushed to the reception desk and hung on to her.

"Mrs. Helen, where is Olivia? Where will I find her now?" I asked full of emotion.

"Did something happen?" the old lady got scared.

"I need to talk to Olivia as soon as possible, it's very important to me."

"She's in her office...she's got—"

"Thank you!" I screamed and ran up the stairs.

"He has an important meeting," the receptionist finished.

I ran upstairs and knocked vigorously on the door of the guesthouse owner's office. I was excited, thousands of thoughts were swirling in my head. It couldn't wait.

"Olivia, we need to talk." I entered the study and stopped mid-sentence.

Olivia was not alone. A young man sat at the desk next to her. They were bent over a project, the man holding a pencil, pointing and explaining. They both looked up when they saw me.

"Sorry, I didn't know you had an appointment." I'll wait." I retreated to the corridor. I scolded myself for carelessness and lack of logical thinking. I didn't normally act like this. I took deep breaths several times. Well, I followed my heart, I wonder what will come of it.

Olivia came out into the hall.

"Natalie, is something wrong?" she asked with concern in her voice.

"That can wait." Continue meeting, sorry to interrupt.

"It can take up to two hours."

"Does not matter. I'll wait."

"You sure?"

"Yes Yes."

Olivia returned to her study and closed the door behind her. I stepped out onto a small terrace, a glass door at the end of the corridor. I sat in the chair and calmed my emotions. Only then did I realize that I had seen the man sitting in Olivia's office somewhere before.

I quickly remembered where I knew him from. While on a walk in the woods with the girls, we saw a Toyota parked on the roadside, we were convinced that the driver had fainted and needed help. And he was just sleeping tired after the long journey from Holland. I smiled at the memory. I peeked over the railing to see if a charcoal Toyota was parked in the parking lot, but I couldn't make out the brands of each car from this distance.

I relaxed a bit.

Why didn't I think of working here sooner? If only Olivia would agree. I was determined to do whatever it took to get her to agree. She had to agree.

An hour later, she invited me into her office.

"What did you want to talk about?" she asked curiously.

"I have a proposition," I said, full of emotion. I sat upright in the comfortable armchair across from her. "I'd like to work for you." I can clean, help in the kitchen, I can assure you that I can cook well, whatever it takes, even twelve hours a day.

Olivia leaned back in her chair and looked at me curiously. For a brief moment, a smile of satisfaction flitted across her lips.

"In return, I'd like to stay here." A small room and modest meals are enough for me. I really want to stay here. This is the only place where I feel very good and I don't want to leave. Helen wants to retire, I know that you have a lot of work here and lots of guests. I can work hard.

I know this isn't what a job interview should be like, but I really cared. I got carried away by emotions.

"Natalie you have to respect your time. You put a lot of energy into your work", Olivia said calmly. "You should appreciate yourself more."

I stared at her dumbfounded.

"You came here with a proposition, I understand that you care very much. Nevertheless, in any such situation, you should take care of your own well-being.

"It will be good for me to stay here.

"You have presented very unfavorable conditions for yourself, this cannot be."

I felt all the euphoria leave me as quickly as it had come.

"You don't agree..."

"I agree, but under conditions that will give you a sense of security. Everyone deserves to be properly rEverded for their work" she said firmly.

I sighed with incredible relief. Then I would accept any offer.

"We actually have a lot of work to do. I'll hire you. I'll think about what exactly you're going to do. You will get a contract of employment, meals, a room in a boarding house and a regular salary.

"Thank you!!" I said happily.

"When can I start?"

"I'm guessing tomorrow?"

"Perfect."

"You will be moved to a room on the ground floor. I have four small apartments for employees there, with a kitchenette and a washing machine in the bathroom. It is definitely less luxurious there, but you will be more comfortable there, you will have more freedom."

"I am immensely grateful to you."

"No problem. I require honesty and commitment from my employees. And two weeks' notice. Do you accept these terms?"

"Of course. I would just like to attend your lectures, sometimes to talk about what I learn. I bought some books on spiritual development…"

"Great. As long as the lectures don't clash with your assigned classes…" She held out her hand to me. "Welcome on board."

"You won't be disappointed," I returned the handshake.

"Okay then, come on, I'll show you your new room."

She got up and we left the office.

I put my suitcases in my new apartment. It suited me perfectly. I was satisfied. It happened so fast. I felt it was a good decision. The only and the best at that moment of my life. I was curious what would come of my decision. Where will it lead me? I wanted to go in that direction. I felt happy, I listened to the voice of my heart. And I could stay there as I wanted. I was bursting with energy. I left the room briskly and went to the lake. I paid no attention to anyone on the way, I was going to my favorite place. I had just said goodbye to him, and now I was able to come again for morning walks to the lake. I joyfully ran onto the pier and felt good emotions bursting through my chest. I stretched my arms up and spun around myself. I felt happy. Great feeling. I looked at the mountain peaks on the horizon. Yes, definitely, that was where I belonged, at least for a while.

I was so blinded by joy that I didn't notice that someone was watching me curiously from the yard.

I was starting a new stage of life.

What was supposed to happen, let it happen, I opened myself to the unknown, I trusted.

CHAPTER 9

In the afternoon I had a conversation with Olivia. We were sitting in her office.

"Tell me, how long do you want to stay here?" asked Olivia.

"Honestly, I don't know. As long as possible. I have no other plans for the future.

"I see. Actually, it's very good that you came to me with a job offer" she said in a calm voice. "In the near future I plan to expand the guest house, I have to focus on this project and I will have less time for my guests. You could take over some of my responsibilities. I think we'll both benefit from it."

"I'd love to learn anything," I agreed with a smile.

"I would like you to work in different positions over the next few weeks, so that you can learn the rules at every stage of the operation of the guesthouse. It's very important. A week in the kitchen. You will learn everything related to food supply. For me everything has to be of high quality. The next week you will work with the cleaning crew, they will teach you everything you need to know, you will get to know each room, all amenities and offers. You'll spend the next week with my mother at the front desk. Once you've learned everything there, you'll come to me."

"I'm available," I declared. I did not expect such a turn of events. I thought I would get a job as a cleaner or a waitress, but here I am - I got an offer to become Olivia's assistant. Incredible. How lucky.

"Once you come to me to learn and help, the first challenge will be to organize a painting show of our participant Asia. I saw her work in the photos. They are wonderful, we will help her a bit, we will boost her creative ego, let the girl develop."

"I can not wait."

"If you have any questions, I'm available." Agnieszka and Adrian already know that they are to train you. And now the employment contract. Read it carefully and if everything is correct, sign it. She handed me the document in duplicate. I ran my eyes over the most important points.

"Initial pay rate. I will upgrade after training."

I was very glad. I signed, thanked and left the office with the feeling of having conquered another peak of fulfilled dreams.

I had to share this joyful event with my sister Eve.

That evening I decided to meditate on the pier. Dressed in a warm sweatshirt, I sat on the wooden planks, crossed my legs and closed my eyes. I focused my attention on the sounds coming from outside. The light sound of water lapping against the shore, the rustling of bushes, somewhere in the distance I heard the croaking of frogs and the barking of a dog. I felt a gentle gust of warm wind on my face. I felt great, my heart was bursting with joy.

It was supposed to be a gratitude meditation. I focused on my breathing. I controlled the flow of air into my lungs, inhaling and exhaling slower and slower, shutting out what was outside. I felt that subtle flow of energy in my body again. I smiled. I had much to be thankful for. Behind closed eyelids I saw images, my immediate future, joyful mornings by the lake, long walks in the forest. Composure. Trust. I saw myself happy. With each changing image, I mentally said "thank you." Thank you that I was there, thank you that I could feel safe, thank you for the wonderful people who appeared in my life and were yet to appear. I thanked you for everything.

Then I focused on my breathing again, let my thoughts drift away, and stayed silent for another quarter of an hour. As soon as a thought sneaked up on me, I would return to my breath. Inhale and exhale. Inhale and exhale. Just enough.

By six in the morning I was ready. I went down to the kitchen, where Adrian, the purchasing manager, was waiting for me. He was a thirty-year-old slim brown man, very energetic, with a sense of humor.

"So, coffee first, or shall we start now?" he asked when he saw me.

"I'd love a cup of coffee, but starting work from a break like that doesn't look good."

"Don't worry, you'll still have time to work out," he said.

And in fact an hour later I was following him briskly and listening to what he was saying. There were lots of specifics. I did not expect that working in a hotel service could be so difficult and absorbing, and this was just the beginning of my learning. During the short break while Adrian went to talk to the head cook, I got myself a notebook and meticulously jotted down everything I had learned so far, not wanting to miss anything.

The first round of guests arrived today. There was a lot of confusion. Helen was clearly tired, so after 2 pm I finished my studies with Adrian and went to help her at the reception. I didn't have to, I just wanted to. I had a lot of energy and didn't feel tired at all.

Helen accepted my help with a great sense of relief.

Mr. Anthony was also clearly pleased. He walked proudly among the guests, greeting them at the entrance to the guesthouse. He brought suitcases single women. When he saw me, he smiled warmly, put his hand meaningfully on his own chest, in the region of his heart, and then blew me a kiss from a distance. I understood the message. I just nodded my head happily and went back to work. I explained to the elderly couple how to get to the room reserved for them.

I was standing here among all these people and I felt very good. Wanted, needed, appreciated. I had prospects, a chance for development, for something new and unknown. I had an overwhelming sense of gratitude. Who would have thought my life would turn out like this.

It must have been good.

Around six o'clock, after dinner, which I ate in the cheerful company of cooks, I went for a walk. I circled a small lake, looked at the distant mountain peaks, breathed deeply and consciously in the clean air, and then returned to the boarding house.

My little apartment was rather sparsely furnished. I had a comfortable bed, wardrobe, table, armchair, colorful curtains. Small kitchenette with stove and fridge. There was also a washing machine in the bathroom. I was very pleased, I didn't need anything else.

I quickly unpacked my suitcases, took a shower and sat down to meditate. Only then did I feel tired. But sleep had to wait, I put Sacred Earth - Ancient Mother music on YouTube. I found that track by accident, calm but quite electrifying music. It affected me in an extraordinary way, I did not understand what was happening to me. While listening to the music, I felt calm and relaxed, and energized at the same time. On the skin of my hands, I felt as if something was gently touching me, enveloping me. I opened my eyes to look at my hands, but nothing had changed. I closed my eyes and let myself feel the joy growing inside me. I watched it with curiosity. For a moment I lost all sense of time and place. I could imagine that I was flying somewhere in space, or flying over the seashore in warm countries. An extraordinary experience. I loved meditating. Consciousness could wander in meditations, to places I had never even dreamed of. I felt really free then.

The following days were very busy. I learned from Adrian the secrets of the functioning of the hotel from the supply side as well as the organization of the work of the entire staff. I met fantastic people, there was a friendly atmosphere here, strongly colored with humor. Problems, and there were a lot of them during the day, were solved concretely and together. Everyone could count on each other. That was my first impression, I was a bit surprised, I did not see that it is possible to build such a well-coordinated crew. It made hard work fun too.

Sometimes I helped Mrs. Helen and Olivia. I attended an evening bonfire for women. It was a spontaneous party. I watched all the guests, I saw how easily they made friends, although there were also gems of a rather heavy nature.

During that evening, I asked Olivia why she usually organizes evening parties separately for women and separately for men.

"It's very simple," she said. – Guys will not understand certain things, you have to talk to them differently. Other values are more important to them. I try to build women's sense of strength, femininity, so that they appreciate themselves, love themselves. I want them to open up, to feel this girly connection. If they were here with their husbands, it wouldn't have happened. The second thing is that single women also come here with friends and I want them to feel comfortable. It often happens that couples make out, hug each other, very for show, and the fact that it is different at home, well, no one sees it anymore.

"You've thought of everything," I said appreciatively.

I had Sunday off. I spent the morning at the gym, sweating out boxing. I used other exercise equipment. After fifteen minutes, I gave up. I was too tired for such a heavy load. I left the gym hot and on a sudden impulse I decided to go for a run. I trotted towards the forest. Not too fast so as not to get discouraged. I was careful to breathe evenly, I already knew how important proper breathing is in physical activity. Half an hour later I returned to the guest house.

After a shower, with a deckchair under my arm and a bag of books, I set off to the lake. I unfolded the deckchair, sat down so that the water gently lapped my feet, and sank into the book. That day I was starting a book in which Joe Dispenza showed a real way of seeing the world, not obscured by an inflated ego. Extremely engaging and interesting guide. I felt extremely uplifted, learning that each of us has incredible potential and unlimited possibilities. It was enough to work a little on your own habits and habits. Not so easy, yet so hard. Well, if you don't try, you'll never know what you're really capable of. And I had a great desire to find mine by limiting My beliefs and consciously change them to those that will support me.

On the same day, I had the opportunity to talk to Olivia about it. She was standing at the front desk pinning the new schedule to the bulletin board. I approached her.

"Hi, don't you rest even on Sunday?" I asked.

"Oh, hi. I also need to use excess energy" she explained. "And how are you?"

"Okay, I just trained with Joe Dispenza."

"Great," she said appreciatively. "Do you want to talk about it?"

"I really do."

How could I not take advantage of such an opportunity.

"Then we'll make coffee and sit on the upper terrace, what do you say?"

A moment later we were sitting in comfortable armchairs on a small balcony, on the first floor, right next to Olivia's office. Nobody disturbed us there.

"I didn't know you were so into the subject," Olivia said appreciatively.

"Your lectures were captivating and thought-provoking, and I bought a few books to educate myself," I explained. "I wanted to learn to understand myself.

"I'm very happy about this. It's a good drug. It may not be easy, but there is no turning back from it. You will see more and more, the blinders will fall off, as they say. You will become more aware of what you do, what you say, who you hang out with. You will choose, decide for yourself, and not take what others give you. Someone may not like it, someone may leave you..."

"I already have that," I said instinctively. "I only have my sister and my friend Simon."

"It has made a lot of room for new people, people who will suit you, you will see, they will appear. Just believe in yourself."

"I have to change my beliefs first…" I said.

"Exactly, and I think the first should be 'I want to', not 'I have to.' It changes a lot. Let me tell you that each of us, without exception, has some traumas, some bigger, some smaller. You have to deal with them. The biggest limitation for everyone is fear. Various forms of fear, such as a sense of security, fear of rejection, fear of the future, fear of ridicule. Look how easy life would be if there was no fear. Unfortunately, it is and paralyzes everyone. To a greater or lesser extent, it takes away the joy of creating, the joy of living and simply being. Fear closes us to our own potential, to our own needs. Out of fear, we stuff our emotions and our truth somewhere deep within ourselves, we have stopped trusting each other. We care about the opinion of society, we live in this world and live up to the expectations of others. Not your own, but others. At this point, everyone will say, I don't care if I don't, and that's a button right. It's just lying to yourself. The ego will not allow you to see the truth. And the truth can be inconvenient.

"So you have to find yourself again," I said, looking ahead at the tre-etops in the distance.

"Exactly. Get your fear out. Dig back to your truth, who you are, what you feel, what hurts, what delights. Support each other every step of the way. Just be the best, most faithful friend. Do what you want and need, not what others tell you to do. As a person changes, gains confidence in himself, the reality around him changes. Stop feeling sorry for yourself, stop judging others, let go of jealousy and envy, just focus on yourself and what you have to do. And don't be afraid. Oh, the whole philosophy."

"Anxiety is really powerful," I said, remembering myself from two months ago. I stood on the edge, without prospects, with a sense of danger. I remember the thoughts that overpowered me at that time.

"You have to gain some confidence in the universe. To myself too," said Olivia.

"And all these brave men?" They are afraid too...

"Yes, of course. It's just that, they put fear aside and act."

"Have you ever been scared?" I asked. Maybe I shouldn't, but I wanted to see Olivia's reaction.

She smiled.

"Yes, of course. I had such a moment in my life, I was very lost. I was afraid to stay in place. I was afraid to look at my life, I was afraid that I had let everyone down. That whatever I do, my loved ones will be unhappy. By me. I was afraid of stopping, but I was also afraid of taking a step forward, of what needed to be done. Nasty feeling. Such enslavement, where you stop believing in anything. It was a hard lesson for me to learn. And this boarding house, I put all my savings into it. The beginnings were not easy."

"Now you look like an indestructible person," I said admiringly.

"There are no indestructible people. I've come a long way to be where I am now. It hardened me. And I traded fear for trust."

"Do you regret something?"

I saw the hesitation in her voice.

"Hmmm, right now I'm just focusing on the now and building the future. From what was, I took a lesson and closed that chapter."

"I have a question. I meditate every evening. Sometimes also during the day. I have this weird feeling inside, like concentration of energy. It is quite subtle, is it normal?" I asked.

"Yeah, sure, it'll get stronger over time," she smiled. "Energy flows, there is power. Have you noticed any changes in yourself?"

"Yes, my thoughts… I don't know how to put it." I have fewer of them, they are calmer, I do not feel mental fatigue at all, I feel lighter.

"You put it nicely." Look, a month ago you were a total mess. I remember your first night, you came to dinner, you were sitting at the table, you were on pins and needles, I had the feeling that you wanted to run away, as if you were here as a punishment.

"Yes," I smiled. You spent a lot of time with me...

"I'm glad you took advantage of this time, gave yourself a chance."

We heard two women screaming from downstairs, they were arguing fiercely with each other.

We looked at each other.

"I have to intervene," said Olivia. She got up and stopped at the glass door. "I have a large private library, you can use it as much as you like.

Thanks, I'll definitely use it.

I leaned back in my chair and took a sip of coffee.

Life is beautiful, I said.

The next week I studied under the guidance of quite serious Agnieszka. She is a very specific person. She managed the entire cleaning team very well. Already on the first day, by noon, we managed to go around all the rooms, I got to know the amenities and standards. What guests like, what they complain about, what are the biggest problems and how to solve them.

As an employee, I no longer had general access to entertainment. I had to forget about the jacuzzi, about group yoga or meditation classes. There was no horseback riding or trips to the forest at noon. There was no time for that. I meditated only in the privacy of my room, and I could look at the horses only in the evenings, on those days when I went to visit Lena. She usually finished her activities with the guests of the boarding house before dinner. Sometimes we sat on the pier to look at the water and the peaks of the Tatra Mountains. Lena was excited about the upcoming trip to Italy, she planned to visit her uncle with her grandfather.

Time flew by quickly, I had a lot of work, but I didn't complain. Damien called sometimes, he was very pleased with the fact that I stayed in "Bella Vita", I also received many messages on Messenger from Sylvia, Daria and Marilyn. It was nice, they were organizing a weekend get-together and they definitely wanted to invite me to it. I agreed right away.

The next week of learning was very pleasant and at the same time the easiest. I sat behind the counter at the front desk and answered the phone. I sent invitations by e-mail, prepared offers and answered every question of our guests. I think I did quite well. Helen told a lot about herself, about her whole family, about her youth, passions and dreams. I listened with great interest. I really liked Mrs. Helen, she is a very cordial, smart and warm woman. I wish I had someone like that around me when I was growing up, then my life would have been easier.

CHAPTER 10

Something happened that day that surprised me.

I just spoke on the phone. I was accepting a reservation for a family of four when the behavior of Mrs. Helen drew my attention. This extremely calm person suddenly jumped up from the chair and moved energetically towards the exit. I glanced at the surveillance screens. A young boy was walking towards us.

Helen, as soon as she was sure of her premonitions, called to me:

"Call Olivia, let her come here quickly!"

I'm done talking to clients. I hung up the phone and looked warily at the scene at the door.

A young boy entered the building. He stopped. He might have been in his twenties, handsome, slim brown, with a penetrating, slightly rebellious look. Nicely dressed.

"Oscar? Oscar?" cried Helen, her voice breaking.

"Hello, Grandma," he said, and gave Helen a slightly awkward hug.

I breathed a sigh of relief. I dialed the extension number to Olivia's office.

"Will you go down to reception?" It's pretty important," I said without preamble.

When the young boy hugged his grandmother, let her look at him from all sides, Olivia appeared in the hall. I saw the surprise on her face. She was serious. She stopped at the stairs and looked at her visitor. It was hard to read anything on her face. She just stood still.

The boy noticed her. They stared at each other for a moment without saying a word.

"Hi mom," he said uncertainly. He took three steps towards her and stopped. "Sorry. You were right. You were right about everything."

Olivia slowly walked over to the boy and hugged him tightly. She embraced and held, not letting go for a long moment.

"Will you stay longer?" asked Helen, standing to the side. She wiped a tear rolling down her cheek with the edge of her scarf. "I'll go to the kitchen, what would you like to eat?"

"Grandma, I'm not hungry," he said, getting out of his mother's arms. He looked at his grandmother and instantly changed his mind. "Or you know, I'd like to eat something."

Helen walked quickly towards the kitchen.

"Shall we talk?" asked Olivia.

"Yes," he agreed.

Olivia gestured to her office.

They left slowly, and I heard Oskar say:

"A beautiful guest house. congratulations."

Half an hour later, Helen came to the front desk.

"I'm sorry for leaving you alone for so long," she said, full of emotion.

"I'm doing fine," I said with a smile. "Would you like some tea or water?"

"No, darling, you don't have to. I'll just cool down a bit - she sat down in a comfortable chair and sighed with relief. Let them talk calmly. Oskar... I didn't think he'd ever come here. That I'll see him again." She shook her head in disbelief.

"I didn't know Olivia had a son," I said.

"She does. They quarreled a few years ago. Oskar could not forgive his mother for buying this boarding house and moving here. He was giving Olivia real hell. When he turned eighteen, he went out into the world to look for happiness. Adam couldn't handle it either. We were very worried about him. But he's back. I wonder for how long. We'll see. Let them talk."

"I got the impression he was remorseful," I suggested.

"May my dear, may he wise up."

The phone rang, so I picked it up. I went back to work. By the way, interesting story. Maybe Olivia will share her observations on this subject someday. If not, that's fine too.

In the evening, after taking a bath, I did one breathing session using the Wim Hoff method and, already very relaxed, I sat on the bed. That day, I decided to look a bit deeper into myself. I turned on some calm music on my phone, nothing distracting, and focused on breathing. I entered the alpha state in meditation when my brainwaves started slowing down. And then, instead of being silent and meditating, I asked myself what I wanted to release. What emotions want to come out of me, show themselves. What needs to be released. I didn't have to wait long. I smiled as the first images appeared. I was in my family home. I saw everything through the eyes of a small child. A scared little girl. I saw my parents sitting at the kitchen table. They were tired. From the next room came the biting voice of Grandma Genevieve, again something was wrong with her. The parents looked at each other, the father got up, this time it was his turn to fulfill the old woman's wishes. I looked at this scene, I went to my mother, I wanted to comfort her, she was worried. As a little girl, I wanted to say something, I called her, but she didn't react, she didn't even notice me. She took care of Eva. Eve was always talkative and knew how to take care of her needs. I've never had such clout, I felt like the least important person in the house, I was a nuisance. My mother often said to me: "Natalie, at least you don't make me worry", so I tried my best to become almost invisible. Nobody ever had time for me. I lived my troubles in solitude. Life at home revolved around grandma Genevieve and Eve. There was nothing left for me.

I got into the feeling For this little girl, I allowed myself to feel her emptiness, rejection and worrying about her loved ones. I knowingly allowed it. I knew it could be hard, but not this hard. A wave of immense sadness and suffering washed over me. It took my breath away for a moment. On the one hand, I tried to be an observer of what was happening, and on the other, I kept repeating to myself: "Feel it, with your whole being, what exactly it is like. You can do it".

I sat on the bed with my eyes closed and the scenes of drama played out under my eyelids. I felt tears running down my cheeks. I didn't wipe them, so as not to break the connection I had made with myself.

Suddenly, a sob shook me. I was sure my heart would burst with grief. I breathed loudly so that crying wouldn't block my air. At one point, I took a pillow in my hand and pounded it hard with my fists.

You can do it, I kept telling myself. Just a little longer, hang on!

It hurt, but apparently it had to be. After a few minutes, I felt my emotions subside. I was slowly calming down. I fell onto the bed and tried to focus on my emotions. I felt relieved. Huge relief. The little girl disappeared from my sight.

I was no longer able to do anything else. I turned off my phone and went to sleep.

In the morning, when I saw my reflection in the mirror, I smiled. Tousled hair, puffy eyes, gray face.

"I love you anyway. I am with you. Always - I said to my reflection, and then I took a notebook, a pen and, warmly dressed, went to the pier."

I sat down on the wooden boards and, feeling the coolness of the water from the lake, began to write. I continued my morning pages. I wrote whatever came to my mind, as long as it took three pages. I liked it. I found some surprising insights in this writing. Sometimes, when asked a question, I wrote an answer right away, and one that I never expected. The amazing thing was that my mind didn't bother me. He didn't suggest, he didn't criticize. It just quieted down and my consciousness took over, the part connected to my depth. I couldn't even name it. But is sticking labels important? The morning pages served their purpose and that was the most important thing. I was learning myself again.

"…I must have gone crazy. It's five in the morning and I'm sitting by the water watching the sunrise. It's beautiful, I can feel the cool air. I always thought I was thermophilic, but here, surprisingly, thanks to the cool air from the lake, I feel alive. It's cool, I feel cool. I wouldn't trade those mornings for anything. Really weird, have I always liked it like that? Sometimes I feel like I've been sleeping like a bear for the past few years, and now I'm waking up slowly. I open my eyes and see more and more, the colors are different, more saturated, and the world is not rushing like crazy. He stands still, he just is. It's just the way it is…".

I closed the notebook and put it on the wooden platform. I supported myself comfortably with my hands and admired the peaks of the Tatra Mountains looming in front of me in the morning fog.

Over the next two days, Olivia devoted very little time to work. She took care of her son. They discussed a lot, sometimes I saw them through the window walking around the boarding house. They were both serious and sometimes argued.

Helen was very happy.

"He's a smart boy. He didn't go down the wrong path, she said enthusiastically. – They both with Lena are the same as Olivia. Maybe each of them is different, but they have their mother's characters.

"That's rather good," I smiled.

"Good good."

"Oscar stays longer?"

"No, tomorrow he returns to Krakow, where the whole family used to live. There's more potential there. School, work. Our Lena will also live in Krakow from October" she sighed.

"It's not going to be easy for Olivia," I pointed out.

"This is the life they chose, supposedly together and separately. It suits them. Don't judge me."

Anthony entered the reception. His emaciated body was visible under his unbuttoned shirt. Confident, cheeky.

"Hi, my lovely girls, have you seen this rascal, my grandson?" - He asked.

"What's up with Oscar? You don't do anything anymore" Helen was annoyed.

"I want to talk, I want to teach him life. Real life" explained Anthony. "Not the computers."

"That's not your role," Helen reminded her.

"How! I'm a grandfather, I have something to say. Now teenagers are stressed, rebellious, depressed. Who, if not grandpa, is supposed to show what real life looks like and teach real values?"

"What kind of values?"

"The most important."

"You will go to the forest to hunt wild boars with an ax, will you?" Helen screamed.

"Woman, you won't understand…" he sighed.

"Have you packed?" You are leaving for Italy tomorrow.

"I packed."

"I'll check your packing." Leave Oscar alone.

"See, Calm Eyes," he said to me. "It's not easy with wives."

"Oh, Mr. Anthony, have I been promoted? For Peaceful Eyes?"

"Yes, my dear, you have many promotions ahead of you, so try your best. Life is running away, it's a shame to waste it on sorrows and regrets. You already understand, but my son of a bitch doesn't yet."

Anthony turned around and, singing an Italian song, went to the yard in search of his grandson.

In the afternoon I helped in preparing a photo session for our female guests. Agatha brought easels, materials, and two cameras to the smaller conference room. I was very happy to prepare the appropriate scenery for the session. I remember participating in such an action quite recently and how amazing the emotions were.

I was pleased to observe the women's behavior, as surprised, they willingly took part in posing for photos. It was nice and fun.

After finishing work, I talked to Agatha, asked about her passion, she let me play with her equipment for a while. She explained how it worked, gave me some tips, and then stood in front of the gray fabric, making funny faces as she posed for photos. It was great fun.

In the evening, I again treated myself to another stage of letting go. I was ready when again, like last night, a wave of grief and pain flooded over me. I gave vent to dark emotions, let them come out of me and exist. I cried. I felt as if something was tearing my soul from the inside, and then there was silence. Emptiness. I went to sleep with a sigh of relief. No one saw me, no one heard me, that's how I healed my inner self. I didn't know what the effects might be, what might happen, but I believed it was the right way.

I was a support for myself in these very difficult times.

I was building confidence in myself.

In the morning, Lena came running to the reception. She was excited about the upcoming trip.

"Hi," she greeted.

"Hi. Ready to travel?" I asked.

"Yes, the luggage is already in the car, I'm just waiting for mom and grandpa. And we go."

"Have fun."

"I intend to. I'll bring you the best wine they have there. I promised you that once when you were at my riding lesson. I'm so glad you stayed here, really."

"I'm glad to hear."

"Just stay here when I come back."

"I will, I'm not going to change anything for now," I said happily.

"But you could find some time for horses, at least once a week," she suggested.

"I will think about it"

A moment later, Olivia, Anthony and Oskar appeared in the hall. The four of them got into the car and left for Krakow. From there, from the Krakow airport, Lena and her grandfather flew to sunny Italy.

The working time as Olivia's assistant has begun. I was very excited, I could learn a lot. Every day I had short shifts at the front desk, but most of the time I spent with Olivia. We prepared various attractions for our guests, invented quizzes, sometimes it was really fun.

"Do you remember when I said that your first task would be to organize a painting exhibition for Joanne?" she asked one morning.

"Of course I remember."

"Go ahead, you have full scope."

"Already?" I was surprised.

"Already."

"Tomorrow I start working with Kamil. We will expand the guesthouse. It's supposed to come with ready-made projects, so I'll focus heavily on this topic."

"What can I help you with?"

"I'll be doing yoga and meditation for the guests in the morning, talks on the workings of the mind twice a week." In the evening I will work for guests, bonfires, dances, but all the rest, such as organizing performances, cabarets, I will leave to you. You have all the necessary data in the computer at the reception.

"Anthony is not here. Who will take care of the male part of the group?"

"And here I have a surprise," she smiled broadly. "Damien will come on Thursday evenings and will stay until Sunday. He conducts trainings professionally, so for him it's just a change in the scope of knowledge, he willingly agreed to help us. He'll be here tonight."

I raised an eyebrow in surprise. I didn't comment. I paid attention to my feelings. There was moderate satisfaction.

"What did Anthony talk about with the men?" I asked. "Was it similar to classes with women?"

"Of course. It's about boosting self-confidence and motivation. Show that a man has a right to bad days too. My father is very direct with his talk, straight to the point, but he gets to the point. For him, there is no whining, no self-pity. It also teaches guys to be more relaxed, communicate, deal with stress and women."

"Do you think Damien will make it?" I asked, suppressing a smile.

"Do you think not?" she asked cheerfully.

After a moment of silence, she added:

"I've got Izabela up my sleeve, just in case." He is a sexologist. A young girl but with a lot of knowledge. He has been working with us recently.

"Promises to be interesting."

"Over the years I've heard so much from women about how their husbands suck in bed that I decided to do something about it. I met Isabella by accident. I asked her for one guy lecture and she was great. She even brought in sets of lingerie to teach guys how to buy such goodies for their women.

"Really, did they tell you about such intimate problems?" - I was surprised.

"The older they are, the less resistance there is. Guys live under the belief that they are perfect lovers, but in reality it is different. They just don't listen, they don't understand that you have to seduce a woman, reach her through the mind, emotions. And not waving your genitals, snorting here and there for a second is not enough. They think that after such a second foreplay, a woman is ready right away. Probably just disappointment."

I smiled, then quickly turned serious. I thought about Greg. Well, there was no rage. Although I didn't have much to compare him to, because he was my first guy in these matters, I felt that it could have been better.

I was sitting on the terrace with a cup of hot chocolate when I saw him. It was already evening. He walked calmly, holding a small traveling bag in his hand. I smiled involuntarily. I was glad to see him.

"Did you misspell the address?" I asked as he reached the stairs.

From here I had a perfect view of the entrance to the building.

He stopped and looked at me.

I got up.

"I'm definitely not wrong." Nice to see you." He walked over to me, grabbed my waist and lifted me up. And then he kissed her right on the mouth.

"Hey, don't get too carried away. We're not a couple," I reminded myself, getting out of his embrace.

"It's just a simple, friendly greeting," he explained with a shrug. He looked at me happily, obviously enjoying this meeting.

"I don't greet you like that."

"Your loss."

"I'm going to get over this loss. Who would have thought we'd see each other so soon," I said.

"Who would have thought you'd stay here?" You look good.

"Thank you."

"Is it okay to date you now, or is it too early?"

"You're fast, you haven't crossed the threshold of the boarding house yet, and you're already waiting for a declaration."

"Okay, I'll ask again. Tomorrow."

"Oh, better now. But don't expect a positive answer."

After a two-hour meeting with Olivia, Damien came to my room. It was very late. I opened the door for him in my pajamas.

"I see I won't take you out for a walk anymore," he suggested, looking at my outfit.

"I don't think so."

"Can I come in?" Talk?

"Talk, yes, but just talk," I suggested firmly.

We stayed in my room until almost midnight. We talked, we joked, it was a very nice time. I felt like our relationship was more casual, or maybe I've changed? I was no longer so tense and principled, I felt light and comfortable.

Damien looked at me with appreciation and delight. He spared me no compliments.

A busy day was beginning. Sleepless but happy, I showed up at the reception desk and took care of solving our guests' problems. I organized a performance of a cabaret known in the area for the weekend. I've taken a few new bookings.

To meet Olivia came the handsome guy I first met in the woods, sleeping in the car. The next meeting took place on the day of my planned departure. He was in Olivia's office when I burst in feverishly.

I remember exactly. And seeing that man again, I felt like we knew each other again. But from where? He greeted with a smile and walked towards the stairs, I followed him with a careful look.

Damien organized an event in the form of a treasure hunt, which was a case of whiskey. He had to work hard to do it, but he managed to say it.

In the evening, everyone enjoyed dancing by the fire. I thought that I would not have the strength after a whole day of intensive work, but as soon as I saw the bonfire, heard the music, I felt like having fun. Damien and I danced barefoot on the lawn. Then we went boating in the middle of the night. I felt satisfied and happy.

"You've changed," Damien said as we lay on our backs on the wooden deck. We stared at the stars in the sky and talked. "It's a very subtle impression, but still."

"What has changed in me?"

"You're happy, you're happy. Recently, you avoided people, it was hard to get you anywhere, and now you are full of kindness. You enjoy interacting with people. I watched you work today. Do you really want to stay here and do what you're doing?

"Yes. Yes, of course. I have everything I need here. Maybe someday, in some time, I will go further into the world, but not yet. This is my place for now."

"And when do you rest?

"I'm resting now."

Saturday passed on a bus trip to the Kościeliska Valley. Both Damien and I were guardians of a whole group willing to go on a hiking trail surrounded by beautiful mountains and even more beautiful views. I started to like my job more and more. I talked to the guests of the guest house, the whole trip went in a nice atmosphere.

I made a very valuable acquaintance, which to a large extent determined the further direction of my professional path.

We took a snack break. We sat on old benches or, if you preferred, on the lawn. I overheard a very interesting discussion between two women. As we moved on, I approached a fifty-year-old blonde.

"Ms. Anna, I just heard a fragment of your conversation… I've never heard of TRE, could you tell me a bit more about it?"

The woman responded enthusiastically.

"Of course. TRE is an abbreviation of the English word Tension & Trauma Releasing Exercises, these are exercises that release tension and stress from the body - she said animatedly. – We make the body tremble, such a body shake, in order to release all the accumulated tension in the muscles. Because as you know, living under stress, negative, unprocessed emotions freeze in our bodies. We don't want to see them, we push them deeper and deeper into ourselves, and they are there all the time, they grow, they are like a bomb that wants to explode. And that's where diseases come from. TRE helps a lot. The therapist leads through exercises to neurogenic tremors. It is quite safe and improves the quality of life."

"Where can you learn it? Are there any schools? Courses?" I asked.

"I'm teaching it. Here's a business card, darling." She pulled a wallet out of her backpack and handed me a colorful business card. – I have my office in Krakow. I also conduct certified trainings.

"I'd like to learn it," I said. I don't know where this sudden interest came from, but I decided to go in that direction.

"When we get back, I'd love to give a demonstration lesson." All you need is a piece of floor.

"Thank you, I'd love to."

Mrs. Anna talked for a long time about the advantages of using this relaxation technique, about her public appearances and satisfied students.

In the evening, after returning from a trip to the mountains, I was a bit tired, but I went to Anna's for a lesson anyway.

"Come on darling, welcome," she said as she let me into her hotel room.

"What should I do?" I asked.

"Practice first."

Instructed, I did every exercise prescribed. I warmed up my muscles, prepared to cleanse my body of emotions.

"Okay, now lie down on the floor." On the carpet, so you're comfortable." She knelt down next to me. "Bend your legs at the knees, oh yes, good, feel with your awareness that you are lying on the floor, that your feet touch the floor. Focus on that. Knees a little farther apart. Very good. Now lift your ass up high, up as high as you can, stay in this position for a minute and a half, that's good. Now lower your hips to the floor. Relax your body. Let what happens."

My body began to tremble. First legs, then hips, arms, even head. The closer I got to my knees, the stronger the tremors became.

"Breathe evenly. Don't hold back, "Anna said. "If you want to stop the process, all you have to do is tense your muscles. It would be good if you could hold on a little longer. You're doing great.

It was starting to get tiresome. I felt my body literally being thrown to the floor, nothing hurt but it was a strange feeling. Hands and shoulders twitched compulsively uncontrollably. Finally, exhausted, I stretched my legs out so that I was completely flat on the carpet. My body was slowly calming down.

Now take it easy, focus on the sensations of your body.

I focused, I felt a strong energy flowing through my body, something amazing. I smiled, feeling as if a great deal of something powerful had been released within me. I don't know what it was, but the feeling is indescribable. I was going to repeat this exercise.

"Thank you, it's been a very interesting experience," I said, getting up off the floor. I asked for more details about the course and went back to my room.

Damien was already waiting for me. With champagne and a little snack.

"Don't you need to prepare for tomorrow's lectures?" I asked, sitting comfortably in the chair.

"I'm ready," he said happily.

"When did you have time for this?"

"I've been in the industry too long to be surprised by anything. It is enough to read a summary of a publication or an article and I can talk about it for hours.

"How is this possible?"

"It's easy. Take, let's say, a mug or a simple stick and talk about that object for three minutes, whatever comes to mind. What does it look like, what is it used for, what can you do with it. Once you can handle a simple stick, practice a bit on other subjects, then later there will be no topics for you on which you would not have anything to say. It's just a matter of practice and the right approach. In speaking to people. It is important not to bore them. They will focus your attention for the first few minutes, and then you have to mess around. Some kind of joke, some question directly to the student, forcing them to give a statement. Everyone has their own techniques."

"Interesting."

Damien gave me some more tips on how to be a good speaker so that people would listen and enjoy the meeting. I jotted down everything in my memory, it might come in handy.

CHAPTER 11

All my days were very intense. I would get up early in the morning, take my notebook to the pier and write my morning pages there. Those early mornings were very important to me, they were times when I could look inside myself a bit, ponder, think, or just enjoy being there. I usually worked until the evening. I wanted it, I learned it, I enjoyed it. After the bath, I usually read books, searched for information on the Internet about spiritual and personal development. I found many interesting videos and publications. Breathing exercises and an hour of meditation are obligatory before bedtime. I was surprised by the duty in what I was doing. I didn't let go even on those days when Damien stayed in my room until late at night. Total commitment and curiosity led me to more and more discoveries. I watched myself, how my attitude and outlook on reality changed. As self-confidence grew, thoughts were no longer so distracting and tiring. I felt light in soul, mind and body. I felt like I weighed less than thirty pounds. The sleep was strong, I woke up in the morning refreshed and full of strength. And when I saw my reflection somewhere in the mirror, I smiled happily. I was already a different person, a completely different Natalie. I liked myself.

The day started with a happy surprise. My friend Simon decided to visit me. He was planning to come to Poland this weekend. I arranged a room for him in a boarding house on very favorable terms. I was happy as a child. During the week I worked even more to have time only for him from Friday.

On Wednesday evening the phone rang. I looked at the display - Marilyn. I answered the call.

- Hi! We have to meet - said Marilyn as part of the greeting. - Necessarily! Olivia will surely give you the weekend off. We meet at Sylvia's in Tarnów. He has a big house, there will be a party. You must be. This weekend.

"NO! NO! Not this weekend," I shouted into the phone.

"It's not?! We can't postpone it anymore" Marilyn was indignant.

"I can not."

"You must be. What's going on?"

"Simon is coming to see me. The one from England."

"Is that your friend?" she asked.

"Yes."

"No problem. Take him with you to us. Sylvia will send you the address in a moment."

"I do not know if that's a good idea. I want to meet you, but Simon is also important to me."

"Oh, don't look for trouble. See you at Sylvia's at seven o'clock. You will arrive in two hours."

"I don't know what Simon does."

"Just ask him," Marlene said. Everything was clear and simple to her."

"Okay, I'll talk to him," I agreed. Is there any special occasion for this meeting?"

"Right."

"I'm listening, tell me...."

Organizing an exhibition of Asia's paintings was an easy task. I decided that all the works would be on the easels in the lobby by the reception. I chose the time so that the guests finishing their stay could enjoy the art and the next group of guests could participate in this artistic event. Already on the third day I had to call Joanne asking for the valuation of the paintings, because there were several people willing to buy. As is often the case, one rich man bought it, the rest decided it couldn't be worse. There was an order for several works for a seaside resort. Asia came to us personally to sign a contract for painting paintings with a wealthy contractor. She was happy, grateful, her biggest dream had come true in such an extraordinary way. It was Olivia who gave her an amazing chance, for her this exhibition was a trifle, and for the young artist a chance for a better life.

Once again, with a sigh, I was glad to be there, to be a part of that good world. Olivia has created a truly extraordinary place. When I asked her about it, she explained it to me in a very simple way.

"It's about intention. I wanted to build a place where everyone would feel good. Where it will be calm, harmonious, but cheerful. Where will you be able to rest. Where no one will judge anyone or look down on anyone, here everyone is equal. In general, the world is not like that, but my world is what I make it. I want to be with people and for people. Everything I do is based on intention.

"You mean the target, right?" I asked.

"Yes. Exactly. The point is that when I do something, I have a specific desire to achieve the goal. I do something for something, I get involved, I get emotionally into it and I believe that the right action will bring the intended effect. It's an order from the universe. I define what is to happen, I go into it with my whole being and I look at the effect. The intentions can be small, for example, I am going to meet a friend and my intention of this meeting is to have a good time. Or I cook something good with the intention of making it healthy and tasty for my family."

"Incredible. How little I know about the world yet," I said in amazement.

Olivia laughed heartily.

"Everything ahead of you." Have fun exploring the world.

One afternoon I went to town to do some shopping. I was supposed to go to a party in Tarnów, so I decided to buy a more feminine, colorful wardrobe. I enjoyed shopping a lot. I had a few smart clothes in my closet, but most were gray and bland. I felt the need to express myself through my appearance and how I felt. I chose a few summer dresses with floral patterns. White jacket, matching light trousers and shirts in pastel colors. Plus a black leather skirt.

On Friday noon I had some free time and decided to use it for a walk around the lake. The August sun was still hot. Dressed in a short dress and a large straw hat, I went towards the lake. I stretched my arms up, clasped them above my head, and relaxed my whole body. I liked this exercise, it was beneficial for the spine. I stood for a moment on the wooden pier, then walked along the lawn by the lake.

I didn't know I was being watched. A young man, Kamil, was sitting on a bench by a flower bed looking at me from an open laptop on his lap. Apparently he needed a break too.

As I walked, I thought about Simon, he could appear at any moment. He was my long-term, true friend, such an older brother, he always stood by my side, always helped. I liked his openness, he took life as it was, he didn't show off, he didn't have to prove anything to anyone. He went his own way and liked people.

As every weekend, Damien came to help Olivia in diversifying the time of the guests of the guesthouse. Everything had to be of the highest quality and there was no question of giving up mental lectures during Anthony's absence. I warned him that I would spend the whole weekend with Simon. I told him a little about our close relationship. Damien wasn't thrilled that I wouldn't have time for him. He's been telling me this since morning. I joked about him being jealous, he didn't deny it.

I glanced at my watch. I had to go back. Taking my time, I returned to the yard. Kamil was still sitting on the bench and working. Sometimes I saw him circling in the place where the extension of the hotel was supposed to be. He was measuring something. We never spoke. He had his job, I had mine. There was no opportunity or topics to talk about.

"Hi," he said as I walked past him.

"Hi," I replied with a smile and continued walking.

A moment later Simon arrived at the parking lot in a rented car. I went out to greet him. What time synchronization. Ideal.

"Simon! I called as I walked over to the car."

"At last. I haven't seen you in ages." He hugged me tight. "How do you feel? All right?"

"Very well." I took his hand and led him to the boarding house. "Come on, I'll show you your room, and after you've recovered from your trip, I wanted you to meet a few people."

"Do they add herbs to desserts here?" Simon asked after dinner. We sat at a wooden bench on the terrace.

"NO. Why?"

"Because you're radiant." Which is a bit odd, after what you went through in May. Wedding... Greg...

"Oh, that's… you know I forgot already?" Really. I'm so busy here that I don't have time to think about what was, what could be," I explained lightly. - And with you? Is there anyone on the horizon, or are you still playing the unrepentant bachelor?

"No one I want to introduce to you," he said.

"I see."

"What attractions do you have here?"

"I will show you around, but first come, you will meet Olivia and Damien. It's a pity that Anthony is not there, you would be delighted."

We got up. I found Olivia and Damien quite quickly, I really wanted Simon to meet them. We chatted for a while all together, then I took my friend for a walk around the guesthouse grounds. I showed the gym, where, unfortunately, I trained less and less often, a jacuzzi, a stable with horses, and then we followed the well-trodden paths to the forest. I was telling how we organize various interesting attractions for our guests, Simon was very interested. At one point he paused with a question.

"And this Damien? Someone closer than I think?"

"This Damien is just my friend. We met in the first week of my stay here. We had the whole package. There was also Marilyn, Sylvia, Daria and Fred. By the way, the whole team is meeting tomorrow in Tarnów at Sylvia's. We have an invitation, both of us.

"We're going. What problem. I'd love to meet them."

"Okay, that's pretty cool.

"What about Damien? What are your relationships? He looks at you like this..."

"What?" I laughed.

"Isn't he too old for you?" How old is he? She must be in her forties.

"And?" He is only a friend.

"Maybe you think so."

"Come on. I don't feel like dating right now. I'm happy with what I have and don't plan to change anything."

"It's nice here," he said, stopping in place. There was a river right next to us. We had just left the forest, in front of us was an open space developed with meadows, and further in the background the peaks of the Tatra Mountains were visible.

"Right? In Warsaw, I would not have such views How did your family react to you staying here?" he asked after a moment.

"It's beyond my mother's understanding that I work at the front desk of a hotel in some 'hole asshole' as she put it. She was very disappointed, you know how she is. She said it was below my qualifications, if

I had any." I laughed. "Eve supports me, I rarely talk to my father."

"And what next, next year? Two?"

"I don't know. I always thought ahead, worried unnecessarily. Now I don't have to. What will be, will be."

"I don't recognize you."

"Neither do I sometimes," I replied lightly.

In the evening I took Simon on a boat trip on the lake. We swam to the center and, looking out over the lantern-lit area, talked until almost midnight. We had no secrets from each other, I could talk freely about anything. From time to time, Simon returned with questions to my ex-fiancé, Greg. Maybe he wanted me to talk and let it all out, maybe he was just curious about my way of thinking and acting. I noticed that talking about Greg was no longer uncomfortable for me, and I didn't think much about him in the weeks that passed. It was just the past.

Simon also talked a lot about his work, planned his next trips, and had lots of interesting ideas. Perhaps someday I will go with him on one of the trips not far away. Somehow I wasn't drawn to the world, I preferred a familiar environment where I could build everyday life with a sense of security, it was more important to me than exciting adventures in foreign countries. Each of us was different and that's fascinating. We can learn a lot from each other, at least there is no shortage of topics for discussion.

Damien wasn't thrilled with the fact that I was spending the weekend with Simon. He didn't hide his disappointment at all. I was a little sad that he reacted like that. I wasn't going to change my firearms. I hoped that this situation would finally make him realize that he was a friend, a warm-hearted, wonderful one, but only a friend. It's about time he realized that, distanced himself and cooled down.

In the evening, he visited Olivia and her husband Adam, had a fun meeting in Olivia's private apartments, and the next day, as promised, he organized attractions for the male part of the guests of the guest house.

"You are leaving me, my dear," he whispered in my ear as we met at the terrace. "I don't know how my ego will take it."

"You will make it. Look around, see how many attractive friends are here. Invite one on the boat", I said humorously. "I don't think they will resist."

"Very funny. An attractive friend is taken from me by a friend here and to a nice party. Give my regards to the whole team."

"You were invited, you had to agree."

"Commitments, my dear, I keep my promises. Today I will teach my friends how to chop wood."

"Can you do it yourself?" I asked teasingly.

"Hmmm, I still have two hours to practice."

Simon came over to us.

"So, are we getting together?" - He asked.

"Yes, I'm ready now."

"Have fun" Damien said and went deeper into the yard.

We went in my car. I was stubborn because I like to drive. The Opel sat in the parking lot for a few weeks and just had to do some work. The trip was very nice. In Tarnów, Sylvia's house was a real madness. A very effusive welcome and we celebrated the rendezvous right away. I haven't laughed so much before. Simon was accepted to the company from the first moment, he felt very good with my new friends. He spent most of his time with Marilyn. They couldn't argue.

We had fun until morning. I was happy that we could meet, reminisce, share plans for the future. It gave me the feeling that I was with the right people in the right place. Then a joint dinner, to which everyone contributed, and before the evening, promising each other soon another meeting, each of us left for home.

When we got back to the guesthouse, Damien was gone. So I could focus all my attention on Simon.

"Great people," he said delightedly as we sat in my room that evening. "You're lucky you met them here." With such a team, I'm not surprised that you recovered so quickly after parting with Greg. Marilyn told us what attractions you had here during your stay. I didn't know places like this existed. Now I understand why you wanted to stay here.

"Exactly. This is where I belong now, at least for a while. You know, Olivia and Anthony kept telling me to follow my intuition, not reason. I thought it was the biggest bullshit in the world. I didn't understand how you could trust your gut, it was illogical to me. Once I got to the point where I didn't have much to do with myself, I trusted my intuition and here I am. Happy and content for now." I told him about an exhibition of paintings I had organized. About the new ideas I was going to present to Olivia. Simon took up the topic and together we started to come up with new attractions for the guests of the guesthouse.

We had a great time with it. And the next day, first thing in the morning, I had to say goodbye to Simon. I watched with regret as he pulled out of the parking lot in a rental car. With a sigh, I wondered when we would meet again...

CHAPTER 12

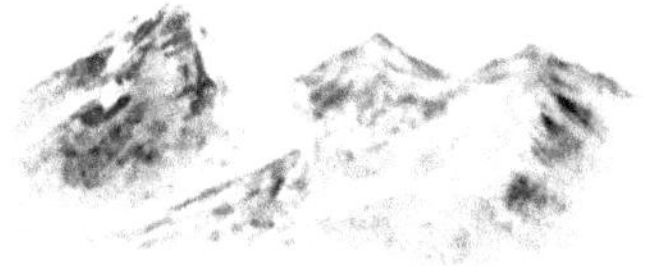

The end of August brought some interesting surprises.

Lena and Anthony returned from Italy, beautifully tanned, happy, full of strength and enthusiasm. They brought many gifts. I got a few bottles of wine from them - with my drinking mode, it was a supply for two years. In the box I also found sweets and a beautiful bracelet.

"This is for you from me, Beautiful Eyes" said Anthony, fastening the bracelet on my left wrist. I was amazed and delighted.

"Thank you, she's beautiful," I said. We were standing in the lobby by the reception. I glanced at Helen, she was smiling kindly, apparently not bothered by her husband giving another woman such an elaborate gift.

Helen also got a lot of sweets, a new, colorful scarf and a necklace.

Lena left her bags and ran to the stables to say hello to her pets. A moment later, through the window, I saw her take off at a gallop on her horse towards the meadows. She obviously missed it very much.

By the evening, not much had been done, we were sitting on the terrace drinking coffee and listening to Anthony's stories. I loved this guy, I could listen to him for hours and not get tired of it. I had the opportunity to see many photos taken by Lena. They were very interesting.

A few days later I received an offer. The job of Olivia's assistant suited me, I had a lot of different activities, and as I fulfilled them flawlessly, I got more and more tasks that Olivia gave me with confidence and faith in my creative abilities. I had full freedom, I could act, invent, look for solutions. Sometimes it was quite a challenge, but also great satisfaction from the successful effect of my work. I dealt diplomatically with the claims made by some guests looking for a reason to be dissatisfied. I patiently put up with their moods, but most of the guests are wonderful, generous people.

I thought nothing could surprise me anymore, but it did.

Olivia approached me while I was printing documents at the reception desk.

"I just spoke with Agatha, our photographer. Remember when I mentioned that she runs an orphanage. The school year is coming up and he is looking for an English tutor once or twice a week in the afternoon to tutor the kids. Would you like to? I mentioned you to her, I promised I'd ask. You don't have to answer right away."

"I would love to, of course I do," I agreed.

"That's great. Agatha will call you and you will arrange the first lesson. Thank you very much."

"No problem," I replied. I sighed contentedly. I got a lot of good things from Olivia, from people I had contact with there, from this place itself. Time is the good received, and in such a large amount, let it circulate further. I was going to teach those kids English, and I'll do the best I can.

Two days later I went to meet Agatha. After a short conversation, she led me to a room where children of different ages were sitting at round tables. They were waiting for me. This was to be the first get-together. So I greeted with a smile and asked each student to say their name.

"The school year hasn't started yet, you still have a week of vacation, so we're just getting to know each other today."

The children looked at me distrustfully, the older ones showed contempt and boredom. I expected that. Agatha gave me a free hand in the teaching method, she wanted to help me with my homework and prepare for tests. I decided to divide the children into groups to make it easier for me to work with them. I had already made a plan in my head, but I was going to implement it only from September, that day I decided to move them a bit.

I asked them in English to get up and gather in the center of the room. They came casually. I started giving each person simple commands in English, like jump on one leg, the next person to draw a big heart on the glass with their finger. I didn't lose my enthusiasm. I tried to be cheerful and funny. After a few tries, the kids opened up a bit and were more willing to take part in the game.

"Gabrielle, I will ask you now, go out the door and shout very loudly the phrase: "I am a beautiful and cool girl.""

Teenage Gabrielle went out into the corridor and did what I asked.

"In English!" I exclaimed indignantly.

All the kids laughed loudly and Gabrielle shouted fluently in English that she was a beautiful and cool girl. Satisfied, she returned to the rest of the group.

"Well, that was something," I complimented. I pulled out board games, dice, and pawns from my bag. I divided the students into smaller groups and proposed a game. The boards had pictures with simple questions in English and you had to answer them.

"Here we go, darlings. Play, and if there are any questions, feel free to ask. I will listen and help.

Two hours later, I left the building very happy. I think I managed to reach the children. I wanted to help them, lead classes in such a way that they would remember and learn as much as possible. In a friendly and cool atmosphere.

Sometimes I was able to attend Olivia's lectures. I didn't always have time for this, but that day I managed half an hour. I came to the conference room a bit late, sat on the side in an empty chair and focused on the life wisdom provided by the owner of the guesthouse.

"When judging another person, we don't really see the full situation, we don't sit in that person's head, we don't really know what it's really like, we only see a partial picture and from our own perspective. We think we can judge others, put labels on it, it comes so easily to us, but is it right? I don't think so. Each of us experiences difficult emotions in our own way, we all have our own dramas and do the best we can. We don't want to be judged either, none of us want that. Let's just accept people as they are. We judge the most when we compare ourselves with another person, a friend, a neighbor. Don't ever do that, comparing yourself to others doesn't lead to anything good. There will always be someone better, there will always be someone worse off than us. Let's save this. We observe beautiful people on Instagram, they post photos showing how they are doing, how great they live, we would like that too. We sigh, we get depressed, we work in vain to look like them. Live like them. And all these pictures are for show, they are just an illusion. You can make cute smiles while posing for photos, flex a great figure, and have a messed up life. The richest man may have a company, money, prestige, but no one can see that he has neglected his family while climbing the career ladder, that he has no true friends, and that the people around him are selfish and dishonest. We only see part of the truth."

Olivia paused for a moment, drank some water, and continued her speech.

"Let's get on with our lives and what we have to do." Let's not waste energy and time judging and comparing ourselves to others. The topic I started is related to the next one I wanted to talk about. We often do not realize that we give our future, security, decisions to other people, sometimes even strangers. I will give an example. When I drive a car, I am amazed at the behavior of people on the lanes. I watch them very carefully. Pedestrians enter the lanes, and once they have taken that first step, they almost never look in the direction from which the cars are coming. They look ahead, to the side, but not at the cars. Amazing. Pay attention to that. They give their security to others without even realizing it. Another example. Traffic jam. Well, it happens. Maybe not here, but in bigger cities, definitely. Drivers honk at each other, curse, challenge, what will it give them, firstly, and secondly, one will honk and ten will get angry, they will take over these negative emotions. An example from my life. My husband and I rode bikes. By bike path, not too fast. A guy was coming out of a side street, stared, braked suddenly. He got scared and got very angry. There was no threat to us, I saw the car, so the situation didn't affect me in any way. The frightened driver honked. He started calling out. I shrugged and drove on, but my husband stopped and got into an argument with the hotheaded driver. It was rough, they stuck some unpleasant labels on each other and it was over. But my husband was furious. I asked him why he allowed himself to take the emotion of being pissed off from a stranger. Why did he let a stranger take away his peace and relaxation. These are very simple examples. Every day we are exposed to giving power over ourselves to other people. We are being manipulated. Let's not allow that. Many examples can be given. Someone will tell us something uncool, and we, instead of taking our side, because we know ourselves best, believe this person, accept what they say about us as true, and we feel sorry. Only we ourselves can have power over ourselves. Nobody can make us do anything. Let's respect ourselves. Let's take responsibility for our lives. Let's not let others decide for us. You don't think you can live like this? try it.

"It's obvious stuff, everyone knows it," said a woman in the front row. – This is nothing new.

"Yes, I am talking about very obvious topics, very simple, but there is a difference between "knowing" and putting this knowledge into practice, into everyday life" said Olivia. "We all deserve a wonderful, comfortable life. At any time, we do everything to ensure your comfort and well-being. Unfortunately, not everyone knows how to do this. Some people are looking for the golden mean, magic tricks or techniques to just change their lives to a happy and perfect one in one minute. There is no such thing, there is no such thing. And the way to happiness lies in simplicity, in noticing these little things. In not judging others, in not comparing yourself to anyone, in accepting yourself and others. In making conscious decisions, in appreciating what you already have today. The essence is in simplicity. And that's the coolest thing about it all, because it's available to everyone.

My phone rang, so I sadly walked out into the hallway and couldn't hear the end of the speech.

Eve called.

"Hi, how are you?" I asked as I walked down the hall.

"Hi Natalie. I have great news! You will not believe! I found you a job. In Warsaw! My new friend's mum is a primary school principal and would love to hire you. I already talked to her. You can start in September!"

She surprised me. I went outside and stopped on the stairs. I looked out into the distance at the sights before me and sighed deeply.

"Eva, I already have a job."

"Hey there. You always wanted to be a teacher, to teach children."

"Yes, but my needs have changed a lot lately," I said. The little mongrel ran up to me, tail wagging happily, twirled around at my feet for a while, then settled down to rest on the tiled steps.

"Natalie, pack up and come."

"I can't. Doesn't want. Eve, thank you very much for thinking about me, worrying and helping me, but I have to go my own way now. I've already chosen. I'm happy. Maybe I'm not doing important things, maybe I won't achieve great success where people will look at me with admiration, but finally I'm doing what I like. They treat me like family here."

"Really?"

"Come, see how it is here. What I do, how I live."

"I don't recognize you, Natasha."

"You know that you are and will always be the most important person for me ... We haven't seen each other in a long time ... Maybe I've changed. It's time to just stand on your own two feet and do something meaningful with yourself."

"Okay, if that's what you choose, fine, but just know that if anything, I'm here."

"I know. And how are you?"

"My career is gaining momentum, I have a lot of new orders, I sign contracts for new collections" there was joy and pride in her voice.

"Fantastic, just don't forget to rest sometimes."

"I don't have time for that right now, but I'll think about it." Maybe I'll even come for a weekend to admire the views you have outside the window...

I heard some noise in the handset, a quarrel of several people.

"What, you have to go..." I said, guessing what was about to happen.

"Life, work, success… you know how it is," she laughed. "I need to see what they're up to."

"They're lying..."

I put my phone back in my pocket and sighed, breathing in the clean, warm air. And then I smiled contentedly.

In the evening, I sat back comfortably in bed, turned on calm relaxing music and tried to recall something that I should process, repressed emotions that sit deep inside me and control subconsciously. Nothing came, no images appeared under closed eyelids, no emotions. I felt calm and content. Certainly, in some time, in a few days or weeks, a wave of pain caused by memories will flood me.

Today, however, I felt light and safe. In one of the books I learned that you can heal your past by giving yourself support in difficult times. Intrigued, I decided to give it a try. I put myself into a meditative state and thought back to the past, to the first day of school. I don't remember exactly what it looked like then, but knowing myself, I could easily imagine it. A nicely dressed girl with long braids and a serious face. I saw myself and smiled kindly. I was an adult now, comforting this little girl, reassuring and supporting her: "You are very brave, I am with you, you will manage," I said to myself from the past. I traveled a little further back in time when I was a child learning to walk. I watched with tenderness at the clumsy steps, falls, when I got up again and tried again. I didn't know the word "failure" back then.

I traveled back in time to my fifteenth birthday. Then I built relationships, made friends, sometimes I experienced disappointments, other times dilemmas and euphoria. I stayed with myself, I saw my life as if from the side, at every stage I gave myself complete acceptance and understanding.

It was an amazing time travel. I thought back to the present and smiled contentedly. I was curious about more such experiences, what else I would find in books and videos on the web. It was just the beginning of the road to greater awareness, but how fascinating.

I thought about a few more events of the day for which I am grateful, and with peace and a sense of accomplishment, I went to sleep.

CHAPTER 13

It was mid-September.

Satisfied, I set the phone down and looked at the doodles on the paper. I circled the most important dates and two addresses with a pen. I just signed up for a TRE course, i.e. methods of releasing stress and tension from the body. I was very interested in these classes. All I had to do was inform Olivia about the three weekends I will spend in Krakow. I went to her right away.

She was in her office, focused on the drawings spread out on her desk.

"Do you have a moment?" I asked as I peeked into her office.

"Sure, come on," she said without even looking at me. "Will show you something."

I walked over to the desk and looked at the plans.

"It's a ready project for the expansion of the boarding house," she said excitedly. "Look, where we now have a sauna and jacuzzi, there will be an additional large swimming pool, upstairs spa and massage rooms, and here, a small squash room."

"Great, you're up and running soon..." I shared her enthusiasm.

"Yes, I can't wait." I just need a building permit and off we go.

"Do you like challenges…"

"Sure, you have to learn and grow all your life. Have a goal, pursue yourself, have passions and follow them. That's why we're here in this world."

"Well said."

"But it is," she looked at me in surprise, then understood something and smiled softly. "I also appreciate your growth and your willingness to know the truth. You search, you learn. You really impressed me with this.

"Oh, thank you." The praise from her lips was very important to me.

"Speaking of science, I just came to you about this. I signed up for a weekend course to release tension from the body, it will be three two-day meetings in Krakow. It won't be a problem if I skip my work these days?

"That's excellent news. congratulations. I'll call Adam, we have a big apartment in Krakow, you'll stay there."

"No need, thank you." I have already booked a hotel and arranged a meeting with Marilyn.

I've heard a lot about this method. Once you are certified, I would be happy to use your skills and provide you with a place for therapy with our guests. What do you think?

"I'll get certified and we'll discuss it," I said, feeling a growing interest in the idea. The course was guided by the intention of self-support and understanding the signals sent by the body, but why not share this knowledge with others? Well, study first, see if that's the way I want to go, then decide. For now, I did not assume anything in advance, although Olivia's proposal boosted my ego a lot.

I was standing on the pier, it was five in the morning. Wrapped in a warm shawl, with untied hair, eyes still swollen from sleep, I admired the mist floating over the lake. The air was crisp, cool. I wrapped myself tighter and sighed dreamily. The perfect moment, peace, quiet, relaxation. Bliss. I absorbed that moment with all my senses.

After a while, I heard the sound of footsteps behind me and the neighing of horses. I turned to see what was going on. Anthony was walking towards me, holding two horses by the bridles. He walked among them.

"Come on, Pretty Eyes, I'm inviting you for a ride." I brought Tina for you, believing that you wouldn't refuse to go on a trip together.

"How could I refuse you a ride, Mr. Anthony…" I said and approached the mare. I stroked her head, just the way she liked it.

"Anthony. Anthony. Call me by my name," he reminded me as usual.

"I have to be a little perverse, Mr. Anthony. It's like those dresses you used to remind me of every day."

"And that's why I like you," said the old man, and easily jumped on his boisterous steed."

I sat comfortably in the saddle and, somewhat hesitantly, tugged on the bridle, letting Tina know we were moving. We drove very slowly, straight into meadows shrouded in mist. It wasn't until after I focused my attention on my surroundings that I relaxed a bit. I inhaled heavy, damp air that smelled of wet earth. From time to time the sun appeared for a few seconds from behind the leaden clouds.

"How is it in winter here?" I asked, looking out over the valley.

"Beautifully. When there is snow, we organize sleigh rides, we have sleighs with torches. There are evening bonfires with warm mulled wine and sausage roasted on a stick. There are walks in the forest, we even have a slide for sledges and on sacks stuffed with hay, as it used to be fun. Three kilometers away there is a small ski lift, ideal for amateurs. We organize feasts with a highlander band. There's a lot going on, you'll see. Every evening we light the fireplace, organize games together, watch movies together."

"Sounds fantastic. Sometimes I wonder if this place has any downsides?"

"You see, my dear, what you want to see. For some it is heaven on earth, others are just looking for what they can attach to. What you have inside you see outside."

"Not many disgruntled guests around here," I remarked.

"Yes, not much. Some people wouldn't be able to last a day here. Somehow it happens that they choose other hotels to rest."

Too much good energy for them…

"Exactly."

We drove on, the peaks of the mountains visible on the horizon were shrouded in mist.

After returning from the horse ride, I got down to work. Full of good energy and vigor, I put on a colorful dress and did a delicate make-up. I was in a good mood, and looked at everything and everyone kindly. I felt happy. Just. I felt great power and joy in myself, regardless of the time of day or thoughts and problems to solve. I knew I was in the right place at the right time. And that was enough for me.

I replied to a dozen or so e-mails, prepared the conference room for the next meeting to chat about life choices that Olivia was supposed to make. Then I came up with the texts for the cards. I really liked these short sentences or quotes of famous philosophers written on pieces of paper with the logo of the guest house. They were left by the cleaners in guest rooms. Seemingly meaningless words, but upon deeper reflection they revealed so much. I've been preparing them for some time, that day I wrote a quote by Albert Einstein: "There are only two ways to go through life. One as if nothing was a miracle and the other as if everything was a miracle. Below, I added my own: "What miracles do you see in your life every day?". I ran the text to the printer, on cream-colored letterhead. Then I cut the paper into smaller pieces. Then the phone rang. I was alone at the front desk, I reached for my cell phone and looked at the screen. Marilyn called via Messenger. Slightly surprised, I accepted the call and after a moment I saw her face on the screen.

"Hi Natalie," she greeted cheerfully.

"Hello Marlene, how nice to see you." How are you? How to find a new job? I asked.

"Very good. I start on Monday so keep your fingers crossed. For now, I'm resting, enjoying the last days off. You know, I've changed a bit, I'm calling to tell you first. For some reason, you should be the first to know. It's quite unexpected, surprising, you will certainly be surprised, but somehow it turned out nice. Do you remember that day when Sylvia organized a party for us at her home in Tarnów…"

"Yes…" I encouraged, waiting for her to reveal the reason why she was calling. I was curious what he had to tell me. Her eyes shone with joy, so it must have been good news.

"It was great, we need to do it again."

"Of course. Of course."

"I am very glad that we met at Bella Vita. You know, thanks to you my life has changed a bit."

I listened to her with growing interest. Marilyn behaved a bit strangely, the more so that in the background I heard a male voice: "Come on, finally tell her". I unconsciously raised an eyebrow.

"Well, it's okay, I had to create the right atmosphere," she said to someone sitting to the side. "Natalie, because you know, I'm dating a handsome guy - and she moved the phone to the left so that I could see the face of her chosen one. it choked me. For a moment I thought it was some kind of joke, a montage of a movie or something. It took me a while to realize who I was seeing. No it is not possible."

"At this party, we somehow liked each other very much and became a couple" added Marilyn, clearly seeing my surprise.

"Simon," I finally managed. "What a surprise."

"Hello sunshine," my friend greeted.

How is it possible that this hardened bachelor got involved with Marilyn? They had only just met, a little over a month ago.

"Everything's all right?" Marlene asked. Apparently my opinion mattered to both of them. Did they expect acceptance? I don't think so, but they'd be happy if I responded positively.

"It's an amazing surprise!" I smiled. "But how? When?"

"We spent quite a lot of time together at the party, then we wrote to each other, called each other, and finally Simon came to me for a few days" explained Marilyn.

"I plan to be here more often, so be prepared to meet more often. From Kraków to Kościelisko, it takes an hour and a half."

"I'm very happy, really. I'm surprised, because it's an amazing surprise" I said honestly pleased. I looked at their happy faces, I just couldn't believe that I saw them together.

"We wanted to inform you right away," Simon said. "We don't want any secrets from you."

"I appreciate it," I said with a wide smile.

"We will say goodbye, we have a bit of catching up to do…" Simon joked.

"You surprised me, thanks for calling." Take care." I hung up, shaking my head in disbelief. Then I laughed out loud. My mood immediately improved. I was alone at the reception, no guests were around, so I got up and went to the stairs of the guest house.

Joy bubbled up in me. Surprise and satisfaction. I stood there for a long time in the sun and laughed to myself. What an amazing surprise The universe is preparing us. Really, I wouldn't have thought of it myself. Marlene and Simon. May they succeed, may they be happy together.

Anthony stopped near me, looked at me and nodded, then came closer, climbed the stairs and stood next to me.

"What's good, Happy Eyes?" he asked.

"Ah, Mr. Anthony. It's good. It's very good" I sighed spiritually.

Anthony looked at me carefully, appreciatively. He lingered a little longer on my colorful dress.

"Now I see. And I believe you… You finally got your legs tanned a bit."

"There's so much good in the world."

"That's right, good to see you finally see it," he said. He immediately added "and remember, you are also the good of this world."

We stood there for a long time in silence, facing the morning sun. Both lost in their own thoughts.

Olivia called me to her office. I walked in, wondering what she had come up with this time. It was never boring with her.

She was always in a good mood, but today I sensed her impatience. She looked at me seriously.

"Natalie, I have a huge request. For me it's very important. Could you go to Nowy Targ? I was planning on my own, but an important meeting came up, and I just got a call that the construction guy might be here by noon today, or it might be a month from now. You have to deliver these documents to Kamil. If these documents are not on his desk by 12:00, the construction start date will be postponed, and I cannot allow that. He himself has appointments and can't come."

"Sure I will," I said calmly.

"Thank you very much. I'm glad I can count on you." She handed me a briefcase and a business card. "Here's the exact address, you'll find it easily. Thank you again."

"I'm going now, since it's so important."

"Take the company car," she ordered.

I left the office.

It was quite chilly outside today, so I changed into warmer clothes in my room. I wore a black leather jacket with skinny jeans and a white shirt. I put my briefcase in my bag and headed to the parking lot. I got in my Opel. I drive less and less and I like driving. It was supposed to be a pleasant ride, so it's best to use your well-worn car. I felt comfortable and safe in it. I punched the address into the sat nav and pulled out of the parking lot. Along the way, I wondered how the construction would go. We had guests, and listening to heavy construction equipment might not be comfortable for guests. However, I was sure that Olivia had already found a way to do it.

I drove slowly, looking around. Lots of tourist houses for rent. The holidays are long over, but there are still many visitors.

I entered Nowy Targ and focused on the road. The traffic was heavy, so a long time later I parked the car next to a multi-storey, modern building. I liked the large windows, it felt like they took up the entire wall. Curious, I got out of the car and entered the building. I was greeted by a huge hall. I looked around because I didn't really know where to go. Right next to the stairs, I noticed a large information board with the names of companies and their assigned floors. Excellent. I didn't use the elevator, preferring to take the stairs.

I got to the second floor. In front of me was a glass wall with glass doors, and beyond were several office rooms. Rather austere style, in grays and whites. Only large pots with palms and fig trees gave a warmer climate.

I opened the door and went inside. I counted five people, and they all seemed extremely busy and overworked. Phones were ringing. I saw Kamil. He was bent over the desk. I walked over to his office and knocked lightly on the open glass door. How do they not mind such a lack of intimacy, walls and doors made of glass? That must have been a bit embarrassing. Everyone saw everyone, I wonder if it bothered them?

Camille looked at me surprised.

"Hi," I greeted. I took a white briefcase from my bag.

"Hello, what a surprise," he said, standing up.

"Olivia couldn't come" I didn't go into detailed explanations. "She asked for these documents, so here you go." I handed him the briefcase.

I looked at him closely. Tall, thin brown haired man with a two-day stubble. Dressed in a black polo shirt and gray elegant trousers. A nice smile and a warm look. Quite attractive. I usually saw him from a distance, or passing each other in the hallway, and it wasn't the same.

"Thank you very much." He placed the briefcase on the desk and focused his full attention on me. He held out his hand. "We haven't had a chance to get to know each other. Kamil.

"Natalie".

The handshake stretched a bit. I smiled confused.

"As a thank you for providing the documents, can I invite you for coffee?" He asked.

"I understand you have an important meeting to get a boarding house extension permit," I said.

"Yeah, but I still have forty minutes to go to my meeting, so I'd like a drink. In good company. There is a cafe on the ground floor, they also have a delicious cheesecake. It's on me.

I was surprised. Where did the idea for a coffee together come from? After all, we've only just met.

I raised an eyebrow, wondering what to say.

"As a thank you," he said.

"Okay," I agreed.

He grabbed his phone and wallet from the desk, put them in the pocket of his smart trousers and, smiling, gestured me where we were supposed to go.

"Elevator or stairs?"

"Definitely stairs," I said.

"I saw you a few times at Olivia's. Will you stay longer? he asked as we walked downstairs.

"For a while, for sure. For the time being, for an indefinite period. I came on vacation and I liked it so much that I stayed" I said lightly.

I looked at Kamil curiously. Again there was that vague feeling that I knew this man, we had met somewhere before. I couldn't explain these feelings. There was something magnetic, alluring about him, something I couldn't resist.

"A big life change?" He asked.

"Something like that."

We entered the cafe, Kamil pulled out a chair for me and asked me to sit down. He went to order and I looked around a bit. The decor was quite different from upstairs. It was dominated by warm colors, candles, pillows on the window sill, where you could sit. The cafe was small but very pleasant. Kamil returned to the table. He sat across from me.

"The last time I saw you, you were walking by the lake. You were wearing a floral dress with a hat on your head. It was one of the last hot days of the summer. Then I thought it would be nice to meet you. Unfortunately, there was no opportunity after that, until today.

"You have a good memory..." I said, surprised by his confession. I looked at him with great pleasure.

"Will you tell me something about yourself?"

A coffee shop worker came over and placed cups of coffee and plates of delicious-looking cheesecake in front of us. We thanked her kindly.

I generally don't say anything about my life to strangers, but Kamil seemed like a sincere and honest guy. I liked it. He looked me straight in the eye and listened to what I was saying to him.

"What would you like to know?"

"Like what do you like?" What do you enjoy the most, what are your personal successes…

I smiled broadly. I did not expect such questions. Usually people were curious about where I am from, how old I am, what I do, and here you go, such a change.

"Recently my priorities have changed a lot, I'm at the stage of getting to know myself anew, so it's hard for me to give a satisfactory answer in one sentence."

"In one sentence, it really won't work, so I encourage you to do a few" there were sparks of amusement in his gaze. "I'd love to hear it."

"I don't know if we have that much time," I said, sipping my coffee. Was delicious.

"Then why don't we start today and continue at the next meeting... What is most important to you?"

"Now? Peace, harmony, time for reflection, pleasure. Building nice relationships."

"Sounds interesting. And what made you come to "Bella Vita"?"

"A series of interesting coincidences. I closed a chapter in my life and opened myself to the unknown. We'll see what it brings" it's quite a personal confession, I don't know why I told Kamil about it, maybe because he seemed trustworthy, maybe because I felt good in his company. Perhaps the fact that Olivia would not cooperate with someone unproven or with a dubious reputation prevailed.

I was also curious about Kamil, so I changed the subject.

"Tell me, how long have you been working here?" - I asked.

"Six years. Two years after graduation, when we had gathered some experience, together with two colleagues we opened a design studio. We were doing quite well, we had quite bold ideas, we were gaining new customers. Over time, we hired two more people. We have a great team here, we're friends."

"Do you have clients from abroad?" I asked curiously.

"No, but I like to travel."

"What about accommodation during such trips?" I teased him a bit. "Do you often take a nap in the car on the side of the road?"

He laughed heartily.

"Maybe it happened three times." I remember the last time very well. It was quite interesting. Thanks to this, I met extremely helpful, lovely women.

"You gave us quite a scare back then."

I was returning from the Netherlands. My parents live there, I visit them sometimes.

"Oh, and what made them move there?" I asked surprised and very curious.

"It's a bit of a funny story." I don't really talk about it." He smiled and looked away for a moment, then back into my eyes. "I'm an only child, unfortunately. On my twenty-first birthday, my parents told me that they were going to go out into the world, explore, maybe stay longer somewhere they liked. They said that over the years they gave me a very good foundation to make it in life. They gave me an apartment, some money, and decided it was time for me to become an independent man. I was fucking pissed. I felt betrayed all the more because I always had their support. They left to pursue their dreams, and I had to pull myself together and stand for life. I learned a lot in a very short time. And I realized quite quickly that they had actually given me a very valuable gift. I don't think I would be where I am today if it wasn't for that.

"Did they have any expectations of you?" I asked.

"Yes. one. For me to be happy."

"Are you?"

He smiled.

"I feel quite fulfilled in what I do. Nothing and no one limits me, I lead a quite satisfying life.

"Are your parents planning to return to Poland?" I asked intrigued, I don't know why, but the answer to this question was very important to me.

"Absolutely not. They are doing quite well in the Netherlands, and they continue to travel the world. We see each other twice a year and that's more than enough."

I looked at Kamil with more interest. Quite an attractive and fascinating guy. Moreover, his mother did not interfere in his life.

I leaned forward slightly, then tasted the cheesecake. It actually tasted great.

"Maybe they'll change their mind when the grandkids arrive..." I suggested.

"That won't convince them to come back," he laughed.

"Or maybe grandchildren have already appeared ... Hence the certainty."

"If they were, I wouldn't invite you for coffee."

His phone vibrated. He glanced discreetly at the screen and muted the call.

"You have to go now…" I guessed.

"Unfortunately yes, I have a friend in the county office who will speed up the building permit, but tomorrow he is going on a three-week holiday to Turkey, so I have to act today."

"Then you can't be late for the meeting," I said with a smile and got up. "Thanks for the coffee."

Kamil also got up from the table. He looked at me with fire in his eyes.

"So when's the next meeting?" - He asked.

"At the appropriate time. You know where to find me," I said and walked out of the cafe into the street. I took a deep breath of bliss and intuitively glanced over my left shoulder. I saw Kamil through the large cafe window. He was still standing at the table watching me walk to the parking lot. After a moment, he turned and strode briskly into the building.

I stood by the car. I felt joy, fascination, certainty. This meeting with Kamil, I don't know what happened, this sudden surge and a range of sublime emotions. I don't know how, but I knew ... I intuitively knew that I would become his wife and bear him children. And I really liked that vision. Finally, I opened myself to the unknown with confidence.

I got in the car and drove away, happy, full of good feelings and emotions.

THE EPILOGUE

Three months later, in the evening, I was sitting in an armchair in my room and studying the material I had been given in TRE lectures. Staying in Krakow has always been inspiring for me. The classes and the subject of the training fascinated me very much, I started the next stage of the course on the coexistence and interdependence of body, mind and soul, because I already knew how important cooperation between these spheres of our being is. It's amazing how little we know in life about what really matters.

During my stay in Krakow, I usually spent afternoons with Marilyn. Now we were not only friends, but also Simon. I still can't believe how they got together. I remember how one day Marilyn dreamed that some guy would come to her from the other end of the world. Maybe England wasn't far away, but it was funny that her dream, maybe thrown so casually, without much attention, had come true. What drives us? Is there such a thing as destiny? I liked to think about such topics sometimes, and I found a lot of answers in spiritual and personal development books that I often bought. The more I read, the more questions and doubts arose. It fascinated me, I saw big changes in my perception of the world, I looked at people, at myself differently, with greater understanding and empathy. I perfectly remembered Aileen, a beautiful, well-groomed woman. She seemed confident, pleased with her appearance. Her perfectionism was just a mask, hiding insecurities, feelings of worthlessness and fear of being judged by others. That's why he reacted so emotionally to the request to remove his makeup. She was afraid that someone might see her true self, which she was unable to accept. It was a perfect example of not to judge others hastily.

It also dawned on me what the sign on the wall at the front desk meant: "It's time to move on and give yourself a chance." Knowledge and willingness alone are not enough to build a good life. We still have to take a step forward, with courage into the unknown. Listen and believe your intuition. She did not disappoint me in the case of Damien. We were still friends, we called each other sometimes. I hoped that someday he would meet a woman who would love him, because he is a really valuable guy.

Coming to the guest house changed my life. I'm afraid to think what would have happened if I had given Eve the voucher for her stay at Bella Vita. I was grateful to myself for this step into the unknown. I learned so much, experienced so much.

I also felt like I felt a lot more. I reconciled and accepted every emotion that came to me. There's been a bit more excitement lately. The good, positive ones.

I looked with emotion at the beautiful gold ring on the ring finger of my right hand. Three days ago Kamil proposed to me. I smiled warmly at the memory. We've known each other for such a short time, but it doesn't matter. I feel like we've been waiting for each other all our lives. I was happy to accept the proposal, we are planning a wedding soon. I have full confidence in myself and the Universe. This time it will be fine. I followed my heart because I already knew that it is never wrong.

"Evelyn, thank you. I said quietly."

I heard a vigorous knock on the door. I looked that way. I got up and let the visitor in. It was Olivia.

"Hey, can I have a moment?"

"Sure, welcome." I gestured for her to come into the room.

"I have something for you," she said, taking a seat in the other chair. "I should have given you this a long time ago."

She was holding a book in her hand. She handed it to me.

I looked curiously. Dr. Michael Newton "Journey of Souls" - I read on the cover.

"What is this?" I asked surprised.

"It's something that will completely change the concept of life, you will find many answers there, you will understand who you really are. Everything will be clear, like puzzles that popped into the right places and showed the picture from a wide perspective."

"You intrigued me. Tell me more," I asked.

"It cannot be told. You have to read."

"Is it about souls?" About what's on the other side?

"It's about what we do here, what we're on earth for, what we have to do. Everything you find there is based on years of research. Take as much of it as you want, as much as you believe… I'll go now, it's late." She got up and walked to the door.

"Thank you," I said, examining the cover of the book.

Olivia paused for a moment. She looked at me with joy and pride, then smiled warmly and left the room.

A wide smile spread across my face, then I sat on the bed, leaned against the wall, and started reading.

Page after page I felt more and more surprised and moved. I've been reading for hours and couldn't stop. It was amazing. I learned that we are energy, indestructible, existing for millennia. Endowed with free will. We come to earth to experience, learn, develop, grow. We ourselves, even before birth, choose the country where we will be y live, family, problems to solve. Everything that happens to us is for a reason. Each event is a lesson for us, and if we do not deal with it, difficult, traumatic problems keep coming back to us, they are simply another chance to face what we are supposed to learn here. Sometimes it's very hard, but that's how it's supposed to be. We are also here to love, to admire every moment, to feel happiness, but also to notice other people, to build relationships with them.

Often focused on the outside, we close ourselves off from contact with our soul, the energy that knows everything and that guides us. It is in us, even if we do not feel it. She wants good for us, she is drawn to love, and we are so lost in the ego, in the illusions that the mind imposes on us, we do not let it act, we do not want to listen to the quiet whisper of our soul.

And then, when time on earth ends, the energy leaves the body and returns home with a sigh of relief. Yes, home. We ourselves have freely chosen this life. Everything is for something. There are no cases.

I closed the book and hugged it tightly to my chest. I smiled with emotion. I looked out the window, it was dawn. It was a beautiful day.

I understood everything. I felt freedom. Fear had no power over me anymore, I had nothing to fear anymore. I could feel, touch, taste, be sad, love, jump for joy, listen to music. It's a great gift. All these little things really mean so much. We are not alone here, we have a lot of help, we don't even notice it. People who come our way are support or a lesson, so now I will look at them a little differently. I hoped that what I read in this book was true. Or maybe I already knew it?

I didn't have to be someone important, great, I didn't have to be rich to feel fulfilled. I could do simple things that make me happy, just be, because I was the greatest value in myself.

How important it was that I just was.

And since I was, I was supposed to experience life, so it should be. Well, I could have fun with it. And that's what I intended.

FROM THE AUTHOR

Dear reader, remember: you are the creator of your life. The sum of the decisions you make each day creates your reality. Only you can make your life better. Choose consciously, watch your thoughts, question your beliefs and seek the truth about yourself. It will set you free. You have access to unlimited possibilities, just believe that it is. Believe in yourself.

I wish you a beautiful journey in discovering yourself.

Celine Walasik

Printed in the USA
CPSIA information can be obtained
at www.ICGtesting.com
CBHW050829201124
17651CB00012B/237